Scribe of the Kingdom

The Art of God Incarnate: Theology and Image in Christian Tradition

The Theology of Joseph Ratzinger: An Introductory Study

Yves Congar

Theology in the Russian Diaspora: Church, Fathers, Eucharist in Nikolai Afanas'ev, 1893–1966

Holy Order: the Apostolic Ministry from the New Testament to the Second Vatican Council

From Newman to Congar: The Idea of Doctrinal Development from the Victorians to the Second Vatican Council

The Shape of Catholic Theology: An Introduction to its Sources, Principles and History

A Grammar of Consent: The Existence of God in Christian Tradition

The Holy Eucharist: From the New Testament to Pope John Paul II

Rome and the Eastern Churches: A Study in Schism

The Panther and the Hind. A Theological History of Anglicanism

Byzantine Gospel: Maximus the Confessor in Modern Scholarship

Scribe of the Kingdom

Essays on Theology and Culture

Volume I

Aidan Nichols, O.P.

Sheed & Ward
London

Comiti almo viarum

Every scribe who has been trained for the kingdom of heaven is like a householder who brings out of his treasure what is new and what is old.

Mt 13:52

ISBN 0–7220–7851 X

First published in Great Britain in 1994 by
Sheed & Ward Limited
14 Coopers Row
London EC3N 2BH

Production editor Bill Ireson
Typeset by Fakenham Photosetting, Fakenham, Norfolk
Printed and bound in Great Britain by
Biddles Limited, Guildford and King's Lynn

Contents

Acknowledgements

The author and publisher are grateful for the following permissions to reprint:

Angelicum, for an earlier version of Chapter III, 'T. S. Eliot and Yves Congar on the Nature of Tradition', in Vol. 61 (1984), pp. 473–85, and of Chapter V, 'The Reception of St Augustine and his Work in the Byzantine-Slav Tradition', in Vol. 64 (1987), pp. 437–52.

Annuarium Historiae Conciliorum, for an earlier version of Chapter VII, 'The Horos of Nicaea II. A Theological Evaluation', in Vol. 20 (1988), pp. 171–81.

The Heythrop Journal, for an earlier version of Chapter VI, 'The Appeal to the Fathers in the Ecclesiology of Nikolai Afanas'ev', in Vol. XXXIII, 2 (1992), pp. 125–45 and 247–66.

Libreria Editrice Vaticana, for an earlier version of Chapter IV, 'The Roman Primacy in the Ancient Irish and Anglo-Celtic Church', in M. Maccarrone (ed.), *Il primato del vescovo di Roma nel primo millenio. Ricerche e testimonianze* (Vatican City 1991), pp. 437–49.

The Month, for an earlier version of Chapter IX, 'Homage to Scheeben: 1888–1988', in Vol. 249, 1452 (1988), pp. 1028–31.

Scottish Journal of Theology, published by the Scottish Academic Press, for an earlier version of Chapter VIII, 'St Thomas Aquinas on the Passion of Christ: A Reading of *Summa Theologiae* IIIa., q. 46', in Vol. 43 (1990), pp. 447–59.

Prelude: A Dominican's Story

The essays gathered together in this book have, I hope, a certain *thematic unity* brought out in the sub-title 'Essays on Theology and Culture', as well as some *unity of approach*, indicated in the title's reference to the 'Scribe of the Kingdom' of St Matthew's Gospel. I draw out below what may be involved in that figure's task and virtues (see Chapter I). However, the reader who is good enough to buy, borrow, or at any rate open this book might reasonably wish to know from where its component materials are derived – to ask after, then, the *personal unity* standing behind them. That, at any rate – together with the opportunity to thank various people who have helped me – is my excuse for a short autobiographical explanation of my work.

I suppose I first became interested in theology on the day when I became interested in Christianity. It was in the summer of 1959. I was on holiday with a friend of my mother (who had died when I was eight). We were in Geneva, on a day excursion from that favoured haunt of the English middle classes of the period, Interlaken, in the Bernese Oberland. The tour of Geneva included a visit to the Russian church. When we entered, no service was in progress. However, some people were praying before the iconostasis. Revelation: transcendence, the holy, the *mysterium tremendum et fascinans* which I would later read about in Rudolf Otto's famous book[1], but above all, embodied in the figures of Christ, our Lady and the saints, the idea that God might appear through the human form. God in man, Emmanuel,

God-with-us. Previously, my religion was a home-made one, based largely on experiences of wild nature in the Lake District and reading bits of *The Prelude* in a copy of Wordsworth's poems belonging to my father. I had been christened in the Church of England, but no attempt was made to give me a religious formation. My parents would, no doubt, have been horrified if told they were not Christians. But Christianity to them would have been a largely ethical reality though, some years later, when obliged by a fire which destroyed part of our house to share a bedroom with my father, I discovered that he knelt down by his bedside and prayed every night like a child. However, this hidden piety had no doctrinal or liturgical expression.

Had I known of an Orthodox parish, I should probably have become Orthodox myself. But Orthodoxy was unknown and impossibly exotic in the part of northern Lancashire where I grew up. On the other hand, there were many Catholics, not only because of the Irish immigration of the last century (in fact, in rural Lancashire that was not a significant factor: immigrants needed work, and work meant, for the most part, the productive towns). There was as well an indigenous tradition of recusant Catholicism, kept alive originally by the squires in their private chapels. My own small town, Lytham, had such a hall and chapel, a family concern, now, alas, converted into the head office of an insurance company.

Such Lancastrian Catholicism was dominated by the memory of 'the martyrs': one did not have to say *which* martyrs these were – they could only be the English martyrs of the sixteenth and seventeenth centuries. Inevitably, then, it was a Catholicism which defined itself over against Anglicanism, the 'State Church', a phrase in no way complimentary. This Catholicism was, aesthetically, far from attractive. Its sense of the objectivity of the supernatural mysteries it handled was such that, apparently, it needed no graciousness, no 'trimmings'. Yet this too, in its own way, was an expression of the glory of God, his *kabod*, or 'weight'. The Christian Latin (which, later, I began to learn) of its prayers housed concepts and images to be reflected on and savoured for a lifetime. Of the plainsong, one could at least imagine how it *ought* to be done. Then, by way of compensation, there were the devotions which were explosions of popular mysticism, the candles and banked flowers of the Forty Hours and the May celebrations: the elements of nature brought in to honour their Lord and his human mother, and the prayer for the dead, which never failed to move me, since I was acquiring a certain number of my own. This was a tradition, if not the only one. It had roots in history; it was a memory in action, not least through the sanctoral cycle. It brought one to surmise the dead generations which, nevertheless, lived unto God.

Before I could accept this Church, however, I required to be argued into accepting its rational claims. I *was* argued into them by a teenage friend – we shared the same piano teacher, or else, owing to separate school systems, we should never have met. Fresh from his apologetics classes (which gave an excellent basis for the questions which exercise ordinary enquirers), full of Roman Catholic conviction, having landed me in the one true Church he proceeded to lapse some years later. Nevertheless, our arguments, in which I supported what I imagined to be the Anglican side, constituted my real instruction in doctrine. It took the death of my father, when I was fourteen, to stir me into seeking reception. I needed a Saviour who could deal with death by triumphing over it, and so affirm the lastingness of what deserved, by its merits, to be for eternity.

Being considered a bright boy at a school with a good academic reputation, I was regarded as a somewhat intimidating potential convert; three priests had a go. By the end of this protracted process, in which I read a good deal of and about Newman, and gave myself quite seriously to spiritual practices (surely much more than now!), I was seventeen. I was received on Holy Thursday 1966. The Second Vatican Council had happened, but no one was any wiser in the parish of our Lady, Star of the Sea, Lytham St Anne's. The documents of the Council, had I read them (the clergy preferred the 'Penny Catechism'), would have posed no threat to my grounds for adhering to the communion in which I expect to die. They were: clarity and certitude of doctrine; a mystical depth in worship and devotion; and a spirituality which could give one guidance, courage and consolation not only in dying but in living as well: the whole being held together in a continuity over time which joined me to the centre of all history, Jesus Christ, the Pantokrator and man of sorrows, in whom the heights and the depths of strength and weakness, joy and grief, are one.

Although I was very keen on my main school subject, History, and gained a scholarship in it at Christ Church, Oxford, the year afterwards, the recent domination of my life by religion made the thought of a priestly or religious vocation fairly inevitable. Having lost the natural community of my parents, and having no full brothers or sisters, I gravitated towards the idea of monastic community. In the north of England, there was only one serious contender, the English Benedictine Congregation monastery of Ampleforth in Yorkshire, best known for its prestigious private school. I liked the monks of Ampleforth very much. Drawn from the English upper, or upper middle, class, they had, for me, shining qualities: gentlemanliness and courtesy. They breathed a sense of belonging to a wider world, despite their vow of stability to one spot (in fact, they had numerous parishes, and one or two daughter houses). I was accepted as a novice, and actually arrived as a postulant, with a clerical wardrobe which, over twenty years later, I am partly still making do with, and the only two books we were allowed: the Bible, and the 'RB', or Rule of Saint Benedict. In fact, I did not stay to begin the noviciate. The conscious, and perfectly objective reason, was the impossibility of combining it with my share

in the tedious and long drawn out litigation which had bede-
villed the settlement of my father's estate. Subconsciously,
however, I had the sense that I needed rather more (and
rather happier) experience before I could say goodbye to the
ways of ordinary life.

'Ordinary' is not perhaps quite the word, since the three
years which followed at Christ Church were typical under-
graduate years and so hardly a statistically typical experience.
They were years I cannot see except through gold, in
radiance. This had nothing to do with super-nature. It had
everything to do with the innocent pleasures of conviviality
with congenial peers, of parties and boating, strawberries and
wine. It had to do, moreover, with friendship, the greatest of
human gifts. After a childhood overshadowed by bereave-
ment, this was the necessary pagan experience of exulting in
the creation, a 'Hellenic' moment which everyone must
know, in some form or other, who shares the faith of Scripture that the world God has made is, as it comes from him,
very good. As I would later learn through reading the
religious philosophy of the Swiss theologian Hans Urs von
Balthasar, I had had a taste of the transcendentals – the
qualities of being which mirror the attributes of the Creator
God. Since, in this sense, paganism is presupposed by Christianity, none of this involved any distance from that Church
which some people nowadays foolishly call 'institutional' –
foolishly, since, the Church being built on those office-
holders, the apostles, there is no other. At Christ Church I
discovered, and admired from afar, the Anglican scholar, and
especially the Anglican patristic scholar, of whom egregious
examples lived around me in the canonries: F. L. Cross, S. L.
Greenslade, Henry Chadwick. In the Catholic Chaplaincy,
the Old Palace, I could find a priest, Michael Hollings,
exemplary in his prayer life, huddled in a kind of ecclesiastical greatcoat however early one arrived at his 'Nissen Hut'
chapel, and ever ready to hear confessions with a *mélange* of
gravity and encouragement which made one aware – as do all

good confessors – of being simultaneously a sinner and a moral agent with potential. At the Ampleforth study house I had been asked to keep contact with the Master, James Forbes, a great collector of (aristocratic) families, but with a sense of a monastic *familia* so strong and warm that all else was easily forgivable.

While at Oxford I discovered the Dominicans, although by a somewhat roundabout route. Having learned a little Swedish through participating in a Legion of Mary *peregrinatio pro Christo* one summer – a mellow Southern Irish exercise in door-to-door evangelisation, something which should not be despised (some people would have become Catholics years ago, but were never asked) – I decided to write my Modern History dissertation at the Charles XII library in Uppsala. From Henry Chadwick I received a letter of introduction to a professor at Uppsala, an expert on the Tractarians, a former Lutheran pastor, now a (married) deacon, Alf Härderlin. His home was a sort of treasure chamber of Catholic culture (Cimabue, I think, on the walls, Claudel on the coffee table, and on the stereo Mozart, which I was obliged to follow with the score, something I did with embarrassing incompetence, as became evident when the page to be turned over fell to my turn).

Dr Härderlin proceeded to prophesy over me that I would become an English Dominican, a thought which had previously not entered my head. They were he said, so far as he knew, very sound. I do not remember ever acting so irresponsibly again, but when I got back to England I took steps to do as he had, on the basis of so little acquaintance with me, proposed.

The noviciate and study house of the English Dominicans being (then) at Oxford, I had little to do, in the autumn of 1970, except move my books and clothes up the road. The Province, and especially Blackfriars, Oxford, had just experienced, unbeknownst to my Swedish friend, a considerable crisis of confidence, nor, despite some of the appearances, was that crisis ended. My novice master, Geoffrey Preston, a walking theological encyclopaedia whose knowledge was, however, always relevant, saw himself as a rebuilder of tradition, who could reassemble the scattered pieces into a mosaic. His spirituality was at once biblical, liturgical and indebted to the Dominican saints, whose writings and legends he dispensed with a mixture of reverence and humour. (I would later edit some of his addresses – chiefly under the titles *God's Way to be Man*,[2] meditations on, alternately, Gospel episodes and the sacraments, and *Hallowing the Time*,[3] inspired by the temporal cycle of the Church's year – trying thus to put some of his wisdom at the disposal of a wider audience.) Geoffrey's attempt to inject not just order but *content* into a situation of some *anomie* – in worship, and spirituality, less so in doctrine – seemed eminently sensible to me, but aroused in others the anxieties, on a tiny scale, in 1970, which would become plain on a much larger canvas in 1980, with the launching of the 'restorationist' (as some would call it) pontificate of John Paul II. The reduction of the round of conventual observance to something of a minimum (but more, no doubt, than would characterise many other communities of the period in Western Europe and North America) made various 'causes', dear to the *bien-pensant* elements of city, university and church, loom even larger by contrast. Notable among these were: Marxian socialism, Irish nationalism and 'gay liberation'.

Marxism has its own intellectual credentials; what was disturbing was not that these might be taken seriously, but that their acceptance could be turned into almost a matter of faith. In the 1970s, though the term 'liberation theology' was not yet known in England, the fundamental dilemma which it denotes was already present. Love for the poor, and the desire to help them effectively, is a distinguishing mark of the Christian. I had worked for a year, after leaving school, in a hostel for vagrants and the unemployed. Delousing the bedsheets, and cleaning out the latrines of Dublin tramps, offer, like many texts of the Christian tradition, a concrete sense of how the abjectly poor are placed; but this does not indicate what, on a macroeconomic scale, should be done about it. That Marxism-Leninism is the answer never seemed to me probable – now, in the wake of the confessions of ideological bankruptcy emanating from the Communist world, a rather widely shared conviction. Not that I would tie my colours to the mast of Thatcherite 'capitalism in one country', for that concept of the individual's freedom is, ethically, largely vacuous. The Church has her own social doctrine, a dialectic of solidarity and subsidiarity, of the person and the common good, which has not been tried and found wanting, but, in Chesterton's words, has been found difficult and not tried.

We shall not be judged, however, on our economic theories, but on the degree to which we have cared for the poor in such practical ways as our particular situation allows. In 1984/5 I would find myself acting as official spokesman for the Apostolic Nunciature in Britain on the occasion of the publishing of the two documents[4] on liberation theology by the Congregation for the Doctrine of the Faith. It was encouraging to find that my reactions in the early 1970s had some resonance elsewhere; but troubling to think of the charitable zeal and intellectual energy that had been to some degree thus misplaced by such movements as 'Christians for Socialism' and the like. Nevertheless, it is important to note, as I was careful to stress in my interpretation of these documents, that the Roman church does not reject liberation theology as such. She welcomes it as an attempt to tease out that which is socially congruent with the life of Christ's redeemed people. But she wants to have it in a form which neither reduces the Gospel to politics nor traduces her own ethos in matters touching the common good of the *polis* – from which 'politics' gets it name. Two of the essays included in this collection (see Volume II, Chapters XVI and XVII) concern such theology – and one takes as its subject an orthodox home-grown liberationist *avant la lettre* – Chesterton himself.

Irish nationalism, secondly, was an ambiguous affair in the 1970s, since the borderline between support for constitutional republicanism, and sympathy for recourse to organised violence was too easily blurred by liberal/radical opinion in England. Distaste for the British State as such was something I could not begin to understand at the time, since, despite the lamentable errors and offences of British policy in Ireland in past generations, the present policies of successive British governments (I do not speak of all the executive actions carried out in their name) seemed decent and fair. However, after I left Oxford and England (in 1977 a year after my ordination to the priesthood) for Edinburgh and Scotland, I came to see things rather differently.

Without embracing Scottish Nationalism, it was possible to see that the British Crown does not function in practice as an *imperial* Crown, a Crown identified with none of the *ethnê* under its rule – English, Scots, Welsh, Irish, non-Europeans – but is, in the common perception, an English affair to which others may make a limited contribution. From this point of view, I came to think that, of all the polities which Europe has known in this century, the Danube monarchy *at the end of its history* offers, pardoxically, the most hopeful pattern for the future. (See especially the *Völkermanifesto*, 'manifesto to the peoples', of the *Friedenskaiser*, 'peace-emperor', Karl, who is now the subject of a beatification process.)[5] I have tried to indicate what I take to be the theologically proper interrelation of nationalism and the international order in Volume II, Chapter XIX.

It was in this spirit that I went to Vienna for the funeral of the Kaiserin Zita (in any case, a great Christian woman) in the spring of 1989, and that I look with some hope to the Pan-Europa Union of which Dr Otto von Habsburg is a prime mover, at a time when the idea of a Europe federally united from the Atlantic to the Urals is becoming a long-term possibility in a way that has seemed impossible since Yalta-Potsdam, and at a time, too, when the papacy is urging the rediscovery of the Christian roots of Europe's nations, and of its civilisation as a whole. For the Union, in taking as the inspiration for its federalism the best of the *Reichsidee* – the 'holy Roman' imperial ideal – is committed not only to Greco-Roman ideals of rationality and the rule of a positive law itself founded on the natural law, but also to the public relevance of the Judaeo-Christian revelation.

The issue of gay liberation, unlike the previous two, affected the pastoral care of actual persons in the vicinity of the priory – the university and city of Oxford – and so required especial care in its consideration. In modern Western society, any movement which exalts yet further the role of the erotic in personal relationships must be met with some degree of suspicion. The psychology of ego fulfilment has played enough havoc as it is with the sense of commitment, and of duty to others. Nor is a religious community, whose celibate yet common lifestyle is already an invitation to prurient comment, the right body to undertake a crusade on such an issue. On the other hand, much unnecessary guilt was felt by Catholics living more or less chastely (at least, no more unchastely than heterosexual Catholics) in awareness of a predominantly homosexual orientation. On the occasion of the 1986 Roman letter reaffirming the Church's traditional stance *vis-à-vis* same-sex activity, I accepted an invitation (see Volume II, Chapter XV), as an upholder of the document, to give a theological interpretation of this aspect of the human condition, which is at once a consequence of the confusion of our powers caused by original sin (and notably between our capacity for the love of friendship, and that for erotic love), and yet can also be, when suitably channelled, and with its energy transformed, a source of valid human affection.

Such issues did not, however, dominate my theological studies, which were cast in a much more classical mould. For Scripture, I had two excellent Anglican exegetes, John Barton and John Muddiman, who introduced me to the English, and predominantly Anglican, tradition of humane, ecclesial and (consequently) relatively conservative biblical scholarship to which, in its combination of learning and a certain *insouciance* towards fashionable ocean-going theories of how to read the New Testament (in particular), I would like to think I adhere. In Francophone and Catholic guise, it is brilliantly reflected in the hermeneutical theory of Père François Dreyfus, O.P., of the Ecole Biblique in Jerusalem, the main lines of which I set out below (see Chapter II). In patristics, I had for teacher Fr (later bishop) Kallistos Ware, in whom Oxford and John the Theologian's island of Patmos come together, with barely visible sutures, in one person. We laid special weight on the early monastic sources, which are vital for the whole tradition of religious life in the Christian church: any recovery of a solid basis for that life, whether in its personal or its communitarian dimensions, must begin with those texts, its fountain-head. Bishop Kallistos – his conferences, tutorials and celebration of the Holy Liturgy – recreated in me the love for Orthodoxy which I had discovered twenty years previously. So did his lay predecessor in the Spalding lectureship, Nicolas Zernov, a saintly old man, breathing the best spirit of the pre-revolutionary Russian church, whose example led me later, when at Edinburgh, to undertake a thesis on the Russian-born ecclesiologist Nikolai Afanas'ev.[6]

A chapter on Afanas'ev's 'Appeal to the Fathers', for which Cambridge University Press could not find room in their book, appears here (see Chapter VI). Unfortunately, I cannot profess, in 1993, the optimism about Orthodox-Catholic relations which seemed relatively realistic in 1981 – for the reasons I laid out in a study of the Eastern schism.[7]

For Catholic dogmatics, my tutor was the immensely erudite and searching Cornelius Ernst, whose Dominican life, like that of Geoffrey Preston, was cut short tragically early. The chief gift of Fr Cornelius, as I experienced it, lay in holding together a sense of the complex data relevant to any truth of faith, with the simple transparency of that truth itself. He was a generous tutor, who encouraged one to roam in the great forest of Catholic thought, from the Pseudo-Denys and Augustine through Thomas and Hugh of Saint-Victor to Rahner and Balthasar, as well as pursuing those modern varieties of the 'liberal arts' which Hugh found it possible to 'reduce' (that is, to lead back) to theology. With the help of this wide, if fragmentary, reading, I was able to write my 'lectoral' thesis on the visual element in revelation – summed up in the Russian icons I had seen at Geneva.[8] I owe a great debt to the example of another of the Oxford brethren in this regard: Fr Gervase Mathew had made the relation of the faith to art and culture the connecting theme of his life, as his highly original studies of both the Byzantines and mediaeval England show. Nor should I leave off an account, however scrappy, of the Oxford Blackfriars of the early 1970s without some reference to Fr Simon Tugwell's work in the retrieval of spiritual sources from the tradition of East and West; Fr Herbert McCabe's frequently brilliant re-pristinisations of the insights of Thomas into the relation of nature and grace in sacramental living; and the readings, at once meditative and rigorous, of philosophical texts offered by Fr Fergus Kerr.

Assignation to Edinburgh in 1976 plunged me into the very different world of the student chaplaincy. It is sometimes said that the ideal Scotland consists of the buildings of Edinburgh filled with the people of Glasgow. This, to a considerable degree, was what a Catholic chaplain to Edinburgh University had, and the vitality of young people from the West of Scotland, and of their Catholicism, tribal yet thoroughgoing, was absolutely rejuvenating to an Englishman (though with a Scots grandfather on his mother's side) too long attuned to the more sophisticated, yet also more languid, university population south of the Border. My aim as student chaplain was to stress three things: the creation of a rich and inspirational liturgy; good speakers on themes of Catholic interest; and social joy. A church of young people should experience the communion of the Great Church in those three modes: adoring, reflecting and recreating. In a form fit for late adolescents, they are the Baron von Hügel's three elements of religion: mystical, intellectual, institutional.

My time in Scotland was interrupted by a call (outer, not inner!) to Norway; where the Oslo priory, canonically part of the Province of France, was currently in some difficulty. I was only too pleased to go, since it cohered so well with the Scandinavian origins of my Dominican vocation. As the French Provincial was aware, I already knew a little Norwegian, thanks to study-evenings in Oxford with the Norwegian Dominican Aage Hauken, a convert from Lutheranism, with whom I read Sigrid Undset's wondrous recreation of mediaeval Norway, *Kristin Lavransdatter*.[9] My year in Oslo gave me some sense of the varieties of contemporary Lutheranism which I tried to bear in mind when writing the short section on Luther in my study of the noted French Dominican ecumenist and historical theologian, Yves Congar.[10] I learned whilst researching for this book that, curiously, Congar had almost volunteered for the Norwegian mission. When in Oslo I did some work on the philosophy of religion, which found a publisher a decade later.[11] That book brought to the *form* for an argument to God's existence suggested by Newman a *content* ranging up and down the story of Christian thought; I also had the experience of chaplaincy work with the diplomatic community in its Francophone incarnation – rather to the chagrin of the French cultural *chargé d'affaires*, the principal theme of whose mission was the excessive influence of all things British in Norway! In a country where the monastic life, though once deeply rooted, was later wholly swept away with Catholic Christianity itself, that life can be a powerful apostolic tool. Out of all proportion in comparison to their numbers is the influence, in the environs of Oslo, of the Dominican *nuns* of Lundén Kloster, to whom I gave a set of conferences on the incomparable 'father' of our common Rule, Augustine. The existence of such communities is an irreplaceable witness to the importance of the contemplative dimension in that of the Dominican friars themselves. That dimension, especially in the creation of environment through silence and the prayerful celebration of the Hours, has been neglected by the somewhat activist reform of the Order since 1965 and needs to be reinstated, so that God may be the conscious centre of our houses and true charity come thereby to reign.

Return to Edinburgh as parish priest presented one, both in theory and practice, with the issue of the local congregational church – as distinct from the particular church, the diocese. Owing to the peculiar history of the Edinburgh Dominican house, its chaplaincy (technically, only a 'personal parish' for university students and staff) was more of a classical parish – incorporating all sorts and conditions of men and women in a blessed rag-bag, a microcosm of the Church universal. To do justice both to this mainly self-constituted reality, and to the Church's own structures, it seemed desirable to stress that 'parishioners of election' associate themselves with the Dominican community on the basis of an attraction towards, or fundamental affinity with, the 'charism' expressed in the teaching and holiness of the saints of the Order, and their desire to share in this and act on it for the sake of others. This may seem an arcane piece of ecclesiology; but it is a kind of thinking which will be necessary if the Order is to be saved from an imperialism of the pastoral, which has already impoverished its liturgical, intellectual and conventual life, though in other respects yielding some gains.

Assignation to the Angelicum, the Roman University of the Order, to lecture in dogmatic and ecumenical theology in 1983 enabled me not only to bring together into lecture form some of the ideas and knowledge acquired on my way, but also to experience the church of the city of Rome, the church that carries the universal primacy among the communities of the *Catholica*, and expresses it, not least, in the hospitality given to such diverse representatives of the particular churches around the world. Of course, not everything in Rome is perfect: how on earth could it be? But the many admirable servants of the universally primatial church that I have met, and the care with which policies for various aspects of the Church's life and mission are there worked out, made it hard to credit the 'anti-Roman affect' which has become so unpleasantly strident a feature of Catholicism in the present pontificate.

In my book on the theology of Joseph Ratzinger,[12] I tried to demonstrate the quality of the leading theological mind of the Roman curia, and not least, that mind's rootedness in Catholic tradition in some quite 'un-Roman' forms. 'Roman theology' barely exists today, since the education of the professoriate of the Roman colleges, and hence of the majority of members of the Roman curia, is too diverse to permit the emergence of a single school. Instead, the Roman church draws to itself, for the expression of its mind, whatever elements of theological history seem most profitable to it. In taking Ratzinger as Prefect of the Congregation for the Doctrine of the Faith, it opened itself anew to his particular sources: patristic North Africa, mediaeval Italy and the southern Germany of the nineteenth and twentieth centuries. This is, in fact, an instance of the Church operating effectively as a communion: circulating materials with different origins in time and space, and where desirable, 'receiving' them. Their reception by the church that presides in the Charity, sitting in the presidential chair of the assembly of churches, is, naturally, more weighty than any other. The book was itself relatively well received, but few reviewers drew the conclusion I had hoped they would reach: the centrality and representativeness, within the Catholic tradition over time, of the theological policies of the present papacy.

Teaching at the Archbishop of Birmingham's seminary, St Mary's College, Oscott, with its *memorabilia* of a happier period of Church history, the nineteenth-century Catholic revival, and concentrating on the everyday sacraments of the Church (later *Holy Order* and *The Holy Eucharist*[13]) made a pleasant antidote to this not very enjoyable excursion into Church politics. For the reconstitution of Catholic identity in a whole variety of areas goes diametrically against the desire of liberal Catholics for a further extension of the ideas of pluralism, hermeneutics, and the never-ended re-reception, in new guises, of what was once thought definitely settled. Having worked out some principles, however, one is not entitled then to ditch them, even for that greatly desired gift which is peace. The variety, then, which rightly exists, culturally, spiritually, theologically, in the Church must always be a *bounded* variety. It cannot be a pluralism without limits, a *jeu sans frontières*, where the Gospel voice would turn, for the community that bears and hears the Gospel, into cacophony. This was the spirit in which I introduced first year students at the Angelicum to theology, in lectures I subsequently published.[14]

More specifically still, positive criticism of the magisterium – which is not only a Roman magisterium, yet, as the wider episcopal teaching office, is nevertheless always a magisterium *cum et sub Petro* ('with and under Peter') – there may be; but it has to be remembered that, in disputed questions, truth in doctrinal form emerges only through the refinement of the magisterial teaching, by a process of homogeneous development. This was the subject of my next book,[15] intended, I hope not too impertinently, as a continuation of Professor Sir Owen Chadwick's *From Bossuet to Newman*.[16]

The American Lutheran (but recently Roman Catholic convert) Richard John Neuhaus remarked that Catholic theologians nowadays sometimes give the impression of having spent the last twenty-five years working out how little, as a Catholic, one need believe, and how little do. A dogmatic theology which becomes a casuistry of the minimal; a moral theology which fails to proclaim the possibility, under grace, of the ideal: these are not, as I read the sources of the Order, the Dominican way. Our task is, rather, to communicate an evangelical and Catholic maximalism of faith and ethos – not over against other values, but incorporating whatever in them is salutary. The model for such a programme today must surely be Cardinal von Balthasar, by whose grave I stood, in Lucerne, on a sub-Alpine February day. As wide-ranging in scanning the historical sources for inspiration as in the issues it deals with, Balthasar's work relates all to the radiant centre of Christianity – at once God's glory, his action and his truth – where the Father plunges the sword of the Spirit into this earth, there to bear fruit in the sacrificial tree of his Son, Jesus Christ. I prayed as one ought for another *sterblicher, sündiger Mensch* ('mortal, sinful human being'), as in the authentically democratic formula of the Hapsburg funeral ritual. Should I return, I shall pray for myself, for the Catholic Church, whose present 'passion' Balthasar experienced so deeply, and for our beloved Continent, Europe, from which, for weal or woe, so much in the world of today has gone forth.

Hounds of the Lord (*Domini canes*) cannot afford to be academic, though they will try to be learned. The sheepdogs must guard the Lord's flock, and today those who would worry it are at the gates of the fold. Secularism; the sects; the resurgent force of Islam: to deal with these powers we must know what it is we are doing. My own work, however, apart from a little ministry to students at Fisher House, Cambridge, lies in historical theology where various projects are, I hope, currently maturing in the serenity of the lovely house and garden of the Cambridge Blackfriars. There a diversity of benevolent shades walk – from Archbishop Michael Ramsey of Canterbury and the aesthetician Professor Edward Bullough (both erstwhile owners of the buildings from which the priory grew) to such friars as the Semiticist Sebastian Bullough (Edward's son by Enrichetta Checchi, the daughter of the classical Italian actress Eleonora Duse), the Aquinas commentator Thomas Gilby, the ecumenist Henry St John, the Dante scholar Kenelm Foster. Historical theology is, not least, a contribution to Catholic consciousness, to awareness of the great lines of the tradition to which we belong. As the single Dominican charism diversifies in each one, he or she must make their own the prayer said at our profession, 'May God who began the good work bring it to completion.' His mercy is, thankfully, more determinative even than our freedom.

Aidan Nichols, O.P.
Blackfriars, Cambridge
Memorial day of St Philip Neri
1993

Part One

Some Fundamentals

I
Intelligent Conservatism as an Ecclesial Stance

The 'intelligent conservative' of my title is the 'scribe of the Kingdom' described by our Lord in the Gospel according to St Matthew:

> Every scribe who has been trained for the kingdom of heaven is like a householder who brings out of his treasure what is new and what is old.[1]

In their original context, these words mean that the Old Testament, God's revelation to the ancient Jewish people, is not to be set aside on the grounds that there is now a *New* Testament, a definitive revelation of the one true God in his universal Logos or Word, who has come among us as the man Jesus, the Messiah expected by Israel, the Christ. In the treasury of the household of faith, both Old Testament and New are to be conserved together. In the Judaism of Jesus' day, indeed, the crucial elements of this vocabulary – the 'old' and the 'new', compared and contrasted – were already in place. The 'old' was the Torah, the written Law of Moses; the 'new' was the words of the scribes – the lawyer-theologians who interpreted, in the light of Torah, the oral tradition of Israel. But though, in historical context, this Gospel text has in mind a quite specific issue, namely, the need to hold in unity both Old and New Testaments, it can nevertheless provide us with a useful general orientation in a search for the meaning of the phrase 'intelligent conservatism'. Intelligent conservatism cannot mean simply the conserving of what is old. Everything which is old to us was once new to somebody – and, as this Gospel text shows, that is true not least of the revelation given once for all in Jesus Christ and constitutively completed in the generation of the apostles who gave us its meaning in the apostolic preaching and the apostolic writings. This we acknowledge when we refer, as we still do, to those writings, considered as the residue of that preaching, by the phrase 'the *New* Testament'. The scholar whose learning is of the kingdom of heaven is to conserve not only what is old but also what is new: that is, the criterion for what is worth preserving, for what indeed, *must*, of religious obligation, be preserved, is not antiquity alone, any more than it is simply what is contemporary. Applying this passage, then, to our own situation today by way of what a long-standing tradition of reading Scripture in the Church has called 'spiritual interpretation': intelligent conservatism, the virtue which Jesus urges his hearers to practise in this Gospel, requires us to be open to the possibility that there is something of value in what is distinctively new in the present generation of his community; it also forbids us from writing off as valueless that which in the Church is old. We can call this combined *openness to modernity with fidelity to the past* 'intelligent conservatism sense A'.

Intelligent conservatism sense A may seem such an obvious virtue to practise that only with difficulty can we imagine those whose religious existence as Catholics has become vitiated by its neglect. However, if we look about us, we find those who, to all appearances, do sin against this implicit command of Jesus in its most fundamental spiritually interpreted sense. At one extreme, among the followers of the late Archbishop Marcel Lefebvre, there are those who claim in effect, that nothing valuable emerged in the Church after 1962: they contrast the 'old' pre-1962 Church, faithful to the apostolic deposit, with the 'new', post-1965 Church which is not only modern but modernistic in its infidelity to the deposit. 'Modernistic': that means, in this connexion, that the 'new' Church may maintain the old words, the ancient language of faith, but its adherents have introduced new meanings for these words in such a way that they now refer to different things. At the other extreme, among progressive Catholics, there are those who claim, in effect, that nothing valuable need be preserved from what they term the 'pre-conciliar' Church. Here the Second Vatican Council is perceived as an event so cataclysmic in its ecclesial significance that everything which preceded it is relegated to the status of mere Church history except insofar as it maintains an explicit presence in the Council documents. That Council is regarded, in a phrase popular in its immediate aftermath, as a 'new Pentecost', which relates contemporary believers to the original Pentecost, the absolute origins of the Gospel, in a manner that overleaps all intervening centuries. That those centuries could contain, in certain regards, a wisdom in the spheres of exegesis, theology, ethics, devotion, liturgy, capable of complementing the emphases of the Council, this is not to be thought of. Among such progressives, the dividing up of the Church's tradition into pre-conciliar and post-conciliar, so apparently simple, turns out on closer inspection to be extremely ambivalent. For of the two principal motivating forces behind the Council only one – *aggiornamento* or 'bringing up to date' – is compatible with the progressivist claim that the Council was, for Catholic Christendom, a new start which justifies the radical relativisation of earlier Church tradition. The other main moving force – *ressourcement*, or going back to the sources, is incompatible with the progressivist mentality so described. And yet, given that the Second Vatican Council canonised a great movement in Catholic theology in French and German speaking countries in the first half of this century to return to not only the New Testament but the Fathers of the Church, and to mediaeval and early modern theology only insofar as it reflected and continued the patristic achievement, it is self-contradictory to maintain that the Council by its innovations left behind a preconciliar Church. This contradiction explains the essential instability of a Council-oriented progressivism, which soon finds it necessary either to impose an abusive reading of the conciliar texts, by dismissing various passages as sops to the conservative minority, or, alternatively, to move on to a projected Third Vatican Council, where the Church will be purified of the archaisms surviving at Vatican II and ushered, unencumbered by the past, onto the broad sunlit uplands of the future.

Of these two sins against intelligent conservatism sense A, the Lefebvrist and the progressive, I have spent more time in describing the second since it is, for the contemporary Catholic Church, by far the more threatening. First, the excommunication of the episcopal leaders of the Lefebvre movement makes it crystal clear that their posture is spiritually schismatic *vis-à-vis* the life of the present Church. As yet, no way has been found of commenting with equivalent clarity on the state of soul of the progressives, whose posture is in fact spiritually schismatic *vis-à-vis* the past Church – a past Church which is the past *of* the present Church, and in that sense *is* the present Church, since the Church, if she be in truth the Church of the Word Incarnate and the Holy Spirit given at the first Pentecost, must be one and identical throughout her history. Secondly, the progressive way of sinning against intelligent conservatism is, on the whole, the one which is more likely to be committed by men and women in our lifetime. That is, although there are elements in contemporary culture which give people, in their secular experience, an orientation to the past – movements for the conservation of cosmic patterns in physical nature, and of human monuments from the societies of the past, the dominant orientation in a culture shaped mainly by technological materialism is towards the scientific and economic future. The sense of historical continuity in secular society, and the practice of historical sympathy for earlier generations, is liable, one supposes, to become feebler rather than stronger for the foreseeable future, and this being so, it is more probable that progressivism, and not traditionalism, will be the greater anxiety for the Church as she enters the third millenium. Before, however, leaving the issue of intelligent conservatism sense A it may be worth pointing out that traditionalism and progressivism do not only have it in common that they are transgressions against such conservatism: they also share a common origin. The origin is the coincidence of the Council with a particular phase of Western culture in the 1960s – a decade which, on the basis of a flourishing world economy and the optimism generated by the benefits of post-Second World War reconstruction, not least in the former colonial territories of the European powers, considered itself to be on the verge of a breakthrough in the consciousness of what it is to be human. The neophilia, or love of the new, in the period had as one of its most influential expressions the movement of revisionary socialism known as the New Left, and one of that movement's most telling images was the moment in the Paris Commune of 1870 when the revolutionaries fired at the city clocks so as to put an end to historical time as it had been known hitherto, and to usher in its replacement. Catholic traditionalism and progressivism as they exist today both originated in the 1960s as responses of quite opposite kinds to that crisis of Western culture which happened to coincide with a great Council of the Church. The one rejected the attempted neophiliac revolution with horror, the other embraced it with euphoria.

Intelligent conservatism sense A, while ruling out both traditionalism and progressivism as vices of the Catholic spirit, since their systematic attachment to, respectively, the 'old' alone, and the 'new' alone, is alien to the scribe of the kingdom in our Lord's parable, does not yet tell us, however, what *positive* criteria we should be applying in our assessment of the possible contributions of past and present to the life of the Church. In the parable, the conservatory where the wisdom of the Christian scribe is laid up is not meant, evidently, to be just a junk-room filled indiscriminately with the flotsam and jetsam of the sea of the world, whether from past ages or from his own. That conservatory is described rather as a treasure house, and so a place where only what is precious is conserved. The question then becomes, how are we to identify what is precious whether of past Judaeo-Christian generations, or of our own time in the Church?

Two criteria can be suggested, and these will give us in turn, two further senses of the phrase 'intelligent conservatism' needed before we can use this concept as a lens through which to focus what is happening currently, in different domains, within modern Catholicism. First, for Catholic Christian faith, the principal criterion of evaluation must be divine revelation, or, more specifically, the special historic revelation witnessed to in Scripture, summarised in the patristic Creeds and both guarded and interpreted as to its doctrinal content by the ecclesial organ brought into being by God in Christ for that purpose – namely the apostolic ministry which now exists in the form of the Catholic episcopate, together with, and in subordination to, its primatial head, the bishop of the church founded on the martyrdom of Peter and Paul, the local church of Rome. This criterion of evaluation – divine revelation as expressed in the apostolic teaching, itself found in Scripture and Tradition, and presented with contemporary authority by the living voice of the magisterium – must be unconditionally the first. That is, it must always take precedence over any other criterion; it is the supreme court of appeal in Christian argument and must be recognised as such; it can never be relativised by reference to any other factor. This follows from the terms of our Lord's saying: the scribe whose attitudes he commends is a scribe *of the kingdom of heaven*. In other words, he is not any artful, learned intelligence, setting to work on the materials of human experience. No, he is a scribe or a scholar dedicated to the kingdom, the reign of God proclaimed by Jesus Christ and to such a degree brought about in his own person as the crucified and risen Lord of history that he, Jesus, could be called by the third-century Christian doctor Origen *auto-basileia* ('the kingdom itself'). He is a scribe *of* the kingdom, a scholar whose understanding is determined by the kingdom, and who therefore, naturally, makes the kingdom the centre of his interpretation of the world. In the language of later theology, the scribe of the kingdom has set supernatural truth above all natural truth as the light in which that natural truth is itself to be seen and appreciated. Intelligent conservatism sense B, then, adheres to this principle: revelation, that is, the special historical revelation given in Jesus Christ and his Church takes epistemological precedence – priority as a way of knowing – over against any other claimants for this exalted position. In this way, intelligent conservatism sense B is immediately distinguished from theological liberalism, as we have come to know it in the Catholic Church since the Modernist crisis of the late-nineteenth-century.

Modernism considered as liberalism is very different from the cult of modernity entertained by progressivism. Thus the founder of Catholic Modernism, Alfred Loisy, was, in his veneration for the inherited forms of Catholic practice – for the old Roman Mass, the Breviary, various traditional devotions and the general ambience of the nineteenth-century Catholic revival – in all respects except its scholarship, its theological life, as much a traditionalist as Archbishop Lefebvre, as was also Loisy's maverick Anglo-Irish disciple, the Jesuit George Tyrrell. The aim of the Modernists, as theological liberals though in other respects defenders of the inherited Catholic religious culture, was to keep everything, or virtually everything, outwardly unchanged in the Church but to transform the epistemological foundation on which it had hitherto rested. That is, the Modernists sought to change the sense in which the Catholic religion was held to be true, the better – in their view – to protect that religion, as lived and practised, from corrosion by the acids of scepticism, secreted by the scientific, philosophical and historical discoveries of the modern world. For Modernism, the teachings, rites and practices of Catholic Christianity are to be preserved insofar as they express great moral truths which can only be effectively embodied in religion, as also certain large and general metaphysical truths, such as the existence of a relationship between the human soul and a divinity not otherwise describable but acknowledged as the mystery behind, or at the basis of, the world. In Modernism, the interpretation of the divine revelation given in history is not a self-interpretation, made by the accredited witnesses of that revelation, the apostles, and preserved and fostered in the community they left behind under its episcopal and papal presidents. Rather is that revelation to be submitted to the epistemological authority of secular science and scholarship – which means of course that it is no longer received in any coherent fashion as a special revelation at all, but is thought of as simply part and parcel of the continuing religious experience of the human race, something which can be explored, studied and analysed by men learned in various secular disciplines so as to ascertain what human truths are to be found within its symbolic forms. Although that kind of theological reductionism is still found today, what is important is not the particular line it takes but the general principle or axiom on which it proceeds: namely, that divine revelation, or the alleged divine revelation, preserved in Catholicism, has no absolute priority over other ways of knowing. Catholic teaching can be submitted to the critiques of philosophy, anthropology, sociology or any other well-founded discipline, and be found wanting as a result. Intelligent conservatism sense B asserts the contrary of this: when something is known with assurance to be Catholic teaching, it may submit the deliverances of contemporary or any other philosophy, anthropology, sociology, etc., to its own rule of judgment, on the grounds that whatever the Church of Christ believes and confesses is founded on the Word of God, who, as Truth itself, can neither deceive nor be deceived.

But there is yet a *third* aspect to the meaning of the phrase 'intelligent conservatism' as it emerges from the pages of St Matthew. The conserver dedicated to the kingdom of heaven and defined by that dedication, is not, in our Lord's parable, a simple Simon. He is, precisely, a *scribe*, a learned man, a skilful man, an artful man. Intelligent conservatism sense C is a conservatism which does not neglect any of the human resources that contribute to being a good scribe, a good student. Divine revelation as we receive it by Catholic Christian faith is not something which remains external to our human faculties. On the contrary it enters into our intelligence, into our hearts, our imaginations, and even our emotions. Because it does so, it comes to provide the members of the Church with a second criterion whereby to evaluate what is precious in what comes to us from the past or from the present. This second criterion for what we should let into our treasure house is less easy to grasp, because less objective, than is the criterion of divine revelation. Divine revelation is utterly objective: though given to the corporate subject which is the apostolic Church it exists in the tangible forms of the Bible and the other monuments of Tradition, and is expressed in its objectivity as the public doctrine of the Church. By contrast, the second criterion used by the intelligent conservative is more subjective in character. It consists in the habitual Catholic sensibility built up over the ages as Christians have sought to respond to the objective divine revelation by appropriate forms of religious practice, and of religious theory – or theology. For example, it is clear from the evidence of Church history that a Catholic sensibility regards Christian worship as necessarily having a ritual dimension. Without ritual, without, indeed, fairly elaborate ritual, the mystery of worship, that is, what is given to us in the Church's worship, cannot be satisfactorily expressed. It is not a doctrine of the Church that worship or liturgy should have a developed ritual expression. It is what Catholic Christians, of East and West, in a succession of historical periods, have found to be required. Again, in another example, it is not a doctrine of the Church that a theology suitable to express divine revelation must be metaphysical in character – that is, to be able to deal with the eternal as well as with time, with the infinite as well as with the finite. However, this requirement is something that, once again, Catholic Christians, in both the Latin and the Byzantine traditions, have found to be a *sine qua non* of an adequate theological life. Though no part of divine revelation says so, though no Church doctrine therefore would have it so, Catholic sensibility in trying to mediate between revelation and the materials of the world around us, whether these be *objects or gestures*, as in the liturgy, or *concepts*, as in theology, has come to see these things as *desiderata* of the faith itself. Through the exercise of intelligence of various kinds over the generations, in the service of the kingdom of heaven, there has come to be a Catholic sensibility which includes, then, a Catholic aesthetics in such areas as liturgy and iconography, and a Catholic intellectual style in such areas as theology and philosophy. Intelligent conservatism sense B, therefore, requires us to maintain the habitual sensibility of Catholic Christendom as a way of judging just what kinds of expression of divine revelation we should encourage and promote.

Intelligent conservatism, then, which, to remind the reader, I am not proposing as one way of being a Catholic among others, even the best way, but as the very teaching of the Lord of the Scriptures himself, has three components. First, in sense A, it is both open to the new and faithful to the old. Whilst remaining open to what is of value in the characteristically new, intelligent conservatism, conscious of the predominantly future-oriented quality of present-day world society, is, therefore, particularly concerned to maintain fidelity, in the name of Christ, to what has been received from the past. Secondly, in sense B, it judges what is to be treasured, whether new or old, by the criterion of the special historic revelation entrusted to the Church, a revelation – now found as doctrine – which enjoys epistemic precedence over other formulations of truth. Taking that revelation as its primary and unsurpassable reference, it refuses to submit it to any other epistemological authority. Thirdly, in sense C, intelligent conservatism reveres the different kinds of intelligence, ranging from the artistic to the conceptual, which, exercised in the past, have formed a Catholic sensibility, or habitual way of judging the 'style' of activities in which divine revelation is appropriately expressed. Considering, then, how to mediate doctrine in the concrete – in a religious way of life, or in the abstract – in religious ideas, intelligent conservatism is guided by an habitual sensibility built up in preceding believing generations and constituting a kind of practical wisdom whose deliverances can be commended though not exhaustively demonstrated. It is along these lines that the Catholic tradition, and its theological exploration, must be creatively continued today.

II
François Dreyfus on Scripture Read in Tradition

Père François Dreyfus, O.P., of the Ecole Biblique in Jerusalem, has worked out a little noticed (in English-speaking countries) account of biblical hermeneutics, which underlies his now celebrated study of the divine self-understanding of the Jesus of history.[1]

The modest aim of this chapter is to set forth this hermeneutics – under the rubric of its central idea, Tradition as the actualisation, in the post-apostolic Church, of the biblical Word – by identifying its salient features, and delineating them in terms which stay close to the original author's own.

Exegesis in the academy, and exegesis in the Church

For Dreyfus, whereas all scholarly study of the biblical text has its own intrinsic value as an activity of the human mind as ordered to that mind's own object – the real, the true – in the special society which is the Church the exegete does not fulfil his task unless his work is ultimately guided by a goal of a *pastoral* nature.[2] In the last analysis, the ecclesial study of Scripture is practised so as to guide the people of God towards the kingdom of God. The question then becomes, does all work on the Bible contribute to this goal? How should exegesis be conducted so as to terminate in such pastoral actualisation of the significance of Scripture? Which readings lead in this direction? And which lead away from it, or lead nowhere?

At the present time, there is a heightened awareness of this problem which, it is true, has rarely gone unnoticed in the history of exegesis, especially where the study of the Old Testament is concerned. Writers have not hesitated to speak of the 'failure of the historico-critical method'[3], and to redeem this failure, attempts have been made to render the biblical text pastorally actual, sometimes at the level of entire commentaries. Thus the Evangelical *Biblischer Kommentar zum Alten Testament* ('Biblical Commentary on the Old Testament')[4] closes its commentary on each section with a paragraph entitled 'Ziel', indicating lines of reflection to follow up for present application. In the Catholic context, *Herders Bibelkommentar* ('Herder's Bible Commentary') has taken as its sub-title, *Die Heilige Schrift für das Leben erklärt* ('Holy Scripture as Throwing Light on Life')[5] in an effort to communicate the message of Scripture to pastors and the laity. The American collection, *The Interpreter's Bible*,[6] operates on two levels, one entitled 'exegesis', the other 'exposition' – but, interestingly, with different authors. The same authorial division of labour characterises the Franco-Belgian series, *Assemblées du Seigneur* ('Assemblies of the Lord')[7], in its treatment of the biblical passages used in the contemporary lectionary of the Roman rite.

But despite these attempts, the consumer, whose opinion counts rightly for more than that of the producer, is dissatisfied. Dreyfus sums up the 'reproaches' levelled at present-day exegetes in three statements:

1 The knowledge possessed by exegetes is a knowledge reserved to a new caste of scribes and doctors of the law, whose teaching alone can communicate the true meaning of Scripture. A simple or *naif* reading of the text is outlawed: above all, never think that the text means what it seems to mean.

2 This knowledge is archaeological in the sense that its principal concern is to show the rooting of the word of God in a

culture which is no longer ours, and belongs to a long-dead past. The corollary of this primary concern is neglect for a message which goes beyond that past cultural rooting, by calling out to our culture and our personal freedom. To have access to the word of God one must uproot oneself and become converted to another culture and mentality, prior to performing the same operation in reverse on the way back. Are such mental gymnastics truly indispensable, and how was it possible that eighteen centuries passed without their discovery?

3   The knowledge involved is a closed knowledge which claims to determine by limiting what the text means, whereas in the various linguistic disciplines which flourish beyond the world of critical exegesis the emphasis falls, rather, on the possibility of new readings of a text in a new situation generative of new meaning. More profoundly, but not unconnected with this, there is for the Christian the innovative rôle of the Holy Spirit, the Spirit of Christ, who on the road to Emmaus, opened the disciples' minds that they might understand the Scriptures.[8]

These complaints lead Dreyfus to formulate the crucial distinction (but not separation) between *exégèse en Sorbonne* and *exégèse en Eglise* – exegesis in the academy, and in the Church.

According to Dreyfus, the starting point of an adequate hermeneutics must be – for a Catholic Christian, and indeed for historic Christendom at large – the axiom that God has caused his truth to be conveyed in the sacred writings for the sake of human salvation, *nostrae salutis causae*, as *Dei verbum*, the Dogmatic Constitution of the Second Vatican Council on Divine Revelation, puts it, summing up the testimony of the Church's doctors throughout her history.[9] The finality of Scripture is that of revelation itself, namely, to lead human beings to their eternal happiness.

Thus, although the specific aim of exegesis in the Church is not the conversion and salvation of the sinner but the understanding of the Word of God, that understanding is not an end in itself, but is, rather, ordered to the beatitude of those to whom the Word is addressed. Dreyfus elects the term

'pastoral' as the most compendious word for this soteriological purposiveness of the Bible: 'pastoral' denotes all aspects
of the Church's ministerial activity – theology, moral teaching, spirituality, catechesis, and so forth, in their global
unity.[10]

For many, however, the question of the pastoral finality of
a text is not a matter for exegesis, but for biblical theology.
As they point out, this finality is not something that is disen-
gaged from the text by itself, but from a given text in its
relation with Scripture as a totality, or even with the Tradition, or traditions, which, in point of fact, have actualised
these texts in the course of the Church's history. And this is a
task for biblical theology or even for theology *tout court*. We
shall see later how the taking into consideration of Tradition
(including theological tradition) forms a part of the task of
exegesis in the Church context, and how it must be integrated
into its research. More specifically we can say, and in the
meantime, that while exegesis and biblical theology may
indeed be distinguished, exegesis can hardly be practised
without a modicum of biblical theology and *vice versa*. In
fact, Dreyfus takes 'exegesis' in a broad acceptation which
includes biblical theology, and the general thrust of his ideas
is to suggest that exegesis, when properly practised, will tend
to occlude some apparently sharp methodological boundary-
lines, and to show that by its own logic exegesis will culmi-
nate in pastoral actualisation.

Another objection which might be lodged at the start of
this enquiry would be that the idea of the necessary pastoral
actualisation of exegesis overthrows or at any rate endangers
its character as a science: a discipline whose affirmations can
be verified and checked, at least by those in possession of the
requisite intellectual and technical tools. We can reply that
exegesis is certainly, in this sense, a science; but is it therefore
only a science? There are some who would say so. W. Richter
insists that scholars must abstain from all that is not 'demon-
strable'.[11]

The demand for demonstration and verification should, no doubt, be met as fully as it can, but when a limit has been reached in this process must the exegete therefore fall silent? The great Old Testament form critic H. Gunkel did not think so. In an article on 'Aims and Methods in the Interpretation of the Old Testament', written in 1904, Gunkel declared that, 'Exegesis in its highest sense is more of an art than a science.'[12]

If this is so then it is because, we can say, the Scriptures are themselves a literary artwork for whose understanding there is required not only intelligence but also sensibility; for the Scriptures are addressed to the entire person, with his sense of values, and to his whole existence which the text is to enrich and whose horizons it is to enlarge. In the narrative of the death of Absalom in Second Samuel, for instance, the reader can discover a new dimension of his own humanity: David, with his father's suffering, becomes, by an act of imaginative identification, a factor in the reader's own life, and, should he be a believer, the suffering fatherhood of David enables him to grasp more deeply the *divine* fatherhood, as D. Barthélemy has so movingly written.[13] Nor is this a lapse into arbitrary subjectivity: for the concord of a large number of readers as to what this text does for their lives is in itself an objective fact which the scientific student must take into account. So Aristotle in his definition of tragedy in the *Poetics* includes as an intrinsic element in what tragedy is the reaction of the spectator.

Moreover, it is in any case too limiting to restrict one's consideration of the biblical text solely to its literary aspect. Literary theory or the science of literature, *Literaturwissenschaft*, is no doubt an indispensable preliminary for the study of all texts, including those of Scripture. But one could not study, say, Ptolemy's treatise on astronomy solely under its literary aspect, neglecting the aim and object of the author which was to inform us about the stars and their movements. So one should not study, for example, the book of Amos

without moving on from literary considerations to that perspective which is proper to the book's object, the discipline
within whose terms its content should be situated – in this
case, homilectics, or religio-ethical discourse. Once a text's
genre is established, the study of its content belongs by right
to the discipline which the genre reveals – whether jurispru-
dence or ethics, philosophy or theology: and, clearly enough,
the 'scientific' – that is verifiable, checkable – character of
each of these kinds of human reflection is something which
varies very considerably.[14]

How then should we sum up the distinction between
exegesis in the academy and exegesis in the Church, *exégèse
en Sorbonne* and *exégèse en Eglise*?

First, whereas exegesis in the academy studies the text in all
of those aspects which can be an object of knowledge,
making use as it does so of all available resources of human
understanding, it does not establish among these various
facets any kind of hierarchy of value. Exegesis in the Church,
on the other hand, limits itself to these aspects of a text
knowledge of which is relevant to the content, transmission
and actualisation of the biblical message, and establishes between these facets a grading, in terms of whether that significance be greater or less. Secondly, whereas exegesis in the
academy excludes the non-rational knowing that is faith, a
knowing which believers see as supra-rational, but others as
irrational, such faith-knowing will play a part in at any rate
certain stages of exegesis in the Church. Thirdly, whereas
exegesis in the academy takes as its finality simply its own
knowledge, considered as knowledge of the real, exegesis in
the Church finds its finality in the salvation of the people of
God, in virtue precisely of the office, charge or mission of the
exegete which he exercises in the midst of that people. Or, as
Dreyfus puts it:

The exegete at the Sorbonne addresses scholars, his colleagues.

The exegete in the Church has *ultimately* in mind the 'little ones'.[15]

And he cites here the dominical word from the Gospel of St Matthew:

> I thank thee Father, Lord of heaven and earth, that thou hast hidden these things from the wise and understanding, and revealed them to babes; yea, Father, for such was thy gracious will.[16]

Earlier in this century, Père Lagrange and others spoke of exegesis in the academy as 'independent' exegesis or criticism: and this term had its point. Such academic exegesis is indeed independent in comparison with that ecclesial exegesis which is quite properly dependent – characterised by a dependence of service, at the service of God's people, its life and growth.

Dreyfus takes further these reflections by enquiring, is exegesis more fundamentally the study of a text, or a search for the intention of an author?[17] Hitherto ecclesial exegesis has, overwhelmingly, identified the quest for significance with a search for the author's intention. This seems to follow from the doctrine of inspiration: if a biblical text can be called the word of God that is because its human author enjoyed the charism of inspiration, writing what God wished him to write. This viewpoint was long shared by non-Catholic hermeneutics, including those students who rejected *theopneustia*, the idea of divine inspiring. Such influential figures as Friedrich Schleiermacher and Wilhelm Dilthey regarded the interpreter's task as one of understanding the author, his psychology, motives, intentions. Gunkel, in the essay already quoted, declared that, in the study of this literature:

> What is truly valuable is the soul of the human being, the

mysterious inner life that discloses itself to the outside world
inasmuch as it gives itself expression.[18]

But the development of *general* hermeneutics has, in this
regard, much affected *biblical* hermeneutics. First, the
possibility of understanding a past author as he understood
himself has been contested. Cultural distancing, it is said,
constitutes an unbridgeable gap. The 'fusion of horizons'
between author and interpreter does not take place by cancel-
ling out the interpreter's standpoint so as to leave only the
author's intact, for that is impossible, but by realising the
irreducible otherness of the two distinct horizons, and in
making of that otherness a key factor in the hermeneutical
act. We find, at the present time, a mounting tendency to
detach the text from the author and his intentions – both in
general hermeneutics and in that special case of hermeneutical theory which is the hermeneutics of the Bible. Whatever
an author may have meant, he wrote what he wrote. Once
promulgated a text is an instrument (*un appareil*) which
anyone can use for his own purposes: it is not certain that its
inventor had a better use for it than anybody else. Structuralism is itself constructed on the foundation of this pushing to
the sidelines of the author. And even where structuralism in
the full sense is not in question, structuralism's aversion to
the notion of authorial intention is often echoed. Thus
Richter, in the study already cited, understands authorial
intention as the intention conveyed by the *structure* utilised
by the author, and R. Lapointe invites his readers to recognise the 'autonomy' of the literary work *vis-à-vis* its creator.[19]

This marginalisation of the author, Dreyfus shows, needs
to be evaluated with some care. While a biblical book may
well include a variety of elements, informational, narrative,
historical, poetic, and so forth, these elements are integrated
within a higher unity, that of a *message*, whose object it is to
generate, nourish and fortify certain convictions, and to

arouse certain kinds of behaviour. Considered as a message, the text necessarily bears a relation both to its author and to those for whom it is intended. In an analogy drawn from broadcasting: its function is to transmit to the receiver – whether individual person, or community – the convictions found on the side of the emitter, who can speak in his own name, or in that of a group, or indeed present himself as the spokesman of the mystery to whom the group gives the name of God.

It follows that reference to the author's intention is part and parcel of the understanding of any text which constitutes a message. What convictions does he wish to communicate? What behaviour does he want to prescribe? Moreover, the text as message always contains in some way instructions for its own deployment. Though it *can* be used for other things, its form indicates the purpose for which it was made.

And yet the biblical text-message does not present itself as addressed to *me*, but to the contemporaries of the author. Only by a free decision do I consider myself as *le destinataire*: the person to whom the message is destined. This free decision has two modalities. The first is ecclesial, a matter of my belonging to a Church whose beliefs I share, beliefs which involve adherence to this message as perpetually valid, and to be proclaimed to all. Secondly, however, there can also be a free decision to regard as valid, or as valuable for me, simply some part or aspect of this message, or a decision to interest myself in it for reasons of a professional, aesthetic or political kind, for reasons connected with the study of Oriental or ancient languages, and so forth.

The fact that the message is not addressed to me but to people separated from me by a huge temporal and cultural distance makes necessary an *interpretation* of the message, and in part justifies, according to Dreyfus, the criticism offered by modern hermeneutics of the positions of such writers as Schleiermacher, Dilthey and Gunkel, often called, thanks to their indebtedness to the heightened interest in subjectivity characteristic of Romanticism, 'Romantic hermeneutics'. But the more adequate understanding of the process of biblical interpretation to which this criticism of Romantic hermeneutics points is not itself undifferentiated. It functions in two different ways, depending on which of the two modalities of the free decision to regard oneself as the recipient of the biblical text is in question.

For, in the *first* case, where the free decision is mediated by my incorporation in the Church, all churches profess in some way that the message of the Bible is truly what they present today to their faithful. There is, they claim, a true identity, constituted by homogeneous continuity within the same tradition, connecting the original act of communication and what is happening now. The task of exegesis in the Church consists in showing that the message which some biblical author addressed to his contemporaries remains permanently valid so long as one knows how to actualise it correctly, and that this message retains the abiding power to guide God's people towards his kingdom. Such continuity of message, Dreyfus goes on, must be located *on the side of the intention of the author* – even though that intention was applied to a situation, epoch and culture different from our own. An understanding of exegesis in the Church which accepted the view that a text is simply an artefact that can be used for whatever purposes a user desires, the author's use being no better than anyone else's, would soon empty the affirmation of continuity of message of all real content.

In the *second* mode of free decision, where I as an individual, and without reference to the Church, choose to regard myself as involved with or interested by the biblical text, this primacy of the author's message can still be recognised, but such recognition is much less likely. If I am only concerned with a part of the message, or with one or more of the aspects of the text in which it is embodied, I will be less anxious to recover the meaning intended by the author.

This distinction between attention to the text simply *qua*

text, and attention to the text *qua* expression of the message of an author does not quite coincide with the distinction between exegesis in the academy and exegesis in the Church, but it serves to make that distinction clearer. In the Church, study of the Bible must find its finality in study of the text seen as the message of an author, and the actualisation of this message as the word of life for the present generation by a 'prolongation' of the sense intended by the author. By contrast: outside the ecclesial framework, whereas such an attitude remains a possibility, just as one might study the texts of Plato or Confucius as helpful for human living today, it is not the only attitude possible, nor can it be regarded as somehow privileged in respect of other approaches, where the text is seen simply as a literary work or is valued for the light it throws on other areas of knowledge, according to the researcher's intentions.

Actualisation within the Bible

The great value of historical-critical exegesis has lain in its emphasising the historical character of the biblical message, as something addressed to the men of a determinate time and culture, speaking to them in the midst of their concrete humanity, with help to offer them in their particular problems. Thanks to this scholarly literature, the Bible has gained in vitality. Its message is no longer treated as something intemporal, but as directed to beings of flesh and blood. The 'biblical renewal' of the years following the Second World War popularised this literature for the Catholic public, which thereby discovered the human features of the men of the Bible, and the incarnation of the biblical work in a concrete history enacted by living human beings.[20]

Only gradually was the reverse side of the coin shown to view. Little by little, the realisation dawned that it was not to us that the biblical message was addressed. Dreyfus finds a helpful example in the Pauline doctrine of marriage and virginity. Would Paul have reaffirmed this teaching had he lived now? Or is it not the case that his principle, 'Let each remain in the state to which he was called'[21] depends on a conviction of the imminence of the Parousia which proved to be ill-founded? Perhaps exegetes might hope to leave the resolution of this question to theologians and moralists, but these gentlemen reply that their rôle is to present in synthetic fashion the revealed *donné* as attested by Scripture, and to seek an understanding thereof by using all the pertinent resources of human knowledge: it is not their place to construe the meaning of some single determinate biblical text.

Yet the problem thus posed – how to render actual a word or text which has in view a situation different from our own – was faced by the biblical writers themselves. They too confronted such questions as: how can the customary law of semi-nomadic tribes be applied in a monarchical polity strongly centralised even in its worship? How can the writings of a prophet addressing himself to the great ones of the kingdom of Judah in a precise political setting be of value to an exiled population on the eve of their return? How can the preaching of Jesus to Jewish hearers be the word of life for a Christian community whose problems are of a markedly different kind? The actualisation of the biblical text by other texts within the Bible can serve as our model for the actualisation of the texts of the Bible as a whole in that Church which lives on after the making of the Bible is completed.

It is generally agreed that, in the Scriptures, we can glimpse a process of adaptation and accommodation, or the renewal and reorientation of earlier texts by later. The book of Deuteronomy, for example, shows the desire to actualise ancient traditions, Yahwistic or Elohistic, in new situations; the work of the Chronicler involves a fresh actualisation of that of the Deuteronomic historian *vis-à-vis* the novel features of the community of Israel at the end of the Persian period; the book of Isaiah consists of successive reactualisations of the message of the prophet, and so forth.[22] What has been less attended to is the *foundation* of this inner-biblical actualising process. Whence did the conviction arise that a word addressed to one group, in one situation, held good for another group dissimilarly placed?

Dreyfus finds the answer in Israel's conviction that the people of God is *one*, with a quasi-organic unity, of such a kind that it forms a single personal reality, despite its dispersion over time and through space. The English Old Testament scholar, H. Wheeler Robinson, who underlined the importance of this notion of 'corporate personality', described it as a 'Hebrew conception', yet it also has its vital rôle in the New Testament where it is resumed and trans-figured in christological terms.[23] The corporate personality of Israel becomes the union between the head, Christ, and his members, whether that be expressed in its Pauline form of the doctrine of the body of Christ or in the Johannine metaphor of the vine and its branches.

Dreyfus recalls the chief characteristics of corporate personality as Wheeler Robinson describes them. First, it reaches out into both past and future. Past generations and those still unborn are alike united in the present generation, the bond of their union being the common ancestor, who lives on in his descendants. Secondly, it is not a matter of a merely 'moral person', much less of a literary personification, but of something far more real. Thirdly, there is a fluidity of passage between the individual as representing the community, and the community as expressing itself in the individual. Fourthly, the idea of corporate personality by no means evaporates at the moment when the individual is recognised in and for himself, and with that new sense of individual identity a new sense, too, of individual responsibility arises.[24]

Whereas for modern readers, the connection between, say, the situation of Hosea and their own had to be demonstrated, for those who lived by the principles of corporate personality it could be taken for granted. For this mentality, the particular situation of the one fraction of God's people to which the message of a biblical author was directed is immediately relevant to that people as a whole. It is the same 'personality' which is addressed at different stages of its life, its transgressions compared either with a faithful past or with earlier sins. And so the present generation experiences itself as involved with the history of earlier ones, concerned with that history as a decisive factor in the determination of its own behaviour. And this is so not just in terms of examples to follow or avoid, but as a matter of preserving the present from the pernicious contagion of the sin of earlier generations and opening the present to the beneficent influences issuing from the friends of God in times past. Pronouncements about the events of the past, and the reactions of the generations engaged by these pronouncements, appeared immediately significant for the men and women of the present generation, an element in their own destiny.

Nor did the growing sense of the individual snuff out this spirit. From the period of the Exile, with its greater individualism or personalism come the Isaianic songs of the Servant, the 'I' of the post-exilic psalms, and the Danielic vision of the Son of Man, at once the corporate Israel and its angelic guardian. Thus in, for example, the prayer of Esdras the sins of the fathers and those of contemporaries are not distinguished; in Nehemiah we read that the Lord 'has been just in all that has happened to *us*', and in Daniel that '*We* have sinned, *we* committed iniquity ... *we* did not listen to the servants, the prophets'.[25] This consciousness of forming a diachronic unity remained very much alive in post-biblical Judaism, and endures today as a striking feature of the synagogue liturgy.

In the New Testament, the force of such language is undiminished. In Galatians, for instance, we read that, 'before the coming of faith, *we* were enclosed under the guardianship of the Law; thus the Law served *us* as a pedagogue'; in Ephesians, 'It was in him that *we* were set apart'; in Romans, Paul tells that church, 'Once *you* were disobedient to God ...' and so on.[26] The concept, as recovered by Wheeler Robinson, is clearly of importance for our understanding of the biblical books. We tend perhaps to think of, say, the post-exilic prophets as *replacing*, by their stress on weal, the emphasis on woe typical of their pre-exilic predecessors. But the contemporary contributions are, it may be, better thought of as *added* to those of the past, manifesting, certainly, new dimensions, but not calling into question the actuality of the older words. The severe warnings of the older prophets remained in vigour. The ancient word stayed ever actual. It was not to be annulled but to be completed, in view of new situations, thanks to the explicitation and exploration of elements always present, at least implicitly, but hitherto little developed.

Within the biblical period, such awareness of the unicity – the unique unity – of the people, and of the presence of the past in the present, was celebrated in the worship of the liturgy which sustained and even perhaps formed this conviction. The festival was a quasi-sacramental presentation of the founding event within the present celebration. It is likely that such a concept has its roots in a widespread religious institution of the ancient Middle East far beyond the boundaries of Israel: in the nature festivals which placed land and people in a position to receive the divine energies which alone could assure fertility to soil and man alike. The historicisation of these feasts, according to Dreyfus, did not so much change these conceptions as give them a new arena in which to be deployed. Henceforth, what was in question was those divine energies which once had been at work in the founding historical events of the past, and now became present again in the cultic celebration. As the Mishnah will put it:

From generation to generation, each man has the duty to consider himself as personally having come out of Egypt, for it is written, 'On that day, you will tell your son, It is because of what the Lord did for me at the time of my departure from Egypt'.[27]

In this perspective, the primary object of actualisation in the Old Testament must surely be the Exodus: the founding event of Israel's salvation, not a text or message but an *act* of God.

In the New Testament this perspective is not abolished but brought to its fulfilment. The Exodus is replaced by the definitive divine act, prefigured, only, by the escape from civil bondage. The Paschal mystery, Christ's saving death and resurrection, has its own cultic reenactment, the Eucharistic celebration; no actualisation of the word of God has truth unless in some connexion with this. As guaranteed by the word, there the Logos made flesh is present, and to him the faithful are actually united in the unity of his body.[28] The parallelism of function here between the Exodus and the mystery of Christ's Passover brings Dreyfus to the important subject, in this context, of *typology*: a key element in the inner-biblical actualisation of Scripture.

In general, biblical typology depends for its credibility upon two postulates: the consistency of the divine action, and the consistency of human behaviour, human response. But more especially, Dreyfus identifies three different ways in which, conformably with these axioms, typological correspondences could be highlighted. First, the task of actualising some scriptural text may be facilitated by the fact that the original author deliberately created, in his description of various figures, models for future generations. Thus, according to the distinguished German exegete, Claus Westermann, in the Yahwist's account of human origins, Adam stands beneath a sign which reads, 'See what Man is!'[29] Each and every *adam* is meant to draw inferences for his own life from the life of the first man in his representativeness: the need for obedience to God, the possibility of victory over temptation, and the recognition that everything is a gift of God. Abraham too is described, implicitly, in exemplary terms, as a model by which all Israel is called to live: in his personal history, all future generations of Israel come into view.[30] Something analogous can be said of Moses, David and others, and this process reaches its climax in, once again, the central figure of the New Testament, the new Adam, of whom Pilate remarks, with Johannine irony, 'Behold the man!'[31] Secondly, we can find in the Psalms a different kind of typological actualisation, which consists in applying to the individual those events of the past which once the entire people had lived out. Psalm 23, for example, applies to the faithful individual what Deuteronomy has to say of the whole people as guided by God, and what second Isaiah declares about the new Exodus.[32] Deuteronomy itself, moreover, had already made the manna of Exodus into a symbol of God's creative word by which the individual Israelite is to live. And yet the context, as always, remains corporate: such attention to individuals is not bestowed in an individualist fashion, but by emphasising, within the corporate whole, the responsibilities and duties of each. Thirdly, we can also trace the workings of what Dreyfus terms a 'spiritualising' kind of actualisation. Certain narratives, institutions and rites are reinterpreted so as to give expression to a reality which is more interior, more spiritual – without, however, ever becoming discarnate. So for instance, in Psalm 51, the psalmist invokes the rite of purification after leprosy (by a sprinkling with hyssop branches) in order to express his desire to be purified from his sins.[33] In Hosea 14, the prophet says, on behalf of the people, 'We offer you our bulls – our lips.'[34] In Jeremiah 9, the circumcision of the body becomes that of the heart.[35] And Joel 22 picks up a similar theme: 'Rend your hearts, not your garments.'[36] In many of these cases, so Dreyfus notes, such a transposed significance may well be earlier in date than texts describing the divine institution of the relevant custom – so that at the moment when the custom appears as divinely originated it already contains its typological meaning. The practice is already 'sacramental' in that its further spiritual actualisation is already prepared. The typological relation of, say, circumcision to Christian baptism no longer seems so artificial when one realises that the priestly codification of circumcision in Genesis 17 is later than the oracles of Jeremiah proclaiming that the true circumcision is that of the heart.[37]

But despite the undoubted importance of such exemplary individualising and spiritualising typology, the most crucial kind of actualisation found taking place within Scripture is, for Dreyfus, the re-reading of a text in the light of some subsequent event. Although the 'promise-fulfilment' schema is the most familiar instance of this, the process concerned does not stop there. Chapters 9 to 11 of Romans, for example, amount to an actualising *relecture* of the great stages of the biblical history in the light of that new (and disconcerting) fact which was the refusal of the majority of Israel to accept the Messiah.

But the central event which concerns us in this perspective must be, as already indicated, the mystery of the Passover of Christ.[38] In the New Testament, the death and resurrection of Christ bathe in the fresh radiance of the Easter light the narratives of Jesus' baptism, his temptation in the wilderness, his transfiguration. The Paschal mystery is presented as that central reality which gives meaning to the entire condition of the Christian: his or her baptism, sufferings, trials, death take on new meaning by their association with the death of Christ. Similarly, the new life manifested in the Christian's various activities, and the shaping of the latter by faith, hope and charity, are the unfolding of a sharing in the life of the risen Lord. Here it is not a question of the event of Easter interpreting a text in order to actualise it, but of the event interpreting the Christian's daily life to give it meaning, and it is this interpretation which is preserved in the biblical text. Here we glimpse an aspect of our subject which will detain us later: not so much actualisation of an earlier text by a later but actualisation of event by event: the central Paschal event giving profound, evangelical meaning to the events of daily life.

Reciprocally, however, the New Testament authors present the Paschal mystery as itself interpreted by events and teachings both anterior and posterior in time, precisely so as to render their message actual. Thus while the earliest kerygmatic speeches of Acts do not present the death of the Messiah in sacrificial terms, that sacrificial interpretation soon followed when the events of the Passion were illuminated by remembered words of Jesus on how his life would be given as a ransom for the multitude.

The event of the death and resurrection of Christ stands in the same relation to the Old Testament as it does to the rest of the New Testament. It is an event at once interpreting and interpreted. The New Testament authors actualised the ancient biblical texts by means of their relationship to the mystery of Christ. In itself, so Dreyfus maintains, the primary thrust of the Old Testament is by no means self-evident. That Testament contains a plurality of messages each of which corresponds to the intention of a different author and the *ensemble* of these messages can be interpreted in markedly different ways, depending on which elements one chooses to privilege. Why should, for example, Isaiah and Hosea be deemed more weighty than, say, Leviticus and Ezra? The selection process concerned has been carried out quite diversely in different communities, stemming from the biblical revelation. Whereas post-exilic Judaism privileged the five books of Moses, the Christian tradition has placed its stress, rather, on the Old Testament's promises, prophecies and eschatological *dicta*, all of which are now seen to have their fulfilment in Jesus Christ and his Paschal mystery. Though the Old Testament's texts can provide a basis for both the one choice and the other, they impose neither. The true reasons for the choice lie in the convictions of the believing community in each case.

As Dreyfus points out, the great majority of New Testament writers actualise the Old Testament texts in relation to the mystery of Christ. Thus when the Letter to the Ephesians recalls the fourth commandment, 'Honour your father and your mother', it is in the context of a general exhortation to life in Christ, and the mention of the Decalogue is immediately preceded by the invitation: 'children, obey your parents in the Lord'.[39] The same is true of the *relecture* of the Genesis texts in Ephesians, on the institution of marriage at humanity's beginnings: these texts are now re-read and actualised in the light of the mystery of Christ and his Church.

Paul too treats such outstanding Old Testament themes as the relation of the Law to the promises, and the doctrines of election and a faithful remnant, in the light of the Paschal mystery. He recognises but one explanatory principle for all of these: Christ as the saviour of every human being, through faith.[40]

Sometimes, Dreyfus confesses, this actualising re-reading of the Old Testament text in the light of the Paschal event highlights what is only a quite secondary aspect of the original text. Thus the citations of an Isaianic oracle of deliverance in St Luke's account of Jesus' preaching in the Nazareth synagogue leaves in shadow the nationalist, and narrowly temporal, quality of the original. And yet, thus repositioned in the new context of Jesus' redemptive mission, the oracle is not thereby de-natured. For, seen in the setting of the book of Isaiah as a whole, where it enjoyed a relationship with the Songs of the Servant (and notably the fourth of these), the original oracle was already affected by concerns not only temporal and national but also spiritual and missionary. Starting out from the conviction that the ancient word is ever valid, and always eloquent with counsel for living in new situations in salvation history, the word of the past is interrogated anew, and with the help of the novel angle of vision, fresh dimensions are discovered within it. Although the biblical authors had not reflected on the conditions of possibility for historical understanding, they realised spontaneously, so Dreyfus believes, what H.-G. Gadamer terms the 'fusion of horizons': that of the ancient word with that of the new situation.

But in so doing, did they respect the primitive message or did they merely exploit it?[41] Some exegetes would accuse the biblical writers of falsifying the message they wished to actualise, whether that of the Old Testament by the New, or that of Jesus by the evangelists and apostolic writers. It is a faith conviction of the Catholic Church, expressed most recently in the Constitution *Dei verbum* that while the evangelists may not have reproduced with material fidelity the words and actions of Jesus they did not deform their meaning.[42] And this Dreyfus extends to cover inner-biblical actualisation in general: if the Holy Spirit is at every point at work in the making of the biblical corpus, it seems improbable that earlier texts and later could be related only by reciprocal contestation or outright contradiction – even though there may be, certainly, some tension between the thought of the original author and that of his 'continuators' and 'glossators'. So too tension can exist, after all, between different areas of the thinking of the *same* author.

The problem is, Dreyfus admits, thorny, yet it is not, he avers, intractable. In the first place, the faithfulness of a later author to a more primitive message is sometimes disputed on the basis of a questionable understanding of the original and its successive re-readings – as, for example, in the case of a root-and-branch rejection of all elements of the prophecy of salvation (over against that of condemnation) in the preaching of Isaiah. But more widely, the faithfulness at issue in inner-biblical actualisation should not be conceived, Dreyfus warns, too rigidly: it suffices that what the actualisation finds in the original was genuinely present in germ, even if in only a secondary fashion. And as is shown by the continuing rôle of the great masters of the past in modern thought, it is quite possible for the fundamental intuitions of an ancient writer to endure even when the limitations imposed by a past culture, with its imperfect apprehension of the real, are left behind.[43]

The post-biblical actualisation of Scripture in the Church

In the post-biblical period, the organic unity of the people of God continues to be the foundation for the actualisation of Scripture.[44] In Scholastic fashion, Dreyfus defends this assertion by reference to final and efficient causality in Scripture's making. Considered from the viewpoint of its end, Scripture exists for the service of the growth of the total Christ, until Christ's Church-body reaches perfect stature in his Parousia. Considered from the viewpoint of its source, the hallmark of the Bible is its divine origin as the work of men moved by God in a unique way, thanks to the charism of inspiration. And here only the Church can be regarded as the adequate *destinataire* of Scripture, since only she is 'proportioned' to its author, raised up by grace as she is to be the Bride of the Son of God.

For Dreyfus, if a word twenty or thirty centuries old remains the word of life for Christians today, this is not, in the main, owing to some universal – in the sense of atemporal – dimension which the biblical word possesses. Rather is it because any partial word forms part of that totality which is the word of God to his Church, a word which, along with other gifts of God, has as its function the nourishing of the Church's life in all her members. Only as a part of the whole does a given verse now possess its meaning, and it only has meaning for me in my capacity as member of the body of Christ. It is the Church who is by nature in a position to discern what is the particular refinement added by a given passage, the proper note which it contributes to the symphony of divine revelation, once reinserted into that totality where the Church hears the word of God addressed to her by the Holy Spirit. It is an abiding conviction of the Church's tradition that this actually valid meaning of Scripture exists. The various interpretative schemes elaborated in the course of her history, from Origen to liberation theology, have always had this aim: the finding of a key which allows us to disengage, beyond an historical sense now *passé*, the 'actual' sense offered to the Church today.[45]

However, in his insistence on the Church as the only adequate *destinataire* of the Bible in its global wholeness, Dreyfus does not intend to prevent each *Christifidelis* from taking the Scriptures as nourishment for his or her own Christian life. Yet the first has, for him, an all-important priority over the second. Drawing on St Paul's biological analogy, Dreyfus insists that the absorption of the scriptural food is done by specialised organs which work for the good of the whole body, transmitting to each cell what is necessary for its own development. Among the people of God there are, in other words, special persons and institutions charged with studying and meditating upon the Bible so as to actualise it for the benefit of the faithful at large, in relation to circumstances, pastoral needs and the capacity of their hearers.[46]

Here Dreyfus pauses to consider an objection. For Ben Sirach wisdom was the privilege of a well-instructed élite with higher education, so that it was scarcely possible for, say, a manual labourer, in his view, to become, by meditation upon God's covenant, a wise man. But with Jesus things stand otherwise. He chose as his apostles men with little education, lacking a high culture, and, as we have seen, declared the 'little ones', *hoi nêpioi*, to be the favoured recipients of revelation. True, such 'little ones' would find it difficult to grasp this revelation in its scriptural form – for lack of the necessary education and culture – although this obstacle is to some extent disappearing in the developed countries of the world, thanks to the progress of education and the democratisation of culture by printing. But does this mean that, in the fifteen centuries or more when these blessings were as yet unbestowed, a means of salvation necessary or at least highly useful to the multitude was available to the learned and well-to-do, but inaccessible to the little ones themselves? The liturgy provided a medium whereby the most important texts might become available to all, yet this was, at best, only a selection. These reflections lead Dreyfus to a statement at once candid and nuanced, of the *relative* significance of the Bible as the written word of God.[47] In its written form, the word is but a letter and, moreover, a letter which, if taken in isolation, kills, even if it be the letter of a gospel. The Scriptures are the word of life for the today of the Church only if they serve other salvific realities of a more fundamental kind: Christ, as Word Incarnate; the divine life brought about by the grace of the Holy Spirit; the sacraments of faith; the life and teaching of the Church, considered as drawing us to the Father. Whereas Scripture has, in permanence, a unique place as the normative and immediately accessible word of God thanks to its written character (*littera scripta manet*), this privileged rôle is exercised at the level of the Church *taken as a whole*, rather than on that of the individual faithful, whether he or she be scholar or illiterate. For the individual believer, pride of place must go, not to the written text but to the word of God as interpreted and actualised by the living community, the body of Christ of which he forms part. And Dreyfus does not hesitate to absolve of error the decision of the Church to restrict the circulation of the vernacular Scriptures at certain times of crisis, when heresiarchs were appealing to the text in a unilateral way. He concludes that the 'normal' form of the actualisation of the Bible is the concrete pastoral activity of the Church, addressing herself to different categories of the faithful according to their needs, in preaching, liturgical and sacramental life, catechesis, and by charity in all its inventiveness.

To illuminate this relative significance of the Bible in the Church, Dreyfus reminds his readers of the classical distinction between the three régimes in the relation of God and his people. First, we have the régime of the Old Testament where

God spoke to his people and acted on its behalf through institutions, events and elect persons, the word of God transmitted by the prophets and sacred writers taking as its particular function the clarification of the meaning of the institutions, events and life-stories which prepared and figured forth the realities to come. Secondly, there is the age of those realities – the régime of glory, where God will reveal himself in an immediate fashion to the people of the redeemed, by face-to-face vision, all other manifestations of the divine becoming thenceforward otiose. Thirdly, there comes the actual régime of the Church, an intermediary state between the first two. Here the definitive reality is truly yet imperfectly present as new life in the Spirit of the risen Christ. In this present régime the divine word and action are realised chiefly in Christ as head of the Church, a head who lives in each of his members by his Spirit. Scripture, the apostolic ministry, the sacraments, are at the service of this foundational reality in which the Paschal mystery is realised in the Church and in each believer who lives out the life of the Risen One and shares in his condition of abiding self-offering to the Father.

To Dreyfus, this distinction is capital for our subject. In the régime of the new Law, Scripture no longer has the leading rôle which it enjoyed in the old Covenant, and this is true not only of the Old Testament but of the New as well. Henceforth God communicates himself to man in a fashion deeper than by words, events or institutions: he gives us himself, a share in his triune life. But, since it is the same God who communicates himself in Scripture and by the gift of his life, and as the first of those communications is ordered to the second, the Church, and each Christian, can discover ever more fully the affinity, or even identity, that holds good between what is heard in Scripture and what is lived out by the sending of the Holy Spirit. And yet the coming of this more fundamental reality does not render Scripture redundant as will be the case in glory, when life in Christ reaches its plenitude. In our present condition, the reality of our friendship with the Holy Trinity is lived in faith. It needs the Bible, as it needs the other means of salvation, in order to be recognised and pursued in conscious fashion. As yet, the divine life is not an object of direct intuition: it is discovered only by the mediation of the historic revelation which manifests to man, after Good Friday, Easter and Pentecost, what, as on the way of redemption, he now is. If we accept the principle of St Thomas that everything contained in the New Testament is relative to this life in the Holy Spirit 'either as disposing to, or as giving precepts about, the use of this grace', then the actual meaning of a scriptural text will not be found, under this intermediary régime of the Church, at the end of a hermeneutical process of a purely noetic type. Rather does the biblical text point us on towards some facet of Christian experience: the experience of Christ, slain and triumphant, living in his Church by the Spirit.

Difficulties arise, however, when we attempt to infer a concrete method of reading Scripture from this general principle that the only adequate actualisation of Scripture is made by the community which shares in this experience. Dreyfus identifies three obstacles. First, there is the characteristic 'temptation of the group': to find in Scripture only a confirmation of what some grouping already thinks and does, neglecting the invitation of the word of God to enlarge horizons, to modify attitudes. This can be overcome only by an encounter with the historically original meaning of the text, the foundation meaning which should govern actualisation in some fashion, since actualisation must be homogeneous with the historic sense and follow from it, though taking into account both changed circumstances and the entirety of the Christian mystery. Secondly, there is the typical 'temptation of the sect': to deny the existence of a variety of sub-traditions which have actualised the text in a different way from one's own. This can be overcome only by the development of an ecumenical spirit – in the broadest sense of that word – which takes up the questions posed by other interpretations of the text, and makes an honest attempt to respond to them. (Later, Dreyfus will have more to say about the distinction, so necessary here, between authentic Tradition and possibly deviant traditions.)

But Dreyfus reserves his sharpest aperçus for a third obstacle: the problem of that inescapable 'pre-understanding'. The relation between the life of the community and Scripture is always read with the aid of a certain grid, which is provided by the distinctive mind-set, and the particular ideological and philosophical convictions or assumptions, of some determinate milieu. This grid, so Dreyfus warns, easily turns into a lens which would filter what we read and distort it. He will subsequently describe the task of Tradition and magisterium in the Church as the reducing – never, alas, the entire elimination – of this danger.[48]

In the meantime, he turns to the privileged locus of the post-biblical actualisation of Scripture, which we have already identified as the liturgical celebration of the events of salvation. In the liturgy of the Church, the presence of Christ and his mystery is celebrated in his body, and it is by that presence that the actualisation of Scripture is chiefly assured. The Constitution of the Second Vatican Council on the sacred liturgy, *Sacrosanctum Concilium*, spells out the essential points.[49] Its centre in the Holy Eucharist, the liturgy realises the presence of Christ in his Paschal mystery, so represented as to render the community contemporary with the Paschal event. The liturgy brings about the unity of the Church as body of Christ with its head: the *totus Christus*. In it, the present community becomes contemporary in and through its Lord with all generations of the people of God, past, present and future. Above all, here the future, definitive reality of the kingdom is not only signified, but is already truly present: the life of the Age to Come is really given.

The liturgy, so Dreyfus points out, has always been the locus *par excellence* for the actualisation of Scripture for

Judaism and Christianity.[50] For the Jewish tradition, it is relevant to note the liturgical translations of Scripture (the Greek Septuagint, the Aramaic targums), which were often an actualising adaptation of the text. Furthermore, much of the Midrashic literature is made up of liturgical homilies on the biblical text, read in the synagogue office of the Sabbath: and, as far as the Christian tradition is concerned, such actualising commentary continued in the liturgical sermons which, for the age of the Fathers, constituted the Church's chief actualising form. Such homilies are for Dreyfus, indeed, the principal aim of ecclesial exegesis. After all, the homily prepares the way for participation in the eucharistic Sacrifice and holy Communion, thus reflecting the fact that, within the Christian community, the actualisation of the Bible takes place by the relating of the texts to the mystery of Christ.

The two main modes of actualisation employed at this privileged place continue those we have already found in the inner-biblical *relecture* of Scripture: *typological actualisation*, and *actualisation by event*, modes distinct, yet not separate, but, rather, in constant interaction.

Unfortunately, so Dreyfus relates, the history of the Church provides us with examples of *typological actualisation* of an unacceptable kind: the justification of the Crusades, for instance, in terms of the Hebrew wars against the Canaanites, or the legitimising of the enslavement of the native pagans of America by reference to the subjugation of Moab by King David. In each case, some situation or kind of behaviour was supported by appeal to an isolated Old Testament exemplar, without asking whether other biblical texts or events with a more central location (because more closely related to the heart of Christian revelation, the mystery of Christ) might not call into question the practices concerned.[51] For Dreyfus, the most finished example of such contestable typological actualisation is J.-B. Bossuet's treatise, *Politique tirée des propres paroles de l'Ecriture sainte* ('Politics Drawn from the Very Words of Holy Scripture'), written for the guidance of Louis XIV and scarcely more than an exposition of the political notions current among the leading classes of the society of the day.[52] In the opinion of Dreyfus, Bossuet's exposition is not greatly superior in method to that of Westermann.[53] From the scene where Joseph resists the wife of Potiphar, Westermann draws the conclusion that, since this story is more concerned with Joseph's refusal to betray the confidence of his master than it is with the triumph of chastity, we should not regard sexual acts as either reprehensible or otherwise *per se*, but only in some wider ethical context. Or again, from Joseph's planning remedial action for the Egyptian famine, Westermann infers that the Church should take a more positive view of the human sciences. A laudable sentiment – but hardly one that follows from the original message of Genesis.[54]

At the other pole to this attitude is the view of Westermann's co-national, Martin Noth, that we can never actualise the models presented by persons or historical situations in Scripture, since these belong ineluctably to the past. To try to do so would be, implicitly, to adopt a cyclical view of time, foreign to Scripture itself. Only the divine acts, so Noth believed, are actualisable. And yet, as Dreyfus underscores, the divine acts are known only in their created effects which are as much caught up in time as are biblical persons and situations.[55]

That Noth is too restrictive here can be seen by reference to what we have already accepted, in the company of Dreyfus, as the basic axioms of typology in the context of the inner-biblical actualisation of Scripture: the permanent commitment of God to his own plan of salvation, and, in consequence of this, a consistency in the relation of God to man, founded not only on this permanence of the divine purpose but also on something invariant from the human side – something about man which mutations of culture, society and religion cannot suppress, though they may conceal. If this twofold continuity is real then it must manifest itself in

some way in the course of the history of God's people by a
perception, at various moments, of some similarity between
the biblical situation and the contemporary one.[56] From this
criterion of continuity it follows that a postulated actualisation of Scripture which lacks antecedents in tradition is sus-
pect, though not wholly disqualified. If it is to be justified it
must show the more thoroughly a correspondence between
the two situations involved.

Reflection on the continuity of human responsiveness in
the context of the Church leads Dreyfus to disengage a
further criterion for the post-biblical actualisation of Scripture: the life of the community. For here the more specific
foundation for human continuity is furnished by the unity of
the people of God, and that people's entry upon the new age
of salvation thanks to the missions of the Son and Spirit.
Consequently, the post-biblical actualisation of Scripture also
turns on ecclesial 'praxis', seen as animated by the Spirit of
Christ living in the Church.[57] Dreyfus gives us as example the
Sermon on the Mount with its interdictions on both divorce
and the making of oaths.[58] One of these texts has been interpreted in Christian tradition as a law, whilst the other
has been seen (leaving aside here certain fundamentalist
groups) as simply an exhortation always to tell the truth: a
simple yea or nay should be as worthy of trust as if it were
accompanied by an oath. Such a distinction can hardly be
demonstrated by the strict exegete. Only the working of
the Holy Spirit of Christ has enabled the Church to discern
whether a given text has the value of law or merely that of
exhortation.

When looking at the basic ground rules for the post-
biblical actualisation of Scripture, Dreyfus has already stated
his fundamental principle that the actualisation of a scriptural word must always be done by reference to that Word of
God *par excellence* who is Jesus Christ, present in his
Church, and more fully grasped there in the measure that,
under the Spirit's influence, the 'total Christ' develops. And

this now brings Dreyfus to the second main mode of the ecclesial actualising of the Bible: *actualisation by event*.

He thinks of this as working itself out in four ways: directly ecclesial events; 'cultural' events; 'historical' events, and 'personal' events.[59] Ecclesial events, the events of the life of the Church, play an important part in the better understanding of the word of God. These events which constitute the appearance of such heretical doctrines as Arianism or Pelagianism, for instance, though mainly negative, also had a positive side in that they brought the Church to refine her grasp of the mystery by which she lives. And because the Church lives in a perpetual symbiosis with the world, secular events too can play a part here. *Gaudium et spes*, the pastoral Constitution of the Second Vatican Council on the Church in the modern world, recognises a rôle here for what may be termed, broadly enough, 'cultural' events.[60] The development of natural science, for instance, has led the Church to actualise Genesis 1 not so much in terms of its explicit cosmology as in those of its implicit theological message. Or again, with the development of the human understanding of political society, there has been an increasing recognition – at first sight problematic for the actualisation of, for example, Pauline texts on civil authority – that human beings should freely and responsibly, in association one with another, arrange the governmental type of their society, choose its leaders, and determine their powers. Here one will want to maintain the principle, laid down in Romans, that obedience to authority is always required, since its foundation lies in the divine origin of power.[61] But the obedience itself will be construed chiefly on the model of that which the legislator owes his own laws. Parenetically, the Romans text will be actualised by inviting the Christian fully to exercise his responsibilities as a citizen, in the perspective of an evangelical renunciation of private interest for the sake of the common good. Such an actualisation links up with the central point of all actualisation of Scripture: the Paschal mystery of Christ.

In place of a passive obedience to authority, the believer is invited to an active collaboration with God's plan, to a share in the kingship which Christ exercises over the world, but with an accompanying recognition of the demand that this brings: imitation of the Christ who came to serve, and not to be served.

After cultural events come 'historical': events in the order of political action, affecting man in his social existence. Such a factor in actualisation recalls the issue of typology, since here we are dealing with events bearing some analogical likeness to biblical events, setting off the dialectic of reciprocal interpretation between event and text. Dreyfus cites the long captivity of French prisoners held by the Germans in the Second World War, an experience which recalled, for the believers among them, Israel's captivity in Babylon. The German captivity interpreted the biblical text thanks to a 'connaturality' between the mind-set of the modern prisoners and the biblical deportees. The prisoners in Germany, it seems, were chiefly interested in what was happening back in France, rather than amongst themselves, inclining Dreyfus to reject the critical suggestion that Ezekiel's pre-587 oracles were pronounced in Judaea, for which hypothesis the argument usually offered is the prophet's lack of interest in the life of the exiles themselves. Again, Ezekiel has been taxed with mental imbalance on the grounds of the Utopian nature of his restoration programme: but such a proliferation of schemes for a thorough-goingly new society was, Dreyfus recalls, common among even the most balanced personalities of the prisoner-of-war camps. The way in which, in turn, the biblical texts interpret the events lived out by the prisoners of 1939–45 is more problematic, since, on our principles, the text cannot be actualised save in the light of the mystery of Easter, the norm of all post-biblical actualisation. In this perspective, the differences between the biblical captivity and the modern situation spring to the eye. The Christian knows only one 'holy land', that of the heavenly Jerusalem; and the privation of civil freedom is relativised for him – as the Letter to Philemon shows – by the liberation won by Christ. And yet the biblical texts *did* invite the captives to live their uprooting and testing as an invitation to conversion. Their distress made them more receptive to the appeal, Return to God!

Lastly, Dreyfus considers 'personal' events: the happenings of a spiritual life story. Many spiritual authors have noted the correspondence between the text of Scripture and what is lived out by the faithful. Even those mystics who, as lay-women, lacked formal education in matters biblical, such as Catherine of Siena or Teresa of Avila, had abundant recourse to the Bible in order to describe their spiritual experience. This Dreyfus ascribes to a connaturality between the personal experience of the living God which such mystics enjoyed, and the experience of the inspired writers discovering the God of the Covenant and taking it as their mission to make him known to the people he had chosen.

If the actualisation of Scripture happens first and foremost not in a new text but in a new life – Christ living in the Church – it will be, Dreyfus supposes, in the most perfect forms of this Christ-life in the faithful that such actualisation should, above all, be sought. As Bernard of Clairvaux put it, *Quae foris audit intus sentit* ('What they hear without they experience within.')[62] Exegesis should not neglect the light brought by the mystics in, for instance, their description of the sequential stages of the way to God as their writings relate that to various biblical texts, notably the Psalms.

And yet the majority of biblical texts are not describing, by any stretch of the imagination, the life of union with God. Should the comments of the mystics on these other texts be regarded as mere accommodation, pious effusions with no real interpretative value? Dreyfus thinks not. He recalls what has been said already about the typological actualisation of Scripture in its three main procedures: individualising, spiritualising and exemplary typology. Following the first, a mystic may apply to the individual faithful in his or her relations with God what the ancient texts have to say about God's relation with his people as a whole, this procedure being based on the principle of corporate personality. Following the second, a mystical writer might highlight the spiritual dimension of certain realities – institutions, events – which *prima facie* seem purely temporal in significance: in this he or she would be emulating the New Testament practice of treating the Old Testament order as preparation for, and prefiguration of, the salvation wrought by Christ. Following the third, it is characteristic of the mystics' use of Scripture to draw on the fact that a number of biblical personalities are presented by the sacred writers as models, whether for imitation or avoidance. To this Dreyfus adds the larger number of texts which can be described as 'open': prayers, hymns, supplications applied by the mystics to spiritual situations which the original author did not clearly foresee, but which he did not exclude either. Beautifully, Dreyfus pictures these three kinds of typological actualisation as converging on the person and mystery of Christ: the corporate personality of individualising typology is rooted in the *Christus totus*; the spiritualising typology finds its fullness in his Paschal mystery; and the exemplary typology offers paradigms which can lead the faithful towards the condition of perfected humanity in Christ.

The next task for Dreyfus is to consider the Holy Spirit as he who effects this post-biblical actualisation of Scripture. Attention to the Spirit's agency will then lead him naturally to the final topic in his hermeneutics: Tradition and magisterium as the context of the Spirit's action.[63]

The action of the Holy Spirit, and the rôle of Tradition

On the road to Emmaus, it is Christ – the Giver, from the Father, of the pentecostal Spirit – who opens the minds of the disciples to the meaning of the Old Testament.[64] In 2 Peter, moreover, we hear that no prophecy can be the object of purely human interpretation since it was through being impelled by the Spirit that men spoke what came from God.[65] Here authentic interpretation is interpretation made by virtue of the same Spirit who inspired the prophets. These are the classic texts for our subject, but others of more indirect significance can be appended. For Paul, sin acts not only on the ethical personality but also on the intelligence which becomes darkened. Israel's infidelities obscured her understanding so that she no longer grasps the true meaning of the Scriptures. In 2 Corinthians, Paul insists that Israel needs to be healed by the Spirit of God who, through the gift of faith in Christ, will take away the veil from her eyes.[66] Again, in the First Letter to Corinth, Paul remarks that a person must receive the Spirit of God if he is to understand the secret things of God, the revelation of the hidden divine purpose, within which the understanding of Scripture is doubtless included.[67]

The principle remains central in the Fathers. As Jerome testifies, 'In explaining Scripture, we always need the coming of the Holy Spirit.'[68] John Chrysostom echoes this, 'To grasp the divine Scripture we need not human wisdom but the action of the Holy Spirit.'[69] Gregory the Great remarks that:

> It was the all-powerful God who for our salvation fashioned the words of the holy Testaments, and it is he also who opens for us their understanding.[70]

The Middle Ages stayed faithful to the Fathers. William of Saint-Thierry, in his 'Golden Epistle', to the brethren of Mont-Dieu, sums up:

> It is the Spirit who gave birth to the Scriptures who must be at work in those who want to understand them. They demand to be read in the same Spirit.[71]

This statement Thomas Aquinas will cite, in abbreviated

form, on two occasions.[72] In the Reformation period, the Jesuit doctor Robert Bellarmine treats this principle as common to both Catholics and Protestants who, he says, disagree only on the question of where the Spirit is to be found.[73] In the modern period, the teaching has been taken up by the magisterium of the Catholic Church, notably in Benedict XV's encyclical, *Spiritus paraclitus*, in honour of St Jerome, and the conciliar Constitution *Dei verbum*.[74] Taking his cue from these, the current president of the Pontifical Biblical Commission, Henri Cazelles, has this to say:

> Scripture would be unintelligible, inoperant, a dead letter, without the presence of the Spirit who alone gives it meaning and life.[75]

Dreyfus admits, however, that it would be anachronistic to ascribe to Fathers, mediaevals and early modern divines a distinction between those biblical meanings attainable by the critical method alone (*exégèse en Sorbonne*) and those further meanings, found through a hermeneutic of actualisation, which the Spirit alone can make available to human minds (*exégèse en Eglise*). But something analogous *can* be found: in the Lucan episode of the journey to Emmaus, for example, the disciples already possessed in all probability that grasp of the Old Testament which was current in their Jewish milieu – something which corresponds more or less to what we would now regard as the literal sense of the Old Testament, but enriched by an inner-biblical *relecture*. Much the same kind of interpretation would have been in the minds of the Fathers when confronted with the Jewish reading of the Old Testament by their own contemporaries. Similarly, for the New Testament, while ancient commentators did not share our explicit distinction between the words of Jesus, the message of the evangelists and the present message of the texts, they were aware of the need to fill the gap between the text on the one hand and, on the other, such matters as current heresies or pastoral problems on which the resources of the text must be brought to bear.[76]

To Dreyfus it is evident that, for the natural (or rational) interpretation of the Bible, the Spirit's assistance is not indispensable. At best, the Spirit might aid the human mind in a task which of itself is congenial to its own native powers. Were the historical-critical method the sole way to establish Scripture's meaning, the Spirit would have no place in hermeneutics, and it would be absurd to claim (with the Second Vatican Council) that the task of interpreting in authentic fashion the word of God, whether written or transmitted, has been entrusted to the living magisterium of the Church, as the beneficiary of the Spirit's assistance.[77]

The main example Dreyfus gives, of how the Holy Spirit functions as a factor in hermeneutics *vis-à-vis* a wider circle of biblical texts than the few whose meaning is determined in (infallible) magisterial definition, is drawn from 1 Corinthians 7, where Paul is concerned with the relative significance of marriage and celibacy as Christian callings. Commentators disagree as to just how much Paul's preference for celibacy was conditioned by his perception of the peculiar needs of the Corinthians' church, his expectation of the Parousia and the influence of a certain popularised Stoicism in his milieu. Not all the exegetical options can be simultaneously true, varying as these would from the minimalising view that celibacy is, at any rate, a legitimate possibility for a Christian to the maximalising view that it is, as a condition, always superior to marriage since closer to the life-form of the kingdom. Now we have agreed so far that the event which, above all, interprets the biblical text as a whole, and finds interpretation by it, is that abiding event of the Paschal mystery present in the life of the Church and in each of the faithful. But what is in question here is one aspect of this Christ-life in the Church-body. Abundant texts of the patristic period on the virgin as spouse of Christ show the Fathers witnessing to that ascetic movement of the early cen-

turies which impelled very many men and women to embrace
a form of life uniquely consecrated to the Lord and his kingdom, a movement whose only source must be the Holy Spirit.
Tradition, accordingly, has actualised the Pauline text in a
certain direction:

1 Contrary to what might be imagined, Paul's message here is
permanently valid, since it treats of an enduring reality in the
Church's life.
2 The eschatological aspect of Paul's message, connected by
him to the imminent end of time, is both preserved and transformed. Virginity now appears as an anticipation of the
eschatological state where 'they will neither marry nor be given
in marriage, being like the Angels in heaven'.
3 A degree of superiority of celibacy over marriage is unani-
mously affirmed. Not of course a superiority of celibacy *per se*
over marriage *per se*, but that of a celibacy for the kingdom, for
Christ: for the tradition strongly underlines the christological
character of celibacy.

No doubt the Fathers exaggerated the 'inconveniences' of
marriage, yet tradition witnesses to an experience of a profound affinity between celibacy and a life totally consecrated
to Christ. With the help of saints and doctors the later
Church can look back at the Pauline text and better discern
what is transient conditioning and what the invariant, abiding element in its message. More generally, then, the Church
in the course of her own Spirit-guided growth obtains a
deeper grasp of the mystery, and finds, as between the biblical
text and the mystery, new correspondences which life in the
Spirit, both personal and communitarian, discloses.[78]
But what of the rôle of the magisterium in this process?
Dreyfus finds it interesting that, in the official documents of
the Catholic Church, affirmations about the special place of
the magisterium in the interpretation of Scripture become
increasingly insistent *pari passu* with an ever more positive
evaluation of rational (or historical-critical) exegesis. It is in
Dei verbum, indeed, that we find the strongest affirmation of

the magisterium's function as interpreter of Scripture, and it is this same document which goes further than any other in an appreciation of the exegetical methods of modern criticism.

Dreyfus records that, in the Catholic context, introductions to the study of the Bible do not fail to deal with both of these courts of appeal. But the generality of such works are not, in his view, very successful when it comes to articulating the respective rôles of, on the one hand, rational exegesis, and, on the other, that of Tradition and the magisterium *within the unity of the interpretative act*. The problem is that, because rational exegesis studies the sacred text in the same way in which it would study any other contemporary text from the same milieu, the intervention of an argument *ex auctoritate* can only appear as an epistemological thunderbolt, an outside interference. Usually, an attempt is made to surmount this obstacle by speaking here of a twofold contemplation, or a twofold light, that of reason and that of faith, both of which have illumination to offer. As a human work, the biblical text is quite properly studied by human means, following techniques and procedures used for other texts with the same or a cognate provenance. But as a divine work, inspired by the Spirit, its only adequate recipient is, as we have seen, the Church. Possessing the same Spirit as a living and active power, she alone has the necessary instinct or tact for the interpretative enterprise.

This is true; yet it leaves untouched the problem of the interrelation of these two equally necessary approaches. It is insufficient, according to Dreyfus, simply to state the principle that God, in inspiring, respects the autonomy of the human faculties of the biblical author, so that there can be no conflict between the interpretation proposed by reason and that offered by faith. The exegete will inevitably become schizophrenic if no internal or intrinsic connexion can be displayed between the two levels at which he is called to work – the level of critical reason – textual, literary, historical, and so forth, and that of faith, where he must operate with very different materials, drawn as these are from the corpus of the Church's doctrine.

Thus for example in the matter of the 'Jesus of history', the critical exegete, working honestly as an historian on the data he possesses, obliged to make inferences from the fragments bequeathed by the past, may find himself coming to conclusions, admittedly provisional and revisable, which conflict with the articles of faith. The extended example which Dreyfus uses concerns Jesus and Mary: the identity of the 'brothers' of Jesus, the perpetual virginity of Mary. A determination of Scripture by the magisterium on this point seems quite extrinsic to the work of the critical scholar, and might be contested if one holds that the rôle of the magisterium in matters of faith is not to be an arbitrary potentate, but rather the spokesman for a tradition.[79] For Dreyfus, the clue to the resolution of the difficulty lies, in fact, in the latter concept, and more especially in the key notion that the tradition issuing from an event or text is an important element in the understanding of that same text or event.

Even before Rudolf Bultmann, with his distinction between *Historie*, mere history, and *Geschichte*, history as meaningful for human life, thinkers reflecting on the nature of historical understanding had opposed the pseudo-objectivity of an historicism which would assimilate historical study to the natural sciences. As Henri-Irénée Marrou has pointed out, the 'history' of the historian is not so much the past plus the present, as the interrelation of two levels, the past of the event and the present of the historian.[80] The meaning which an event or a text had for contemporaries can and must be distinguished from the meaning it has for me – though it cannot be separated from it. A certain pre-understanding, in Bultmann's term, is inevitable: the crucial thing is to make it as explicit as possible, and to handle it in such a way that we do not close ourselves off from all interrogation by the past of the text or of the event. But what is the rôle of tradition in such *Vorverständnis*? However understood, whether in the existentialist analysis favoured by Bultmann, or in the idea of a fusion of horizons between event or text and interpreter, as in Gadamer, or in the notion of a universal history within which belong both interpreter and interpreted, as with that other giant of a philosophically-alert exegesis, Wolfhart Pannenberg, it is always conceded that the tradition which comes from the event or the text is of value, permitting as it does a better understanding of the object of study and, ultimately, a capacity on the part of the student to criticise and correct his pre-understanding.[81]

Now we have already accepted that, from the moment when the Word became flesh, the actualisation of every biblical text is achieved primarily in the *totus Christus*. This actualisation is not unconditionally new: it is, rather, an aspect of the fullness at which the original text aimed. For this reason, it can never suffice simply to determine the meaning of a biblical text by historical-critical exegesis alone, since this would neglect those dimensions of the Bible which only diachronic study of the tradition deriving from the Bible can make manifest.

And this allows Dreyfus to place his finger on what is specific about the biblical hermeneutic. What distinguishes that hermeneutic from a general literary hermeneutic is that here we are dealing with the interpretation of a text which refers onward to the reality of a mystery. Knowing better that mystery as revealed in the living tradition of the Church, I understand better how a given biblical author, in some passage, has only expressed a part of the mystery, and how his expression was conditioned by his culture and mentality. I also understand better why the communication of God's plan, throughout the biblical period, had to limit itself to whatever its interpreters were able to comprehend and assimilate.[82]

If now we return to the question of the relationship between rational exegesis and that reading of Scripture which is found within the Church's faith, we can say that an act of self-enclosure would be, for rational exegesis, a legitimate step were no other source of illumination of the text available. But in fact the biblical student is able to situate himself within the tradition which stems from the realities that he studies, and in such a way that another, supra-rational, light is constantly available to him. In such a case a self-enclosed critical exegesis is not so much rational as rationalist. And given that the conclusions of rational exegesis themselves claim no absolute certainty, they are open in advance to the modification brought them by new elements.[83]

Having thus established, at least to his own satisfaction, the ground rules of the subject, Dreyfus turns once more by way of exemplification to the issue of the brethren of Jesus. He points out that, first, I enjoy the certitude of faith that in the new and definitive economy of salvation it is primarily the living Christ in his Church who is for me the Word of God, the written biblical word being secondary or relative in comparison. But then, in the second place, within this 'principal Word', I receive through the faith of the Church the certitude, too, of the perpetual virginity of the Mother of God. Suitably fortified, I return to Scripture. There I affirm that, thirdly, granted the dubiety with which rational exegesis must express its conclusions, my certitude is not opposed to the text of Scripture. On the contrary, fourthly, it can lean on arguments whose value historical-critical exegesis must itself recognise. Since I remain therefore within the ambit of critically possible exegetical options, my ecclesially oriented position can hardly be written off as 'eisegesis'.

A dogmatically weightier example is provided by the question of whether Jesus ascribed redemptive significance to his own death. Using the criterion of difference from both the Jewish environment and primitive Christianity, the historical critic arrives at a small number of texts which offer the maximum guarantee of transparency to the *verba et acta ipsissima* of Jesus – his very own words and actions. On their basis, the critic discovers that it cannot be said with certainty whether Jesus regarded his death as a means of salvation for the many, or not. But as Dreyfus points out, it is illegitimate to conclude from this that we have no means of establishing whether Jesus was in fact conscious of offering his life for the salvation of the world. To move from the first position to the second is to pass over from rationality to rationalism. When we realise that we have to do here with a divine mystery, we appreciate that its deep significance need not have been understood straightaway by the most immediate witnesses. The fullness of its meaning would only be found out little by little in the actualisation of the words and deeds of Jesus in the Spirit-directed tradition of the Church. 'I have many things to say to you, but you cannot bear them now.'[84] It is, then, a serious mistake to take the most archaic expressions of the mystery and personality of Jesus as the basis for the reconstruction of doctrine, or for a novel pastoral programme in the Church.[85]

We are moving here towards the application of hermeneutics to the problem of the self-consciousness of the Jesus of the gospels which Dreyfus will carry out in so magisterial a fashion in his *Jésus, savait-il qu'il était Dieu*? But meanwhile he interjects a comment on the patristic notion of *sunkatabasis* or 'condescension', so serviceable in this connexion. *Dei verbum* speaks of the marvellous condescension of the divine Wisdom whereby the words of God, passing through the medium of human tongues, have taken the likeness of the language of men, just as the consubstantial Word, taking upon himself the weakness of our flesh, became like unto us.[86] Here the conciliar constitution refers explicitly to John Chrysostom's commentary on Genesis, and his doctrine appears to be one of the most complete statements of the theme among the Fathers.[87] Constructed in the first instance in the context of anti-Jewish polemic so as to justify the abandonment of the Old Testament ceremonial law, it was taken up by such later Jewish writers as Maimonides, as well as by a wide variety of Christian theologians, not least Calvin. The re-expression of the teaching of Chrysostom, Dreyfus believes, allows for a greater awareness today of the social, historical and cultural mediations whereby the people of God received the revelation of its Lord. For Dreyfus:

1   God has revealed himself in the life and history of his people by inspired men who had as their mission the manifestation of the meaning of this revelation of the divine plan, the goal of which is the eschatological fullness of the kingdom, and the centre of which is Christ.

2   This manifestation of meaning was limited and even countered by the circumambient group mentality of cultural currents with their own dynamism, a dynamism frequently foreign and sometimes actually opposed to the proper dynamism of the divine plan.

3   The tendency of the charism of inspiration is by means of a deeper perception of that plan, to push forward the boundaries of discourse and formulation characteristic of the epoch.

4   That charism contributed therefore to the gradual formation of a new mentality within which the plan of God could be more adequately set forth.[88]

And this enables Dreyfus to state his own conclusions as to the conditions of possibility for the revelation to man of the mystery of the Holy Trinity in the incarnate Son. The disclosure of this mystery encountered three obstacles: a religious mentality which, first, saw the *unum necessarium* as obedience to the Torah, and regarded speculation abut the divine nature as useless, impossible and even sacrilegious; this same mentality, secondly, was importantly shaped by the struggle with idolatry and so with everything which did not coincide with a strict monotheism; thirdly, it was affected by eschatological and apocalyptic expectation – by a certitude that the end of all things is close and a passionate hope for God's triumph over Israel's enemies. In such a situation, the revelation of the mystery of God in Christ could only be piecemeal. In a first moment, only that could be assimilated which corresponded to the mentality of the earliest disciples. Jesus was obliged to run the risk that this mind-set could deleteriously affect his friends' memory of what they had seen and heard, coarsening some points, making too little of others. As a result, between the Word incarnate and what criticism can establish about Jesus of Nazareth, there intervene not only the uncertainties of historical criticism itself, given the fragmentary nature of its materials and the conjectural quality of its criteria for their assessment, but also the fact that the disciples passed on an understanding of Jesus' words and deeds formed within a mind-set often strange to the reality to which they witnessed. And yet the divine condescension throughout limited revelation to what could be humanly understood and accepted.[89]

But here is where the actualisation of Scripture by Tradition comes into its own. Despite these negative features, divine revelation by its very facticity creates a new situation where those who live by what has been transmitted become receivers of the mystery in ways that are gradually made less imperfect. Bit by bit, revelation acts on their mentality, purifying it and attuning it to itself. The Church by her Tradition assures faithfulness to the original deposit among the inhabitants of the always mutating culture in which it is handed down. Tradition, by conserving both the texts and their apostolic understanding in its gradual development, acts as a remedy against the culture-induced malady of syncretism, whose earliest expression was Gnosticism. Where this sickness reigns, Christian specificity is absorbed by the surrounding non-Christian mentality which itself remains unchanged – rather than the Gospel doing the changing. Tradition, inasmuch as it carries what is authentic and abiding, always contests the dominant mentality of an epoch.[90]

For Dreyfus, while the revelation of the word of God is now closed, it continues for the whole timespan of the régime of the Church to develop its virtualities, to pass from the obscure to the clear, from the implicit to the explicit, from the seed to the fruit. Through the growth of the body, the *sensus fidei* of Christ's people discovers more of the Gospel's fullness. But this sense of faith needs a qualified organ if it is to attain to the dignity of propositional expression where truth can be communicated with authority. Though few doctrinal determinations of the Church's tradition claim to determine the sense of an individual biblical text, the *ensemble* of the declarations of the Church's magisterium do permit an actualising *relecture* of many biblical texts. The Church's doctrine points to a deeper dimension of these texts than that which rational exegesis can reach. The magisterium however, invites the exegetes to show the homogeneity between what the Church lives and believes today, and the voice of Scripture itself.[91] If I understand him aright, Dreyfus thus invites his readers to step within a virtuous circle – Tradition, articulated by the magisterium, provides the necessary context for the Christian reading of Scripture, yet Scripture, invoked by the magisterium (frequently enough, no doubt, under the stimulus of Church reformers), and explored within its watchful care, permits the distinguishing of authentic Tradition from deviant (human) traditions. This places on the bishops an awesome burden, but, in the Great Church, was it not ever thus? Catholic dogmatic theology is indebted to Père Dreyfus for his original re-statement of its own exegetical foundations.

III

T. S. Eliot and Yves Congar on the Nature of Tradition

T. S. Eliot's status as the great poet-critic of this century is 'generally acknowledged'.[1] In 1920, he published an article entitled 'Tradition and the Individual Talent' which amply repays theologically-informed attention.[2] In this article, Eliot argued that poetic talent, literary creativity and critical energies were all being misused and misdirected in the literary writing of the time. The reading public looks for originality, novelty, personality in authors. It insists upon those aspects of a writer's work in which he or she least resembles anyone else. Whereas, Eliot asserted, the truest originality of a poet may lie in those parts of his work in which 'the dead poets, his ancestors, assert their immortality most vigorously.'[3] This, he went on, was not at all a question of blind or timid adherence to the generation immediately prior to one's own. The relationship involved encloses, rather, the entire past of the literary tradition. The sphere of life in which the poet and critic should live is this past tradition in its presence: the total past as now. The historical sense

> compels a man to write not merely with his own generation in his bones, but with a feeling that the whole of the literature of Europe from Homer and within it the whole of the literature of his country has a simultaneous existence and composes a simultaneous order.[4]

Far from dulling one's sense of one's own time, it is precisely this situating of one generation within the totality of the whole that makes a writer most acutely aware of his contemporaneity, his particular and unique moment in time.

To ignore or devalue tradition is to enthrone the subjectivity of the poet in a pejorative sense of the word 'subjectivity'. It is to enthrone the isolated self, a self dependent on its own posturings for making a mark in the world. This little self is thus thrown back on its own resources, without full access to the wider realm of meaning in which its experiences and utterances take on their proper status and value. Ideally, personality is transmuted into the aesthetic 'world' of the literary work, a world which is, or can be, an evocation of the order of being itself. Such transmutation is, admittedly, a difficult process. When it fails, we become conscious of the speaker, rather than of the situation or reality about which he is trying to speak. As the 'First Epigraphy', ascribed to Heraclitus, in Eliot's poem *Burnt Norton* puts it:

> Although there is but one Centre, most men live in centres of their own.[5]

Whatever 'most men' may do, however, there is a kind of immaturity, Eliot says, in having personal preferences where tradition is concerned. At least, one may have them, as one may have tastes in painting, but one should not make them decisive. The poet

> can neither take the past as a lump, an indiscriminate *bolus*, nor can he form himself wholly on one or two private admirations; nor can he form himself wholly upon one preferred period. The first course is inadmissible, the second is an important experience of youth, and the third is a pleasant and highly desirable supplement.[6]

Eliot anticipated a number of objections that might be lodged against this account of tradition in the literary sphere. First, it may be asked: Does it not demand an impossible erudition of every writer and reader? No, replied Eliot, he was not appealing for the replacement of creative writers by pedants. He was simply asking that the poet's awareness of the past should grow throughout his career. The writer must make 'a continual surrender of himself as he is at the moment to something which is more valuable'.[7] Secondly: Will not this lordship of tradition make the free personal spirit into a serf? Will it not, in other words, de-personalise author and critic alike? In answer to this, Eliot speaks with two voices. In one voice he agrees with the assertion but tries to turn its vice into virtue. De-personalising is exactly, he says, what he wants to attain, for

> the poet has not a 'personality' to express but a particular medium, which is only a medium and not a personality, in which impressions and experience combine in peculiar and unexpected ways.[8]

I do not propose to endorse this remark for several reasons. To begin with, Eliot's own poetry and criticism make it clear that his sense of the individual was in fact alive and flourishing, in concert with his sense of tradition. As he wrote in an essay on the dramatist John Ford:

> A man might, hypothetically, compose any number of fine passages or even of whole poems, which would each give satisfaction and yet not be a great poet unless we felt them to be united by one significant, consistent and developing personality.[9]

A second reason for rejecting Eliot's language of de-personalisation here is that while Eliot lived in a 'moment' of Western culture in which the cult of personality, excessive individualism, was a grave temptation, our culture today is faced not only with this temptation but also with its extreme opposite, the cult of structure, excessive anti-individualism. A generation which has witnessed the Structuralist attempt to reduce personhood to the intersecting of structures, and the personal voice to the 'speaking of the structures', will see too many perils in Eliot's language at this point to want to make it their own. A third and final reason for questioning the wisdom of making depersonalisation a necessary and desirable consequence of the primacy of tradition is that it simply does not cohere with the main thrust of Eliot's essay to do so.

For Eliot's aim, kept steadily in view throughout, is to suggest how the truest individuality is nurtured by tradition, and only exists where tradition is revered and cherished. More strongly, where a work of art is fostered by the sense of tradition, it can be more than merely novel. It can shed a light powerful enough to modify subtly all the works of art which preceded it in the tradition, what Eliot calls 'the order of the monuments'. Eliot's real enemy is not individuality, but a sentimental and anti-traditional version of what individuality involves. This seems clear from a remark to the effect that the greatness of a piece of writing does not flow from the greatness or supposed originality of the *emotions* which produced it, but from the 'pressure' under which a fusion takes place of elements, meanings, drawn from tradition in the 'now' of the poet's own place and time.

Theological bearings of Eliot's theory

Eliot himself believed that poetry could serve as an analogue of religion.[10] In both, he thought, truth is accessible through the medium of images. Here he drew on a line of reflection in English literature and theology going back in essentials to S. T. Coleridge.[11] The unity and distinctiveness of this English contribution to theology has been affirmed by Hans Urs von Balthasar in his comments on the theological aesthetic of Hopkins in *Herrlichkeit* ('The Glory of the Lord'),[12] but its clearest statement is surely to be found in J. H. Newman's *Essay in Aid of a Grammar of Assent*. For Newman, although reason may penetrate the intelligible content of revelation and to some degree demonstrate its rationality, nevertheless, revelation in itself is primarily expressed in images which 'rest' in the imagination.[13] In Eliot's *Four Quartets*, the analogue between divinity and poetry is all-pervasive, for the entry of the Uncreated Word into the finite realm is refracted in the words of the poet.[14] Insofar as theology is an exploration of revealed images it resembles the work of the poet and critic.[15]

There is nothing fantastic, therefore, in the suggestion that Eliot's account of poetic tradition may serve as an illuminating analogue for what Christians mean by tradition in the theological sense. More especially, Eliot's essay, once transposed into theological terms, indicates directions for theology that are peculiarly apt at the present day. To risk a simplification of an egregious kind, we can say that Western Christian theology and sensibility in the last hundred years has veered wildly between the two poles of individualism and authoritarianism, between the free, unfettered life of the enquiring spirit and appeal to authority, however conceived. It has never found that integration, balance and wholeness in the relation between the tradition and the individual talent which Eliot's essay evokes.

In Protestantism, the period of liberalism was replaced after the First World War by the Neo-Orthodox revival, an exaltation of the authority of the Word of God in Karl Barth and his European disciples, an exaltation of the authority of the early Councils in Anglicanism. These in their turn have been replaced by a new liberalism which is more tired and more desperate than the old. In Catholicism, the epoch of Modernism, with its extreme stress on experience and religious feeling, was succeeded by an age of imposed theological constraint working through an unprecedentedly powerful papacy, what Karl Rahner called 'the "Monolithism" of the popes named "Pius".' The lid was, of course, removed at the Second Vatican Council, an attempt by the papacy partially to repatriate decision-making in the Church to the episcopate with whom it had been very largely originally lodged. But the behaviour of the stored-up contents have made the theologian's chest look more like Pandora's Box than the cupboard of the Gospels from which the wise householder brought forth treasures both old and new. Needless to say, theological confusion breeds its own sicknesses, in missionary outreach, in pastoral care and finally in the intellectual life itself, which in no discipline can ever progress if it is continually obliged to re-make its own foundations.

Curiously enough, the plea Eliot made for a recovery of the sense of tradition has acquired its extraordinary relevance to Catholic theology just at a time when the theological idea of Tradition, and the history of that idea, is better understood in scholarly terms by Christians than ever before. A large number of monographs on the notion of Tradition in various writers and periods have been penned by historians of doctrine. A number of fine syntheses of this secondary material have also been produced, notably Père Yves Congar's *La Tradition et les traditions* ('Tradition and the Traditions'), published between 1960 and 1963 and all the more notable for its author's influence as an accredited *peritus* on the Second Vatican Council then sitting.[16] A comparison of Congar's study with Eliot's essay is illuminating, and can indicate some criteria for a programme of theological reform.

Congar's theory of Christian tradition

After an exhaustive survey of references to the word 'Tradition' and its cognates in Scripture, the Fathers, the mediaeval doctors and the writings of Catholic theologians from the Counter-Reformation to the nineteenth-century Catholic revival, Congar plunges into what he calls 'an analysis and synthesis of the idea of tradition'.[17] Etymologically, Tradition must mean 'the handing on of things received'. It implies then, as Eliot had affirmed, a receptive ('things received') but also an active, indeed creative ('handing on'), attitude to the past. In the case of Christian Tradition, however, this essential relationship with the past does not simply establish a corpus of human meanings, as with Eliot. More than this, it makes possible the transmission of a *doctrina salutaris*,[18] a teaching about divine salvation actually drawing us into the sphere of that salvation. The salvation in question Congar has already defined as a mutual relationship of knowledge and love between God and ourselves. Nevertheless, insofar as this *doctrina salutaris* is still *doctrina*, the analogy with a corpus of human meanings stands.

Congar further suggests that this transmission of a 'covenant-relationship' in Tradition takes up by grace a prior feature of the general human condition, namely inter-dependence or *la médiation fraternelle*.[19] We depend on each other at the natural level; in studying the idea of Tradition we see that we also depend on each other at the supernatural level; and in addition we can glimpse through this aspect of the divine Economy, something of the self-giving of the Triune God. This is well said, but surely 'fraternal mediation' suggests an entirely *syn*chronic process, whereas what Congar really needs at this point is a comparison with a *dia*chronic process. More appropriate here, in fact, would be an appeal to something like Eliot's theory of poetic tradition which sees the literary culture of a society (a reality operative on all levels, from the most to the least sophisticated) as the taking up of individuals into a life-giving chain of succession in which the long-dead are immortal and become articulate in their successors here and now.

Congar, like Eliot, regards Tradition as transformative of human interiority, not simply something situated in the exterior, public realm. For Eliot, incorporation into the public tradition means the re-casting of the interiority of the person so incorporated, in such a way that the bounds of merely individual perception, expression and interpretation are broken through. For Congar too the social and even the juridical structure of the transmission and acceptance of faith is a sort of sacrament of the most mystical and spiritual reality.[20]

And echoing the dialectic of 'Tradition and the Individual Talent', Congar has it that the Christian life of faith is

something entirely personal and interior; quite definitely, however, this is not an individualising force, but one which incorporates; and it is something received, in which one joins and participates.[21]

But whereas in the case of poetic tradition, the 'force' or power concerned is the creativity of finite spirit, in the case of tradition theologically defined, Holy Tradition, it is the (Holy) Spirit of God himself who energises the entire process of transmission and incorporation.[22]

Congar now turns to the section of his work which provides its title, the establishing of a distinction between 'the traditions' and 'Tradition'.[23] The 'traditions' are the kind of thing discussed by the Council of Trent in its debate with the Reformers: aspects of Christian faith, the *regula fidei*, or the Christian life, *institutio christiana*, not contained formally in the canon of Scripture. Trent had in mind such things as the oral teaching of the apostles on the interpretation of the Old Testament, its christological and ecclesiological significance, and their equally oral worship, the sacraments as liturgy, as language-in-action.[24] It was these limited, though important, matters that post-Tridentine theology envisaged when it spoke of Tradition as a separate *fons revelationis*, alongside and parallel to Scripture.

But these are not Congar's primary focus. He is concerned to shift our attention to a more comprehensive sense of Tradition. This concern is explicable in terms of three factors. First, historians of the Catholic Reformation had become (on the whole) dubious as to whether Trent really intended to canonise a 'two source' view of Tradition, not least because

of the Council's rejection of a *partim ... partim* formula
which would have made such a dual source theory clear.[25]
Secondly, historians of doctrine had made it abundantly clear
that a more holistic view of Tradition was temporally prior.[26]
Thirdly, Congar's own theological penetration – and the
breakthrough here is comparable to that of Eliot's essay
– suggested to him that this temporal priority should be a
theological priority as well.

Congar presents Tradition, therefore, as the whole within
which Christian life and reflection are situated. It is

> the transmission of the whole Gospel, that is, the whole Chris-
> tian mystery, in any form.[27]

The reiteration of 'whole' here picks up the same emphasis in
Eliot's picture of literary tradition as what I have called a
'corpus' of meanings. The primary expression of Tradition is
Scripture itself, willed by God as the internal norm of the
Church formed, sustained and extended by Tradition. But the
meaning of Scripture (compare for Eliot the meaning or refer-
ential range of any great text) is to be found only in connexion with a whole host of other enactments or monuments
(compare Eliot's 'the order of monuments') which make up
the fabric of the Church's life. In a diversified but integrated
whole, the liturgy and the teaching of the Fathers, conciliar
and papal definitions, and the witness of the ordinary Christian life, the Christian saints and Christian art all play their
part in traditioning the Gospel.[28] Of this total process, the
Holy Spirit is, as we have seen, the transcendent cause or
Subject. Relying on a happier predecessor of Dr Hans Küng,
Johann Adam Möhler, Congar concludes that the Spirit
creates from within both the unity of Tradition and also the
expressions of its special genius.[29] The transcendent subjectivity of the Spirit enters our world through the corporate or
inter-personal subjectivity of Christ's Church – which, as we

have noted, should be characterised diachronically, not simply synchronically, and so along the lines of Eliot's essay.

It is by conformity with the Church's self-awareness and her memory of what she has received that any putative expression of the Christian faith must be judged authentically normative – or not. As Eliot says of the work of the poet, 'Its fitting in is a test of its value', pointing out at the same time that the test can only 'be slowly and cautiously applied' and requires sensitivity, respect, tact and patience.[30] The English Benedictine Cardinal Aidan Gasquet is said to have remarked to Pope Leo XIII in a moment of abstractedness in defence of a colleague: 'After all, Holiness, none of us is infallible.' Eliot certainly remarks of the coherence of a literary work with the tradition: 'We are none of us infallible judges of conformity.'[31] The remarkable infrequency with which the Roman magisterium attempts such judgments in the contemporary Church is a model of the restraint desirable in this area.

Conclusions and proposals

If an Eliotic-Congarian theory of tradition is valid, then it follows that the first prerequisite of the theologian is not originality so much as docility: an active, eager, lively willingness to be formed, instructed and inspired. The monuments of Tradition are mediations of a prior and greater presence. Through them, the Word and Image of God is given words and images that he may speak and show himself.[32] This in turn suggests some more particular criteria for theological writing.

First, the epistemology of theology, its distinctive mode of understanding, can only be found within Tradition, that is within the historical communion of the Church. Theology cannot be written without, much less against, the society of the faithful.[33]

Secondly, as Scripture is the primary expression of Tradition, there can be no sound theology which is not rooted in

Scripture and irradiated by it. Scripture in this sense is not primarily an ancient text as historically reconstructed, but the Church's book. This recalls the need to keep in perspective the significance attached to the findings of the methods of contemporary biblical exegesis. The meaning of Scripture is not simply to be found in its historical genesis, but also over time, within the order of the monuments that follow from it.[34]

Thirdly, theology must be fed by all the Christian generations, each of which was open to God and whose voices, in the words of Eliot's *Little Gidding*, are 'tongued with fire beyond the language of the living'. Their teaching, literature and art should be seen as enabling, not disabling, factors in the theological quest. How is it that Küng's *On Being a Christian*, for all its merits, can formulate its account of Jesus by way of a deliberate overleaping of these generations, accompanied by unhappy metaphors of 'peeling off layers of encrustation'?[35]

Finally, theology must be informed by the witness of the mystics and the saints for it is in their lives and awareness that the transforming power of the Spirit of Tradition is at its clearest and most palpable. Theology must regain the quality of being *scientia sanctorum* – because it is the saints who are the principal explorers of the mystery of God. We may then find that the best part of the theologian's work is that in which these ancestors of his 'assert their immortality most vigorously'.

This programme amounts to a revolution as radical as Eliot's, the abandonment by the theological artist of his romantic status as a loner in the garret – nowadays all too well carpeted and furnished – of a latterday *quartier latin*, and his re-insertion into the tradition and common life of the *plebs sancta Dei*, the holy people of God throughout the ages. The individual talent must be the servant, not the master. In Hermann Hesse's *The Glass Bead Game* our age is criticised as the 'Age of the Feuilleton', an age that 'appears to have had only the dimmest notion of what to do with culture' and given over to an untrammelled individualism. For Hesse, the mental culture of our time, 'squandering its strength in excessive vegetative growth' (one thinks of the extraordinary length of some recent Christological studies!), could only be brought back to its senses by 'a new, monastically austere, intellectual discipline'. Through that renunciation, the vigour of the free personal spirit might be united with the universality of reason. Could not the same be achieved for theological reason? Should we not wish to echo Hesse and say:

> We moderns, on the other hand, do not even speak of major personalities until we encounter men who have gone beyond all original and idiosyncratic qualities to achieve the greatest possible integration with the generality, the greatest possible service to the suprapersonal.[36]

Part Two

Exploring
Theological History

IV
The Roman Primacy in the Ancient Irish and Anglo-Celtic Church

The ancient Irish church took its origin from pre-Germanic Celtic Britain, and any account of it, and its knowledge of, and attitude towards, the Roman primacy must necessarily begin from this mainland British background.

The background: the Church in Roman and sub-Roman Britain, and its Welsh continuation in the First Millenium

Christianity arrived in Britain along with other exports, both spiritual and material, from the continental Roman empire of the early centuries of our era.[1] Carried by such categories of individual as soldiers and traders, it gained its first martyrs in the imperial persecutions of the third and early fourth centuries.[2] During the latter century, the British church was organised on the same basis as the Church elsewhere in the empire. It was governed by urban bishops who attended Church councils at Arles in 314, at Rimini in 359 (where their expenses were paid from out of the imperial treasury), and, possibly, Sardica in 347.[3] In the fifth century, surviving Christian inscriptions in Britain betray signs of close contact with the Gaulish church,[4] leading a *première* historian of this subject, the late Kathleen Hughes, to write:

The educated Briton felt himself more at home in Mediterranean lands than among the barbarian Picts and Scots. His frontiers were the imperial frontiers, and Rome's special significance for him was as the heart of the empire to which he proudly belonged.[5]

During this earliest period, British Christians, prior to the Anglo-Saxon invasions in the southern and eastern portions of their island, must have been aware of the pope as Bishop of Rome, imperial capital and burial place of the apostles Peter and Paul. But our earliest secure evidence for any direct contact between the papacy and the British West (leaving aside, then, the appeal for baptism from a British ruler, 'Lucius', to the second century pope Eleutherius, apparently based on a misreading, by Bede's Roman researcher Nothelm, of the [Mesopotamian!] 'Birtha' for 'Britium') comes from the pontificate of Celestine I.[6] This pope, disquieted by the spread of Pelagianism, sent to Britain in 429, for the purposes of combating heresy, the Gaulish bishop Germanus of Auxerre. So records a contemporary chronicler, Prosper of Aquitaine, in his *Chronicon*, itself written in Rome.[7]

The same source tells us that Celestine also sent to Ireland, two years later, a certain Palladius, to be the first bishop of 'the Irish believing in Christ'. Hughes accepted that Pope Celestine sent with Bishop Palladius relics of the co-apostles Peter and Paul, and of the deacon martyrs Stephen and Lawrence treasured by the church of Armagh some two or three hundred years later.[8] That this papally sponsored mission to Ireland was not forgotten is demonstrated by the belief of the seventh-century Irish missionary Columbanus that the Christian faith had first reached Ireland from a papal source.[9]

However, the Irish recognised as their own 'apostle' not a pope (as the Anglo-Saxons would later regard Gregory the Great) but a British Christian whose mission was, unconventionally, self-adopted: Patrick. Although the 'Patrician documents' in the Book of Armagh claim that Pope Celestine originated the mission of Patrick, such claims entail either confusing Patrick's advent with the earlier venture of Palladius, or a deliberate attempt to play down the latter and to point up the former, since Patrick's own writings – the *Confession* and the *Letter to Coroticus* (a British king, either in North Wales or Strathclyde) – make no such pretension to papal support.[10]

It seems, indeed, that the conversion of those Celtic areas which lay outside the civil zone of Roman Britain was initiated by British Christians themselves, or, in a second stage of the same process, by the resultant converts taking up the missionary torch and carrying it farther afield. Thus Dubricius (Dyfrig), the father of the saints of Wales, remembered in the earliest Celtic saint's life, the *Vita Samsoni*, as ordainer of Samson of Dol, and among the chapter of St David's as consecrator of Dewi of Mynyw, traditions which led, respectively, the bishops of Llandaff and St David's (Menevia) to claim a local primacy, appears to have worked mainly in Archenfield (Gwent), the Romanised region on the borders of south-east Wales and western Hereford.[11] Ninian (Nynia), who founded a church at Whithorn (Galloway) and later converted the southern Picts, was a British bishop, and, though Bede tells us that he was 'regularly instructed' at Rome, there is no suggestion that the pope in any way inspired his mission.[12] True, the first conversions among the Irish may have arisen from *casual* contacts, presumably of a commercial sort, with both Britain and Gaul, in what Dr Henry Mayr-Harting, of St Peter's College, Oxford, has termed the 'Celtic thalassocracy of the Atlantic seaboard',[13] and, as already noted, a Roman pope appointed their first bishop. Yet the main work of evangelisation was performed by a Briton, convinced of a personal call to missionise among the Irish and consecrated bishop, very probably, at the Gaulish see already deeply involved in British affairs, Auxerre.[14] Furthermore, when, in 569, the west Scottish island of Iona became a monastic centre, its founder Colmcille (Columba) started a mission to northern Pictland.[15] Understandably, therefore, Hughes concluded:

> It would seem that the foundation and expansion of Christianity in the Celtic areas was to a considerable extent, though not entirely, independent of Roman initiative.[16]

During the fifth century, the century of Palladius and Patrick, the position of Britain underwent a profound change. Early in the century, the Roman legions were withdrawn and the Britons were forced to take up their defence against both Celtic raiders from the north and west, and Teutonic settlers from the east.[17] Against the Picts and Scots they were, on the whole, successful, but by about 500 the Anglo-Saxons were occupying the eastern half of the island. However, archaeological evidence, and notably epigraphy, shows that the British church was not cut off from the Continent by the invasions as was once thought: communications between, for example, Wales and Gaul continued.[18]

The attitude to the papacy of the British church in this period may be exemplified in the writings of Gildas, who belonged to the new movement of ascetic monasticism. Though Gildas, writing in the mid-sixth century, has nothing explicit to say about the papacy, he does refer to Peter as *princeps apostolorum* ('prince of the apostles'). However, he uses the phrase *sedes Petri apostoli* ('the seat of the apostle Peter') to mean the office of any *sacerdos*, any bishop.[19] The whole episcopal order exercises, for him, spiritual authority, inheriting the power Christ gave to Peter; he lays especial emphasis on the importance of holiness of life in the bishop. Hughes comments:

> It is likely that anyone educated in the Gildasian tradition would set a very high value on purity of life and that, in any dispute, he might be expected to appeal to the spiritual quality of the protagonists rather than to papal judgment.[20]

This expectation is amply borne out by events at the meeting between Augustine of Canterbury, acting as the legate of Pope Gregory the Great, and representatives of the British (effectively, Welsh) church around 600. Augustine had called a conference of the bishops and doctors of the British border regions, with a view to securing their adhesion to the Roman dating of Easter.[21] Indecisive, it was followed up by a second, attended by seven British bishops and many 'learned men', chiefly from (the Welsh) Bangor. The issue of the primacy was not explicitly raised, although as Augustine in attempting to gain the adhesion of the Welsh to Roman customs was acting on papal bidding, it was implicitly present. At the first conference, which deferred a decision to the second, Augustine tried to settle the matter (so Bede tells us) by a competition in thaumaturgy; at the second, the British bishops made their decision turn on a test of Augustine's sanctity, and more especially, humility.[22] This he failed, perhaps through concern for the *gravitas* enjoined by Gregory in the *Regula Pastoralis*.[23]

Bede's account makes it clear that the synod composed of bishops and *viri doctissimi* [most learned men] held authority in the British Church, an authority more decisive than that of a foreign bishop sent by the pope, whose advice he was attempting to follow.[24]

Politically, Augustine's approach to the Welsh church could scarcely have been less well timed. The Welsh, engaged as they were in an attempt to expel the Anglo-Saxons from the British island, would hardly look with unalloyed pleasure at the prospect of ecclesiastical control by the leader of the newly established Anglo-Saxon church. Throughout the century and more which separated Augustine's abortive conference from Bede's time of writing (c. 730), the Britons were fighting a losing battle against the Saxons, in a bitterness of spirit which not even the advent of a common religion could extinguish. Thus, in 705, Aldhelm of Malmesbury wrote to King Geraint of Dumnonia (the modern Cornwall) that in Dyfed (south-west Wales) priests will not worship in the same church as Saxons, nor sit at table with them.[25] The Welsh scriptoria existed 'behind an iron curtain'.[26] Nor is there any record of contact between the Welsh church and Rome throughout this century of British defeat.

In the eighth, ninth and tenth centuries, once the Welsh attempt to reclaim the whole of the erstwhile Romano-British territory had ended, relations with Rome were resumed. In 768, King Elfodd of Gwynedd introduced the Roman Easter; the King of Powys, Cyngen, visiting Rome, died there sometime between 854 and 856; Dwnwallon, the north-British Prince of Strathclyde, arrived in 975. After the close of the millenium, a Welsh pilgrim 'sums up for us the Celtic recognition of the Petrine powers', even while praying to be buried in his native soil, the Isle of Bardsey:

> May I, the poet Meilyr, pilgrim to Peter, gatekeeper who judges the sum of virtues, when the time comes for us to arise who are in the grave, have thy support. May I be at home awaiting the call in a fold with the moving sea near it, a hermitage of perpetual honour, with a bosom of brine about its graves.[27]

These were, however, the actions of individuals. Corporate ecclesial contact between the Welsh church and the papacy on an official level seems to have been re-established only after the acceptance of regular diocesan organisation, on the Continental pattern, in the twelfth century. From this time on, the jurisdictional powers of the papacy were exercised *vis-à-vis* Welsh affairs, as bishops, like those of Llandaff and St David's, brought their appeals to Rome, and their local chroniclers sought in the popes the origin of the British church, elaborating Bede's account of the appeal of Lucius to Eleutherius.[28]

Ireland

In turning from the ancient British background (and its Welsh continuation in the first millenium) to the situation of Ireland, we must make some decision about the vexed question of the interrelation between the Palladian and Patrician missions. Although Irish churchmen were acquainted with Prosper's chronicle, and the traditional date of Patrick's arrival in Ireland, 432, may be an inference from the *Chronicon's* dating of the mission of Palladius, no memory of Palladius as an active missionary bishop survived in any Irish church. It must be assumed that his mission proved abortive, and was early abandoned. At any rate, Palladius disappears from history, and some other bishop takes his place, since an organised Irish church comes into existence at this time. That the bishop was Patrick, who had been held as a prisoner in Ireland in his youth, had escaped and then dedicated himself to the task of converting his former captors is an unbroken Irish tradition.[29] The familiar story rests on Patrick's own *Confession*, whose Latinity is closest in grammar and vocabulary, as Christine Mohrmann showed, to that of mid-fifth-century Gaul.[30] Unfortunately, while Patrick's family background, as son of a decurion in sub-Roman Britain, and his probable training in a Gaulish milieu, renders explicable his evident devotion to the Roman imperial civilisation, and the imperial church, his literary remains throw no direct light on his attitude to the papacy. In the *Letter to Coroticus*, Patrick laments that he cannot regard the latter's soldiery, Christian in name but rapacious in deed, as 'fellow-citizens of the holy Romans' – but only as fellow citizens of the devil. In the same letter he holds up the contrasting example of the Roman Christians of Gaul, *romanorum gallorum christianorum*, who have sent money for the ransoming of Christian captives. It is in this perspective of adhesion to *the imperial church of the West at large* that we should, in the first instance, interpret the saying preserved among the *dicta Patricii* in the Book of Armagh:

> Church of the Irish, nay, of the Romans, in order that you be Christians as are the Romans [or, 'that you be Romans as well as Christians'] you must sing in your churches at every hour of prayer that praiseworthy utterance: *Kyrie eleison, Christe eleison* . . .[31]

According to the historian of Western liturgy, J. Jungmann, the *Kyrie* was brought to the West by such early-fifth-century pilgrims to the Holy Places as Egeria.[32] The Patrician scholar Ludwig Bieler points out that the threefold *Miserere*, which opens the second of the hymns of Marius Victorinus may imply the use of the triple *Kyrie* at Rome in his time (c. 360).[33] In Patrick's usage, we cannot exclude, therefore, the possibility that a secondary referent in the term *romanus* is, in fact, to *the usage of the Roman church proper* – but this is not explicitly brought out in the sources. The *Annals of Ulster* maintain that Patrick himself visited Rome in 441 – but this is unconfirmed.[34] Patrick's attitude to Rome in jurisdictional terms is even harder to assess. The canons laid down for the guidance of the Irish church by Patrick and his co-bishops Auxilius and Iserninus led Thomas O'Fiaich to write:

> The ecclesiastical organisation which Patrick introduced into Ireland was obviously the one which he found in Gaul and Britain, namely, a Church placed under the rule of bishops, each of whom had authority over a particular district and was attached to a particular church ... That Patrick, after preparatory missionary work, finally chose a particular church as his own – and thereby constituted it his episcopal see – is exactly what we should expect from a fifth-century missionary in Ireland.[35]

With circumspection, then, the tradition of the Patrician local church of Armagh may be used to throw light on the understanding of Patrick's attitude to the primacy.

Within the Book of Armagh is a text known as the 'Book of the Angel', an account of claims, both territorial and juridical, set in the hagiographical framework of an angel telling Patrick that these privileges have been divinely granted to his church. They include: the *terminus* (territory) of Armagh itself; the promise that all the Irish tribes shall belong to Patrick as his *paruchia*; and a number of personal prerogatives attaching to the *praesul*, or office of presidency, of Patrick's city, including one by which all disputes in other churches are to be brought before the see of Armagh, from the authority of whose *praesul* there is appeal only to the apostolic see. This provision cannot, it seems, be later than the middle of the seventh century, since after that time it appears to be assumed by Tirechán of Tirawley who wrote with a view to providing documentary evidence for these claims in the *Liber Ardmachensis* ('Book of Armagh').

> If any difficult cause shall arise beyond the competence of all the judges of the tribes of the Irish, it is duly to be referred to the see of the archbishop of the Irish, that is, Patrick, and to the examination of that prelate, *antistes*. But if, in the examination of that prelate with his *sapientes* [wise men], such a case as we have mentioned cannot be easily decided, we have decreed that it shall be referred to the apostolic see, that is, to the chair of Peter, having authority over the city of Rome.[36]

In the *Collectio Canonum Hibernensis* ('Hibernian Canon Collection'), dating to the early-eighth century, this canon appears in a simplified form, viz. 'If any questions arise in this island, let them be referred to the apostolic see', and is, in this form, ascribed to Patrick himself.[37] This shows, at any rate, a belief that Patrick had authorised some such ruling, c. 700, but the attribution of the command to Patrick himself cannot arouse much confidence, since other sayings ascribed to him in this collection are known to be from non-Patrician sources.

Here, however, 'hermeneutical suspicion' may enter in, since the *Collectio Canonum Hibernensis* is clearly the work of the pro-Roman party in the Irish church at the time of the friction caused by the Paschal controversy in both Ireland and Britain, whilst the canon in the *Liber Ardmachensis*, by its use of the term *archiepiscopus* for Patrick, proclaims its own post-Patrician dating. To what degree do these sources reflect the specific beliefs of the Romanising party in Ireland during the quarrel over the dating of Easter? The three letters to Rome of Columbanus are an expression of Irish attitudes at a time when the Easter crisis was only just beginning, and the formation of parties had not yet taken place. Columbanus, master of the school of Bangor (founded by Comgall in c. 558 in the earliest flourishing of Irish monasticism on an organised scale), arrived on the Continent in 591 with a group of monk companions.[38] He was soon on bad terms with the Frankish bishops, who, irritated by the criticism of their worldly ways on the part of the austere Irish ascetics, concentrated their return fire on the divergent Irish reckoning of Easter. In his first letter to Rome, addressed to Gregory I, Columbanus asks in effect, for a decision in favour of the Irish practice, since the table of Victorinus of Aquitaine, used in Gaul (a modification of the table of Dionysius Exiguus favoured in Rome), is unscholarly.

> (It) has not been accepted by our teachers, by the former scholars of Ireland, by the mathematicians most skilled in reckoning chronology, but has earned ridicule and indulgence rather than authority.[39]

His tone in this letter is independent. Columbanus even insinuates that, in the event of a papal determination that goes against the Irish practice, the Irish may abandon the pope's person, on the grounds that one who sets himself over against the views of Jerome – who had accepted the calculations of Anatolius of Laodicea on whose ante-Nicene, and so less than fully canonical, dating of Easter the Irish relied – must have departed from the Scriptures, on which Jerome always took his stand.

> Anyone impugning the authority of saint Jerome will be a heretic or reprobate in the eyes of the western churches, whoever that man may be.[40]

No reply is recorded. Gregory may have thought the argument so contrived as to not worth discussing. Or he may have felt it best to maintain a discreet silence, sandwiched as he was between Columbanus and the Merovingian bishops. In the second letter to Rome (Columbanus is writing during a period when the see was vacant), the tone is less assured – not surprisingly since in the meantime the Frankish bishops had summoned him to a council which he refused to attend, preferring to seek for papal support. This time he asks rather for toleration for the Irish position, begging the pope

> to grant to us pilgrims in our travail the godly consolation of your judgment, thus confirming, if it is not contrary to the faith, the tradition of our predecessors.[41]

Hughes finds here 'a much clearer recognition of papal authority than in the previous letter'.[42] The third and last surviving letter Columbanus wrote to the apostolic see was addressed to Boniface IV in 613. In it, Columbanus implores the pope to clear himself from the imputation of heresy which had attached to him as a result of his part in the 'Three Chapters' controversy. In so doing, he defines more specifically still his attitude to the primacy. The letter is addressed:

> To the most fair head of all the churches of the whole of Europe, to the most lovable pope, the most exalted prelate, shepherd of shepherds ...

and it contends that

> all we Irish, inhabitants of the world's edge, are disciples of
> saints Peter and Paul and of all the disciples who wrote the
> sacred canon by the Holy Ghost, and we accept nothing outside
> the evangelical and apostolic teaching; none has been a heretic,
> none a Judaiser, none a schismatic; but the catholic faith, as it
> was delivered by you first, who are the successors of the apostles,
> is maintained unbroken.

Columbanus has explained to Rome's critics among the
Western supporters of Justinian's actions at the Fifth Ecumenical Council that 'the Roman church defends no heretic
against the Catholic faith'. He asks the pope to accept this
intervention on his behalf, since after all, 'if a son speaks
wisely, his father will rejoice', and the credit will be Rome's –
appropriately, because 'it [i.e. orthodoxy] was delivered by
you; for purity is due not to the river, but to the spring'.[43]
Invoking the nearness of the Lord's second coming, and the
confusion current in the Church, Columbanus calls on the
pope to demonstrate his leadership:

> ... for it is you that are concerned with the danger of the Lord's
> whole army in these regions ... You are awaited by the whole,
> you have the power of ordering all things, of declaring war,
> arousing the generals, bidding arms to be taken up, forming the
> battle array, sounding the trumpets on every side, and finally of
> entering the conflict with your own person in the van ...[44]

– a rhetorical expression of the *plenitudo potestatis* ('fullness
of power') theme. Although Columbanus seems rather confused about the location of the various heretical divines he
mentions on the spectrum of patristic Christology, he appeals
to the pope to summon a synod which will clear the name of
Rome in christological orthodoxy. Otherwise, those who
were Boniface's subordinates will become his judges, since
they have kept the orthodox faith and the pope (if he fails to
amend his ways) will have not.

Apologising for his freedom of speech, Columbanus moves into a great paean of Christian (over against pagan) Rome.

> We ... are bound to Saint Peter's chair; for though Rome be great and famous among us it is only on that chair that her greatness and her fame depend. For although the name of the city which is Italy's glory ... has been published far and wide through the whole world, even as far as the Western regions of earth's farthest strand, miraculously unhindered by ocean's surging floods, though they leaped and rose beyond measure on every side, yet from that time when the Son of God deigned to be man, and on those two most fiery steeds of God's Spirit, I mean the apostles Peter and Paul, whose dear relics have made you blessed, riding over the sea of nations troubled many waters and increased his chariots with countless thousands of peoples, the most high Pilot of that carriage who is Christ, the True Father, the Charioteer of Israel, over the channels' surge, over the dolphins' backs, over the swelling flood, reached even unto us. From that time you are great and famous, and Rome herself is nobler and more famed; and if it may be said, for the sake of Christ's twin apostles (I speak of those called by the Holy Spirit heavens declaring the glory of God, to whom is applied the text, 'Their voice is gone out into every land and their words to the ends of the earth') you are made near to the heavenlies, and Rome is the head of the Churches of the world, *omnis terrarum caput est ecclesiarum*, saving the special privilege of the place of the Lord's Resurrection.

But on this ringing affirmation of the Roman primacy, qualified as it is by a reference to the residual rights of Jerusalem, there follows a warning:

> Even as your honour is great in proportion to the dignity of your see, so great care is needful for you, lest you lose your dignity through some mistake. For power will be in your hands just so long as your principles remain sound: for he (Peter) is the appointed key-bearer of the Kingdom of heaven, who opens by true knowledge to the worthy and shuts to the unworthy; otherwise, if he does the opposite, he shall be able neither to open nor to shut.[45]

If the pope fails in faith, the whole Church must rise to correct him.

> Therefore, since those things [i.e. the necessity for sound doc-
> trine in a pope], are true and accepted without gainsaying by all
> who think truly, though it is known to all and there is none
> ignorant of how Our Saviour bestowed the keys of the kingdom
> of heaven upon saint Peter, and you perhaps on this account
> claim for yourself before all things some proud measure of
> greater authority and power in things divine; you ought to know
> that your power will be the less in the Lord's eyes, if you even
> think this in your heart, since the unity of the faith has produced
> in the whole world a unity of power and privilege, in such wise
> that by all men everywhere freedom should be given to the truth,
> and the approach of error should be denied by all alike, since it
> was his right confession that privileged even the holy bearer of
> the keys [i.e. Peter], the common teacher of us all ...[46]

Thus Columbanus ascribes to the Roman bishop an effective primacy of governance. Yet he does not hesitate to rebuke a pope whom (he fears) may be departing from good doctrine, nor to ask for the recognition of divergent liturgical customs where no matter involving orthodoxy is concerned.

It is the latter issue which, during the Paschal debate, led to the formation of two parties within the ancient Irish church. Fintan Munnu, speaking in defence of the Irish dating at the synod of Mag Ailbe (c. 630) pleaded for toleration of diverse practices: 'Let each of us do what he believes, and as seems to him right'.[47] The 'Celtic' party, that is, recognised no obli-gation to conform to the Easter dating advocated by the *Romani*. As Hughes puts it:

> The Celts were diverging from Roman *ritual*, not deliberately
> withholding obedience to an order of the pope on a matter of
> belief.[48]

The Roman party, however, considered that the matter was one in which the Irish church had already recognised, by

canon, Rome's right to decide. That this is so emerges from
the Paschal letter sent by Abbot Cummian, c. 632, to Segene
of Iona and Beccan the Hermit. Cummian describes how a
group of Roman-sympathetic abbots had met at Mag-Léna,
in the vicinity of the major Columban monastic centre of
Durrow, so as to discuss the Easter question, and had determined to celebrate future Easters with the rest of the Church.
One abbot, however, had reneged on the decision, having
recourse to the traditions of the 'elders', i.e. of earlier Irish
churchmen. But Cummian finds this an historical self-contra-
diction:

> It seemed to our elders ... that if there should be more important
> cases, these must be referred to the chief of cities, according to
> the synodal decree.[49]

We have already examined the canonical tradition (claiming
to be Patrician in origin) which is alluded to here.

Between c. 630 and the middle of the eighth century, the
Scotti progressively modified their liturgical practices to bring
them into conformity with Rome, and Irish canon law, as we
have seen, came to recognise Rome as a supreme court.
Nevertheless, the organisation of the Irish church was little
affected until the eleventh century.[50] The monastic system
had become too strong for organisation of a Continental type
to be expected, for diocesan structure had, with the development of the monastic confederations from the seventh century onwards, yielded to *paruchiae* of monastic confederacies
– perhaps because family property, sacrosanct in Old Irish
law, suggested to the aristocracy the desirability of having a
member of one's own family as abbot founder, with successors of his kith and kin, or again because the monastic confederations, whose chief abbots were analogous to tribal
over-kings, were widely scattered, ideal for the Irish love of
wandering, *peregrinatio pro Christo*.[51]

By the sixth century, the great abbots, who were usually presbyters, had completely overshadowed the bishops in authority
and prestige. Indeed, in the larger houses, a bishop was often
retained for those functions which he alone could perform, as
one of the monastery's major officials, with high honour, but
without jurisdiction. Seldom if ever among the Irish monasteries
do we find any power of visitation vested in an outside diocesan.
And though these arrangements can be paralleled from Mount
Sinai, Monte Cassino, and Fulda, outside of the Celtic Church
they were extremely rare: Bede is correct in describing the
quasi-metropolitan authority, enjoyed, for example, by the
presbyter-abbot of Iona, as *ordine inusitato* ['by an unaccus-
tomed arrangement'].[52]

In these circumstances, no metropolitical see, on the model
of, say, Canterbury, could emerge. And consequently, no
bishop of the *Scotti* travelled to Rome for the *pallium*; no
legatine commission reached the Irish church. Irish Christians
of the eighth, ninth and tenth centuries went to Rome, rather,
to visit the shrines of the apostles and martyrs, the idea of
Rome as burial place of the saints becoming so powerful that
the word *róm* in Irish gained a secondary meaning as a burial
ground. Not until the Hildebrandine reform did the papacy
take active steps to concern itself with Irish affairs.[53]

England

The conversion of Anglo-Saxon England is a complex story,
which cannot simply be reduced to the two main evangelising
forces, the Roman mission of Augustine, whose effects spread
through Kent to the South and West Saxon kingdoms, and to
East Anglia, while the Irish mission of Aidan, directed at first
to Northumbria, spilled over to the East Saxons and the
middle kingdom of Mercia. These are, however, the chief
factors involved.

When we consider figures like Birinus, Fursey, Agilbert and
others, it would appear that the Anglo-Saxons were the object of

much private missionary enterprise in the seventh century and that their conversion was by no means a matter only for those sent or summoned officially from Rome or Iona. And it is beyond doubt that the influence of Gaulish Christianity was stronger, at least in the conversion of Wessex and East Anglia. But our knowledge of all this is somewhat shadowy. However much can be said about Gaulish and other influences after about 650, in the first phase of Anglo-Saxon Christianity our attention is necessarily focused on the primary creative forces of the Roman and Irish traditions.[54]

Between those two traditions, the issue of attitudes to the primacy was aired thanks to, once again, the Easter dispute. The Roman party maintained that the pope was *heres Petri*, the heir of that Peter who kept the keys of heaven, and whose word could not be disobeyed. The Irish agreed that the Church was founded on Peter the key-bearer – and would come to use the *heres Petri* terminology: 'comharba Pheadair' (compare the Armagh bishop's title, *comharba Phádraig*, 'heir of Patrick'). Yet they refused to adopt the Easter dating advocated by the Romans. In 664, representatives of the (Gregorian) Anglo-Roman church and the (Columban) Anglo-Celtic church met at Whitby. In Bede's account of this synod, the Anglo-Roman spokesman, Wilfrid, addressed the Anglo-Celtic bishop Colman:

> If you and your fellows, having heard the decrees of the apostolic see, nay of the universal Church, confirmed as they are by the sacred Scriptures, if you scorn to follow them, without any doubt you sin.[55]

The Northumbrian king Oswiu decided for the Roman position precisely on the grounds that Peter is the key-bearer, and so his own entry into heaven would be jeopardised by a refusal to hearken to Peter's voice. This same 'eschatological' understanding of jurisdiction recurs in the letter of Aldhelm of Malmesbury to Geraint of Dumnonia.

If then the keys of the kingdom of heaven have been entrusted by Christ to Peter (of whom the poet says, 'Heavenly key-bearer, opening the gate of the sky'), who could enter welcomed through the gates of the heavenly paradise, his church spurning the main decisions, *statuta principalia* [of Peter] and scorning the mandates of [his] teaching, *doctrinae mandata*'?[56]

This was, moreover, Bede's own understanding of the matter. As he tells us, writing as homilist rather than historian:

To the Church of the elect, authority of binding and loosing is given. But then blessed Peter, who confessed Christ with a true faith and was attached to him with a true love, received in a special way the keys of the kingdom of heaven and the primacy of judicial power, so that all believers throughout the world might understand that those who separate themselves from the unity of his faith and society cannot be absolved from the chains of sin, nor enter the door of the heavenly kingdom.[57]

As Mayr-Harting has written, the triumph of unity and order based on papal authority and symbolised in the victory of the Roman Easter, forms 'one of the principal themes' of the *Ecclesiastical History*.[58]

Whilst we have no rejoinder to Aldhelm's letter, and no report of the Celtic arguments at Whitby by an historian who agreed with their views, it is reasonable, on the twofold basis of our knowledge of the actions of the Celtic leaders and the letters of Columbanus, to suppose that the Anglo-Celtic party, like their Irish forefathers, regarded the date of Easter as a matter of ritual, not of faith. But, at the same time, the deep attachment of the Northumbrian church to the memory of Columba discouraged them from accepting that he could have led them astray in what was no *mere* ritual question but a matter of the proper orientation of a Christian in time. Wilfrid's response was to draw attention to the implausibility of preferring *ille Columba vester*, 'that Columba of yours', to the prince of the apostles on whom, as on a rock, the Lord had promised to build his Church.[59]

King Oswiu's success in winning over the Anglo-Celtic churchmen – though not Bishop Colman himself,[60] while at Iona opposition to the Roman dating continued until 716, despite the conversion of Columba's biographer Adomnán to the alternative computation – stands in sharp contrast to Augustine's failure with the South British churchmen sixty years before. Margaret Deanesley, the historian of the Anglo-Saxon church's relations with the papacy, explained:

> The hatred between Celt and Angle in Northumbria was much less than that between Celt and Saxon in the south. In Northumbria the Angles were few, and had fused with the population they conquered, in the south the Romano-Britons had retreated to the west and continued their long frontier fight with the invaders. The southern Celts had seen in Augustine the representative, not of Peter but the hated *bretwalda*.[61]

From this point on (664), the question of the attitude of the Anglo-Celtic church to the Roman primacy is subsumed under that of the Anglo-Saxon church itself. Under Archbishop Theodore, the Greek monk sent from Rome who, after an interregnum, succeeded Deusdedit of Canterbury in 668, the two traditions of Church government were fused. The monastic and missionary devotion of the Celtic clergy was ordered within the structure of a territorial episcopate as planned by Pope Gregory. Bede remarked of Theodore that he was the first archbishop whom *omnis Anglorum ecclesia*, 'the whole church of the English' willingly obeyed.[62]

The warm, even eager, acceptance of the Roman primacy by Bede, unmistakeable in his references to *apostolicus papa*, became, in the remaining Anglo-Saxon centuries, the Anglo-Saxon norm. That acceptance was expressed in multifarious ways: by a series of major papal interventions, or confirmations, in the reordering of episcopal sees; by the regular passage of letters to and from Rome; by the sending of *pallia*, as well as the granting of papal privileges for monasteries, and the journeys of royal and episcopal messengers to the

Lateran for diplomatic reasons, as of pilgrims of every rank to the Vatican for devotional ones – to implore the aid of St Peter, as well as to obtain authorisations from his *vicarius*. This attitude, rooted as it was in the circumstances of the Canterbury mission, and the care shown by the Holy See for the reunited Anglo-Roman and Anglo-Celtic communities from the time of Theodore onwards, survived even, at the end of the millenium, the Danish conquest of England by Swein and Cnut.[63] And, importantly for wider European history, it was this same spirit which the Anglo-Saxon missionaries in pagan Europe would take with them to the Low Countries and to Germany.[64]

V
St Augustine in the Byzantine-Slav Tradition

The topic which the title of this chapter identifies is so enormous, and comparatively little studied, that no more than some reportage, occasional soundings, and suggestions for research can be offered here. Apart from the intrinsic historical interest of the subject, it possesses considerable ecumenical importance in the context of Catholic-Orthodox relations. After indicating what that importance may be, some account of the slow process of appropriation of Augustine's works into the Byzantine-Slav (effectively, Greek and Russian) tradition will be attempted. The article concludes with an enquiry into the attitude of contemporary Orthodox theologians to the saint and his teaching.

Ecumenical importance

It is increasingly recognised that the reconciliation of ecclesial traditions cannot take place through the theological reformulation of doctrine in 'agreed statements' in such a way as to bypass the question of the standing, within the Church's communion, of the doctors with whom particular traditions are identified. Thus, as J. D. Zizioulas has pointed out, in the dialogue between the Eastern Orthodox and Non-Chalcedonian Orthodox churches, it could not be considered sufficient to produce an agreed formula which would reconcile at the level of confessional statement the modern heirs of the Chalcedonian and Monophysite parties.[1] There cannot be full reconciliation between two such historic bodies without some kind of common reception of the holy doctors of each.

Because of Augustine's outstanding significance in the development of Latin Christian doctrine and piety, it is especially vital not to rest content with the mere hermeneutical transposition of Augustinian elements in the Western tradition into some other conceptual key which the Orthodox may find more sympathetic. The question of the explicit Orthodox reception of Augustine's ecclesial contribution must be broached. Analogously, in what is perhaps the closest parallel issue in the reverse perspective, Catholics must find some way of appropriating the figure of Gregory Palamas who, however neglected in the 'Turkish' period of Greek-speaking Orthodoxy, is increasingly regarded by mainline Orthodox theologians as providing the classical 'moment' of their tradition.[2]

Yet many Orthodox have considerable reservations in Augustine's regard. In a nuanced expression of these Père Placide Deseille has commented:

> Augustine was an admirable saint, and one of Christianity's most powerful geniuses. But his thought, which was sometimes too personal, should have been balanced and complemented by the contribution of all the other Fathers, and especially of the Greek Fathers. A too exclusive resort to Saint Augustine is certainly one of the factors which has most contributed to the later separation of the West from the rest of the Christian world. It can be said that, in large measure, Roman Catholicism and Protestantism are Augustinianisms.[3]

Such views can also find less gracious expression, so much so that Archimandrite Chrysostomos of the Greek metropolia in North America informs us that, in certain Orthodox circles in the United States

> there has developed an unfortunate bitter and harsh attitude

toward one of the great Fathers of the Church, the blessed (saint) Augustine of Hippo.[4]

This remark is offered by way of review of a study designed to dissipate or at least neutralise, such hostility: Fr Seraphim Rose's *The Place of Blessed Augustine in the Orthodox Church*.[5] I shall suggest at the close of this chapter that the *American* experience of Orthodoxy is particularly relevant to the presence of anti-Augustinian feelings in the Eastern Orthodox Church today. Meanwhile we may note, in extenuation of *individual* Orthodox who exhibit such attitudes that even Chrysostomos and Rose feel obliged to use the more common epithet 'blessed' (from the Russian, *blažennyj*), and not 'saint' (*svjatyj*), for Augustine, just as, no doubt, they would similarly follow custom in referring to another patristic theologian of somewhat uncertain standing, Theodoret of Cyr. Though the rationale of this nomenclature in the Byzantine-Slav tradition is by no means clear, its existence testifies to the existence of a problem.

Eastern appropriation of Augustine's work

As is well known, Augustine never set foot on the soil of the Eastern part of the Roman empire.[6] The years 394–5 witnessed his first relations with the Christian East insofar as he initiated at that time a correspondence with Jerome, by then definitively established in his Bethlehem monastery. Berthold Altaner speculated that Jerome may well have drawn attention to Augustine's existence in the 'Greek circles he befriended'.[7] In 415, during the Pelagian controversy, Augustine despatched the young Spanish presbyter Orosius to the Levant with a view to combating Pelagian propaganda there. But the resultant synods are more likely to have consisted for the most part of Latin clergy living in the Holy Places than of native Greco-Palestinians.[8] Certainly, John of Jerusalem showed himself unenthusiastic about Augustine's concerns, whether through a certain distance from their subjacent soteriology or perhaps feeling that one who had borne the heat and burden of the day in the Origenist controversy did not need to be instructed in orthodoxy by a Latin bishop.[9] Nevertheless, the exculpation of Pelagius by the synod of Diospolis induced Augustine to send to Jerusalem, in the name of the bishops of Africa, his *De natura et gratia* as well as, for the purposes of instructive comparison, Pelagius's *De natura*.[10] Two letters, only recently recovered, were also addressed to senior Oriental hierarchs: Atticus of Constantinople and Cyril of Alexandria.[11] In 418–9 the imperial proscription of Pelagius probably served to make Augustine's name better known in the East as the fallen theologian's arch-opponent.[12] Since Julian of Eclanum took refuge for some time with Theodore of Mopsuestia, the latter must have known of his work. However, it seems that the concept of original sin which Theodore attacked on his own account in a no longer extant treatise was drawn from the anti-Pelagian writings of Jerome, rather than from Augustine himself.[13] Although Augustine was not a metropolitan, he was invited to the Council of Ephesus by Theodosius II in a manner which, according to Capreolus of Carthage, betokened that ruler's personal esteem.[14]

Yet the *florilegium* of patristic texts read at the first session of the Council contain no text by Augustine, though portions of Cyprian and Ambrose were included. No Greek bishop or theologian ever wrote to Augustine, though in 412 a Greek student, Dioscoros, sought his advice on some philosophical questions.[15] Possidius would claim that one or more of Augustine's books were translated into Greek in the saint's lifetime.[16] If this is not a rhetorical flourish in honour of his hero, it may be that its reference is the anti-Pelagian work mentioned by Photius of Constantinople: *Augoustinos en tois pros ton Aurelion ton Kartagenês pappan diexeisin* ('Augustine in his Discourses to Aurelius, pope of Carthage').[17]

Altaner's survey of possible translations of fragments of

the Augustinian corpus into Greek between the Bishop of Hippo's death and the schism of Photius concludes with the judgment that such materials are meagre in the extreme. 'A high wall of separation' separated East and West in theology, not least because of Greek distaste for the Latin language.[18] The Greek ecclesiastical historians of the fifth and sixth centuries are silent on Augustine. Yet both individual authors and the compilers of anthologies show a marked familiarity with the writings of Augustine's elder contemporary Ambrose of Milan. The Eastern-based writer with the fullest knowledge of Augustine, and notably his doctrine of grace and original sin, is John Maxentius – but in all likelihood he was a Goth belonging to a Latin-speaking milieu in the East Roman capital.[19] Beyond the range of John's circle all we hear is the occasional faint echo. Thus Byzantine *florilegia* include a tiny collection of Augustine texts relevant to the Incarnation of the Word and sent by Leo the Great to Theodosius II and Leo I in connexion with various stages of the Monophysite crisis.[20] A sixth-century Greek catena on Mark, represented by *Codex graceus* 1692 in the Vatican Library's collection, contains a passage from the *Enarrationes in Psalmos* ('Homilies on the Psalms').[21] Justinian's defence of the Theopaschite formula to Pope Hormisdas uses two Augustine citations probably borrowed from *florilegia*.[22] In the course of his apologia for the (two) edicts against the 'Three Chapters', in 543–4 and 551 respectively, Justinian found occasion to quote Augustine's Letter 185,4 as part of his case for the posthumous condemnation of the more radical Antiochene doctors.[23] At Constantinople II, a representative of the Bishop of Carthage produced more Augustinian texts to support the imperial position.[24] And in announcing his own change of mind, or at least of policy, on the matter, Pope Vigilius cited the example of Augustine's *Retractationes* to Eutyches of Constantinople as an argument in favour of second thoughts.[25] But the age of the Seven Councils ends with a single, pseudo-Augustinian reference in the documents of

Nicea II.[26] In the following century, Photius will defend Augustine, as other Latin fathers, against their Frankish Filioquist interpreters, without having any of the actual texts before him.[27] No wonder, then, that Altaner rounded off his great essay in words which I translate:

> So my enquiry has brought out evidence that makes it plain how appalling the intellectual isolation of the linguistically differentiated Greek East and Latin West really was. No Greek theologian or hierarch from the fifth to the ninth centuries had even the most modest claim to an adequate acquaintance with the writings and theology of the great Augustine. If somewhere or other in the literature of the Greek church the name of the greatest Western theologian is mentioned, or we come across a citation from his writings, this in no case implies a serious study of the works of the bishop of Hippo. It must be finally stated that the life and work of Augustine constituted for the Greek church a scroll sealed with seven seals.[28]

Nor is the position at first sight much improved when we move on to the middle and late Byzantine periods. As Michael Rackl commented in his account of the mediaeval Greek translations of Augustine:

> In reality ... one has to perambulate vast stretches of Byzantium's theological literature before so much as bumping up against the name of Augustine.[29]

Translation of, and enthusiasm for, Augustine's writings was confined in the Byzantine world to the little circle of Latinophrone theologians who played such a major part in sustaining Unionist hopes in the period between the two reunion councils of Lyons and Florence. The cue for this surge of interest in Latin patristic theology had been given during the Second Council of Lyons by the Dominican Master-General Humbert of Romans. In his *Liber de his quae tractanda videbatur in concilio generali Lugduni celebrando sub Gregorio*

Papa Decimo ('Book on the Matters for Treatment at the General Council of Lyons to be Celebrated under Pope Gregory X'), Humbert had listed, among the prerequisites for a lasting reconciliation between Greeks and Latins, 'the translation of our books into their language, in which they excel'.[30]

The suggestion was rapidly taken up on the Byzantine side. It seems that, almost immediately, the emperor, Michael II Palaeologos, who supported the Union on both political and ecclesiastical grounds, invited the scholar Maximos Planoudes .to undertake a translation of Augustine's *De Trinitate*.[31] For his knowledge of the Latin language and its literature, as well as the skilfulness of his work as a translator, Maximos would receive graceful compliment from Cardinal Bessarion.[32] A number of MSS of the Greek *De Trinitate* still remain in Eastern libraries, notably on Athos and in the library of the Jerusalem patriarchate.[33] Unfortunately, the good offices with which Maximos had assisted the Byzantine appropriation of Augustine were cut short by the advent of the anti-Unionist Emperor Andronikos II with whom he became both professionally and personally connected.[34]

The work of Maximos Planoudes was taken further in the mid-fourteenth century by the brothers Demetrios and Prochoros Kydones.[35] As prime minister of the Emperor John Cantacuzenos, Demetrios Kydones had already undertaken the translation of one of the principal works of Thomas Aquinas, the *Summa contra Gentiles*. In the moving statement of his own veneration for the Dominican doctor which he wrote for Nilus Cabasilas, Demetrios included a warm encomium on Augustine also, praising him as the wisest of the Latin doctors, outstanding in virtue, wise judgment, and 'theology', exceeding other teachers in the Church of God by the quantity, richness and superiority of his works.[36]

His zeal as a translator was considerable. By way of providing, or so it seems, a general overview of Augustine's theology, Demetrios put into Greek Prosper of Aquitaine's *Sententiarum ex operibus sancti Augustini delibatarum liber* ('On Opinions Drawn from the Works of Holy Augustine') which has been described as a *Summa* of Augustine's thought.[37] But Demetrios was somewhat ill-starred in his capacity to elect for translation what were in fact only pseudonymously Augustinian works. Thus he translated *De fide, seu de regula verae fidei ad Petrum* ('To Peter, on Faith' – or, 'On the Rule of the True Faith'). This was regarded throughout the Western Middle Ages as a genuine piece of Augustine owing to its resemblance to the *Enchiridion* (or 'Handbook') on 'faith, hope and charity.'. It was, in fact, the work of Fulgentius of Ruspe.[38] Again, a number of inauthentic monologues were given priority. Probably by Demetrios, at least in part, are translations of three Letters: 142, *ad Marcellinum*, and 28 and 82, both *ad Hieronymum*, as well as extracts from the *Libri contra Julianum* and the *Tractates on John*.[39] Prochoros Kydones was rather more fortunate. He managed to hit on two major authentic works, the *De vera religione* and the *De libero arbitrio* as well as two letters *ad Volusianum*, 132 and 137. But a homily chosen for special attention is not genuine.[40]

In the post-Byzantine period, a trickle of translations were made, generally by Catholics or, in one case, by a Lutheran. This latter was Joannes Cassomates, the translator of the *De gratia et libero arbitrio*, who was condemned for heresy in Venice in 1571.[41] The *Rule* of Augustine exists in a seventeenth-century Greek translation by a certain 'Adelphos Augoustinos Chalkis kanonikos', but 'Chalkis' appears to have been a Bavarian *Augustiner Chorherr* (canon regular of St Augustine), presumably named Schalk![42] Still in the seventeenth century, the recently founded Congregation *De Propaganda Fidei* commissioned one 'Neophytos Rhodinos Kyprios' to translate yet another inauthentic version of the *Enchiridion*, the so-called *Manuale*. The *Soliloquia*, also in a pseudonymous guise, were appended.[43] The work was directed to Greeks at large, as its preface makes clear. The thin results of the work of the Byzantine translators and their successors speak for themselves when one considers that the translation of such a vital part of the Augustinian corpus as the *De civitate Dei* was not undertaken until 1954.[44] Nor would Byzantine Greeks and their Ottoman descendants have heard the name of Augustine in the liturgy: the Greek *Synaxarion* (the Byzantine liturgical book detailing the celebration of saints' days and certain other feast days) contained no office for him, and it was left to one of Cardinal G. F. Albani's liturgical experts, Domenico Regollotti, to compose a supplement to the *Menologion* (or 'Book of the Lives of the Saints') *of St Basil* for Latin Church fathers, including the Bishop of Hippo. Though Albani was to become pope as Clement XI, the supplement remained unpublished.[45] However, the Greek liturgy of St James does appear to include a mention of Augustine in its diptychs.[46]

In the nineteenth century Augustine's low profile in the Orthodox world underwent a facelift. An early harbinger was Eugenios Bulgaris who in 1806, as director of the patriarchal school in Constantinople, published a biography of Augustine, still extant in two Athonite collections. The title appended to *Codex* 153 in the holdings of the monasteries of Mount Athos betrays no hesitations about Augustine's standing as a genuine Church Father: *Bios entheos tou en hagiois patros hêmôn Augoustinos episkopou Hipponos Lubiês Aphrikês* ('The Divinised Life of our Father among the Saints Augustine, Bishop of Hippo, of Libya in Africa').[47] This favourable treatment of Augustine as a common Father is reflected in the 'characterisation', *charakterismos*, of the saint offered by D. S. Balanos in the *omnium gatherum* of modern Greek culture, the *Megalê Hellênikê Enkyklopaideia* ('Great Hellenic Encyclopaedia').[48] It would be valuable to learn how he is viewed by modern Greek historical theologians and ecclesiastical historians more generally.[49]

In the last hundred years of Tsarist Russia, Augustine was

given much more lavish attention than in the (in any case, somewhat impoverished and educationally limited) Church of Greece. Even before the nineteenth century opened, interest in Western literature, philosophy and religion had encouraged the translation of some central Augustinian writings: the *Confessions* were published in Russian at Moscow in 1787, as was the *De spiritu et littera*. The *De agone christiano* followed at St Petersburg in 1795. But such isolated occurrences pale into insignificance in comparison with the project of putting into Russian the entirety of Augustine's output, which was undertaken at the Ecclesiastical Academy of Kiev between 1879 and 1907 under the direction of A. I. Bulgakov and, in the project's final active year, A. J. Čekanovskij.[50] This monumental task was simply a part of the wider programme of translating all available patristic literature which, agreed on by the Russian Church and government in the wake of the early-nineteenth-century Russian patristic revival, was only baulked of completion by the outbreak of the Revolution of October 1917. However, the following works of Augustine were duly translated: *Confessiones* (the 'Confessions'); *Contra Academicos libri tres* ('Against the Academics'); *De vita beata liber unus* ('Life in Happiness'); *De ordine libri duo* ('On Order'); *Soliloquiorum libri duo* ('Soliloquies'); *De immortalitate animae liber unus* ('On the Immortality of the Soul'); *De magistro liber unus* ('The Teacher'); *De civitate Dei* ('The City of God'); *De vera religione* ('On the True Religion'); *De Genesi ad litteram liber imperfectus* (the 'Unfinished Commentary on Genesis'); *De Genesi ad litteram* ('Literal Commentary on Genesis'); *De consensu evangelistarum* ('The Harmony of the Evangelists'); *Enchiridion ad Laurentinum, sive de fide, spe et charitate* ('Handbook Concerning Faith, Hope and Charity').[51] Martin Jugie's researches into the secondary studies which accompanied this flow of texts unearthed no less than seven general works and twenty monographs along with two major encyclopaedia articles. The monographs explored widely in the themes offered by Augustine's corpus but three topics were preferred:

1 The Trinity and trinitarian analogies (N. I. Ostroumov, who interestingly, presents Augustine as *obličitel' racionalističeskago vozzrienija na Xristianskoe učenie o sv. Troice*, 'an opponent of a rationalist conception of Christian Trinitarian teaching').

2 The *City of God*, as both apologia (M. Krasin) and a piece of Christian philosophy (Hieromonk Grigor), as 'religio-social ideal' (E. Trubetskoy) as well as providing a model for Church-State relations (N. Rodnikov), and a theology of Providence in history (A. P. Lopuxin).

3 The Pelagian controversy, in relation to Augustine's anthropology (D. V. Gusev), to the issue of predestination (Archimandrite Sergei) and to original sin (A. Kremlevskij).[52]

The particularly heavy concentration of interest on the *De civitate Dei* reflects the search of the pre-Revolutionary Russian intelligentsia for the proper form of a Christian society.[53] A detailed investigation of these works would provide the materials for an assessment of Augustine's image in the pre-Bolshevik Russian tradition. However, that image would have been little perceived among the clergy and layfolk at large since, as Jugie sadly concedes, 'Up to now no trace has been found of any cultus in his honour in the Russian church.'

Contemporary Orthodox theological attitudes

The attitudes of contemporary Orthodox theologians to Augustine and his work vary considerably. Yet the novel element in the twentieth century, compared with the admittedly sluggish and often fragmentary appropriation of his writing in the past, is the emergence of a bleakly negative image of Augustine as the bane of the Western Christian tradition and the primary theological source of its ills. But as we shall see, this tendency is by no means representative of twentieth-century Orthodox dogmatics, despite the critical note many Orthodox theologians may sound in regard to limited aspects of Augustine's thought.

At least one writer, N. N. Afanas'ev (1893–1966) has only positive remarks to offer on Augustine, whose *De civitate Dei* he regarded as the necessary theological antidote to a Eusebian 'imperial theology' which had entered only too pervasively into the Byzantine-Slav tradition.[54] S. N. Bulgakov (1871–1944) though taking Augustine to task for what he termed an 'impersonal subordinationism', in which *deitas* is the sufficient foundation of the Trinitarian hypostases, was also indebted to Augustine for the notion that the Holy Spirit's distinctive rôle within the Trinitarian communion is to be its *vinculum amoris* (bond of love).[55] V. N. Lossky (1930–1958), while regarding Augustine's thought as perhaps insufficiently apophatic, roundly declared that without him (as well as other Latin Fathers) the Orthodox Church would not be what it is – a somewhat inflated appreciation![56] G. V. Florovsky (1893–1979), although criticising Augustine's 'extensional' concept of the Church's catholicity, considered his view of history as exemplary in liberating the Church from the temptations of a Greek 'cyclical' view of the historical process.[57]

It is, then, the more surprising to discover such a virulent anti-Augustinianism as that presented by John S. Romanides in various works, and notably in his interpretation of the events surrounding the Photian crisis, *Franks, Romans, Feudalism and Doctrine*.[58] His attack on Augustine is embedded within his own slightly idiosyncratic reconstruction of the *conjunctures* of ninth-century Europe, in which he downplays the considerable tensions between the papacy and the Byzantine imperial power in order to highlight those between Rome and the Franks. His contention is that the Frankish monarchy used the divergences between Augustine and the common patristic tradition, Eastern and Western, as a tool to prize apart 'West' and 'East' Romans. This was possible since, according to Romanides, Augustine had forsaken the *pars sanior* of the Latin Fathers, to his own perdition, on a whole variety of issues:

> ... the questions of the Old Testament appearances of the Logos, the existence of universals, the general framework of the doctrine of the Trinity, the nature of communion between God and man, the manner in which Christ reveals his divinity to the apostles, and in general the relation between doctrine and speculation, or revelation and reason.[59]

Though each of these points may be worthy of discussion, the drawing up of a series of capital charges in order to justify Augustine's exclusion from the company of orthodox Fathers is something new. For Romanides, Augustine is quite simply a stranger to the patristic tradition, being rather a student of the Bible 'interpreted within the framework of Plotinus and under the pressure of his Manichean past'.

It may be no coincidence that, just as much of the teaching work of Romanides has been among the American Orthodox, so it is in the United States that, as mentioned above in connexion with Fr Rose's study, the most widespread disaffection with Augustine can be found. George Every of Oscott College, Birmingham, has suggested that the Orthodox in the United States may have acquired their anti-Augustinianism from an element in the theological life of their Episcopalian neighbours.[60] It was, he suggests, the preference of the eighteenth-century 'Yale converts' to Anglicanism for other Fathers than Augustine, partly in the light of the extreme Augustinianism of their Reformed rivals, which injected a virus into the American theological bloodstream, initially mildly, but now, in the case of the modern Orthodox, conscious of Augustine's defective appropriation in their own tradition and in eager pursuit of their confessional identity, in acute form.[61]

Conclusion

If this is so, the desirability of an Orthodox study of Augustine and his thought, in the round and not under some purely partial aspect, is great indeed, not least for the future of Catholic-Orthodox dialogue. Perhaps such a future study will prove able to echo Florovsky's extraordinary remark, 'I would say that Augustine is really an Eastern Father':[62] a comment not lacking in irony yet borne up, surely, by a surge of recognition which it might be possible to call also love. In such charity towards those who, though dead, still live in Christ, and not in theological dialogue alone, the reconciliation of the traditions may be achieved.[63]

VI
The Appeal to the Fathers in the Ecclesiology of Nikolai Afanas'ev

The Russian Orthodox ecclesiologist N. N. Afanas'ev (1893–1966) is widely regarded as one of the most influential figures in ecclesiological thought this century – both in his own communion, and, through the interconnected notions of the 'local Church' and 'eucharistic ecclesiology', in Catholicism as well. I have presented elsewhere an overview of his thought.[1] Inheriting from his Slavophile predecessors the notion of the Church as a community of love structured by the pattern of its sacramental life but owning no authority of a strictly legal kind, Afanas'ev, struck by Russian Orthodoxy's difficulties in disengaging itself from the protective embrace of the Tsardom as well as the jurisdictional conflicts which plagued it after the Revolution of 1917, worked out an ecclesiology in which the concepts of legal authority (whether civil or canonical) and of an organisationally unified *universal* Church would play no part. Instead the Church must be re-thought as a communion of local churches, each founded on the eucharistic assembly of an episcopally gathered congregation. The relevance of these ideas to the ecclesiological work of the Second Vatican Council, and the ferment of its aftermath, scarcely needs underlining – even if, at the same time, they include certain imbalances and unilateralisms, to which attention was drawn in my study.

This did not contain, however, an evaluation, in terms of patrology, of Afanas'ev's main claim – in his own eyes – to the attention of his peers, or posterity. For it was by appeal to the Fathers, as a contributor to the movement of patristic *ressourcement* (or, 'going back to the sources'), that Afanas'ev's most characteristic ideas were set forth. That *lacuna* I hope to fill in this chapter.

The heart of Afanas'ev's appeal to the Fathers lies in his evocation of the life of the ancient Church as, in the words of the late Byzantine Nicholas Cabasilas, 'life in Christ', a life finding its source and goal in the liturgy but expressing itself in charity at all levels. It is clear from the tone and manner of Afanas'ev's writing that he does not regard this appeal to the patristic age as simply a matter of an empirical comparison, more or less illuminating, between two periods of Church history. The appeal to the Fathers is made by way of being an appeal to authority, even though Afanas'ev by some other criterion also finds himself able to criticise the teaching of individual Fathers.

There follows here the presentation of a gallery of portraits of the patristic ecclesiologists drawn on by Afanas'ev. Some will be lightly sketched, others more fully depicted, depending on the extent and quality of Afanas'ev's concern with them. We may imagine him as a frequent visitor to this gallery of the ancient Church, struck now by one feature, now by another, attracted by some traits, repelled by others. They appear here in their chronological order – although in the case of the first one discussed, the Didachist, Afanas'ev would have dissented from the present-day consensus of scholars as to its dating.

The Didachist

The *Didache* is one of the most controversial of early Christian documents, and it is not surprising if Afanas'ev manifests a certain ambivalence in its regard. It was discovered at a time when scholarship had come to something of an impasse in the study of Christian origins, and as the only major discovery of the period (the 1880s) in early-Christian literature it was made to support everyone's favoured theories. As C. Bigg wrote, it was the 'spoilt child of criticism'.[2] The Cambridge scholar F. E. Vokes, whom Afanas'ev will follow closely,[3] defined the 'real problem' of the Didache as being

> whether it is a picture of the Church at the time when it was written, an antiquarian picture of the Church as it was at some time in the past, or an imaginary picture.[4]

Vokes came down with some force, in company with other scholars of the time, on a combination of the second and third of these three possibilities. The author of the *Didache* tries to express in New Testament and 'apostolic' language what is common to his church and that of the New Testament itself. His church supported a 'moderate Montanism' which it expressed in 'as respectable and apostolic a form as possible'. This explains the mixture of primitiveness and development to be found in the document. This hypothesis of Vokes is far from being merely impressionistic. He argues from a close analysis of the relations between the Gospels, the *Letter of Barnabas*, Hermas and the *Didache* that the *Didache* was written after Hermas, and thus no earlier than c. 150. In general – and surely correctly – Vokes held that the proper procedure for dealing with the *Didache* was to fit it into the known framework of early Christian history, as its finder and other early students tried to do. However, because it was the 'spoilt child' this was not done. Instead, its early date was exaggerated and its significance for a revision of the accepted picture blown up out of all proportion by those whose purpose was to demolish traditional Christianity by postulating a primitive Eucharist like that apparently described in *Didache* ix and x, and a primitive 'charismatic' ministry like that inferred from *Didache* xi and xii. Theologically liberal Church historians thought they saw in the 'Two Ways' section of the *Didache* a superficially Christianised Jewish pamphlet, and in chapters ix, x and xiv a primitive, pre-Catholic Eucharist still closely connected with the *Kiddush*, while in chapters xi–xv at large they found an absence of ministerial organisation which they ascribed to the preponderant position of spiritually gifted 'prophets'. In the entire text they divined a preoccupation with ethics and a lack of interest in dogma, two characteristics which to scholars of the school of Adolf von Harnack and Paul Sabatier were signs of primitive Christianity.[5] For Vokes, by contrast, the *Didache*

> gives in the form of a summary of apostolic teaching a description of what can be called the 'apostolic element' of Montanism; ... its purpose is the defence of the 'New Prophecy'.[6]

Precisely this statement enables Afanas'ev to present those features of the Didachist's Church order which he dislikes as 'deviations' from the 'norm'. For the *Didache* is certainly not one of his favourite works. True, in the early chapters of *Tserkov' Dukha Sviatogo* ('The Church of the Holy Spirit') its author is commended for his awareness that a local church may sometimes lack the service of 'prophets'.[7] This awareness seems to support Afanas'ev's own insistence that a church, to be a church, may lack many gifts, but it can never fail to have its *proestôs*, the Eucharistic president. However, a fuller *ex professo* discussion in this main monument of Afanas'ev's ecclesiology produces a much more negative estimate. Indeed, Afanas'ev has composed a veritable catalogue of the Didachist's offences. Thus, the latter's stress on the prophesying of the genuine prophet as always *eo ipso* true prophecy, without the need for any confirmatory reception on the part of the believing community, is said to cut off the prophetic individual from his proper context, the Eucharistic assembly. In this, it is woefully unlike the Pauline account which sees prophecy as a gift to the whole local church via the individual. The assertion that the prophet can absolve from sin displaces the bishop. The ascription of the right to 'give thanks', i.e. preside at *agapê* or Eucharist, to the prophet also gives to him what is rightfully the bishop's, namely the rôle of *proestôs* (president). Above all, the *Didache*'s ministerial prophets do not belong to a local church but wander from one such to another. In them the *Didache* testifies to its own adherence to a universalist account of the Church, an account made explicit elsewhere in its pages. It is, in fact, according to Afanas'ev, our earliest example of such an ecclesiology.[8]

In order to nip this nascent universalist ecclesiology in the bud, what could be more effective than the deft appropriation of the hypothesis advanced by Vokes, thus relegating the *Didache* to a milieu outside the Great Church? In terms of later scholarship, the principal defect in his presentation lies in his denial that the *Didache* has any characteristic Jewish-Christian qualities. Vokes explicitly says that

> the *Didache* shows, like any Christian writing of any period, the Jewish origin of Christianity, but it shows no special knowledge of Rabbinic writings or Jewish customs. Its knowledge of Judaism is in no way greater than that of any other Christian writer. So far as its knowledge of Judaism and its partaking in the Jewish legacy to Christianity is concerned, the *Didache* is quite timeless.[9]

That the author of the *Didache* is innocent of detailed knowledge of Rabbinic thought and practice may be conceded. Nevertheless, the wider conclusion which Vokes draws from this no longer carries the same conviction. In the present state of scholarship, where the portrait of Jewish-Christianity is now much better filled out, the *Didache* seems to belong firmly within this particular 'world', one of several, as Jean Daniélou pointed out, that together constitute the patristic Church.[10]

As early as an essay of C. H. Dodd in 1947, important reservations were announced about the late date ascribed to the *Didache* on the Connolly-Vokes hypothesis.[11] But in 1958 the most substantial study of the *Didache* yet to appear emerged from the French Canadian Dominican Jean-Paul Audet.[12] Partly by demonstrating that the 'longer title' of the *Didache*, 'Instruction of the Lord to the Gentiles via the Twelve Apostles', was inauthentic, Audet replaced the work firmly into the Jewish-Christian milieu to which, from every indication, it belongs.[13] He reversed the arguments of the earlier scholars on the dependence of the *Didache* on Barnabas, *The Shepherd* and the canonical gospels,[14] proposing that the date of the work is around the year 60 and its place of origin Syria or Palestine, probably Antioch.[15] Naturally, it is not possible to enter here into the details of this controversy, but it may be said that Audet's thesis has won wide support and this of itself necessarily sets a major question mark against Afanas'ev's use of the *Didache*. If the text is as early as the earliest gospel, then in terms of empirical antiquity the universalist ecclesiology must be allowed to be as ancient as its 'eucharistic' counterpart.

Nevertheless, Afanas'ev's portrait of the *Didache* and its place (or non-place) in the tradition may be saved if it is expressed in a more nuanced form. Granted that the *Didache* may well be of the highest antiquity, it may still represent a sub-tradition rather than the mainstream. If it could be shown that Montanism is itself of Jewish-Christian inspiration, then the itinerant Jewish-Christian prophets of the *Didache*, belonging to no one local church but only to the Church at large, rather as the mediaeval friars were 'exempt' from the jurisdiction of local bishops, may be seen as quite marginal in any attempt to re-draw the outline of the ancient Church in its central manifestations.[16] Alas, the links, if any, between Montanism and Jewish Christianity remain indecently obscure. And in any case, to suppose that the specifying qualities of Jewish-Christian churches can make no contribution to a normative ecclesiology is to accept the disputable thesis that theological history must belong unconditionally to the victors. What *is* clear in all this is that Afanas'ev saw in the mirror of the *Didache* those features of a possible ecclesiology which he most distrusted.

Ignatius of Antioch

Ignatius of Antioch is without doubt the hero of Afanas'ev's *oeuvre*.[17] Although his vocabulary is often imprecise and even exotic, Ignatius was nevertheless the first figure in the history of doctrine to speak about the constitution of the Christian *ecclesia*, the preeminence of the bishop in each local church and the priority of the church, though not bishop, of Rome. A number of aspects of Ignatian ecclesiology are dear to Afanas'ev. First, there is the principle of the co-inherence of bishop and church.[18] Secondly, there is the stress on the indissoluble union of president and people, forming together 'one choir' in the liturgical gathering.[19] Then, thirdly, there is the consequent dependence of the Ignatian pen-portrait of the Church on the eucharistic assembly and, behind that assembly, on the Last Supper.[20] Fourthly, although the Ignatian letters may well permit mere presbyters to preside at the Eucharist, their more fundamental tendency is to hurry on the transformation of the 'proto-presbyter' of apostolic times into the classical figure of the 'monarchical' bishop of the patristic period,[21] thus presenting in high relief what Afanas'ev takes to be the key to the pattern of the Christian ministry, the man who presides by giving thanks.[22]

In one sense, however, the arrival of the monarchical episcopate in Ignatian Syria was an ambiguous development in Afanas'ev's eyes. The emergence of the classical episcopate also involved the emergence of a 'high priestly' symbolism in which the bishop was taken to be the efficacious sign in the Church of the high priesthood of Christ as presented in the Letter to the Hebrews. The bishop occupies, after all, the place of Christ the high priest at the Last Supper when he presides at the Eucharist which, to Afanas'ev's mind, is the fullness of the Church of God. However, Afanas'ev deems such sacerdotal symbolism to be of distinctly questionable value. Insofar as it expressed the high significance for the local church of its eucharistic 'president in the Lord', well and good; insofar as it created the possibility of regarding the bishop's eucharistic presidency as flowing from his 'priesthood' and not *vice versa*, not so good or rather, very bad indeed.[23] The price paid in separating the Eucharist from the ministry by postulating a (non-eucharistic) pontificate of the apostles, was a heavy one. The willingness to pay it can only be explained, so Afanas'ev opined, by fear of fragmentation within the early communities. The centrifugal force of early heresies moved the Church to exalt the bishop, as guardian of the faith proclaimed at the Eucharist, to the highest level of authority it could find.[24]

But whatever germs of later exaggeration there may be in the presentation by Ignatius of the figure of the bishop, all are pardonable to Afanas'ev because of the resolutely particularist doctrine of the Church advanced by Ignatius – and this is the final, and most significant, reason for Afanas'ev's commendation of him. For Ignatius, each local church manifests the one Church of God in Christ. The Church of God is not the sum-total of local churches but is fully given in each. Nevertheless, at the empirical level, the local churches do of course form a union, based in Ignatius on charity, and therefore in a derivative way this union of churches may also be spoken of – but very secondarily – as the 'one Church'. It is on this last point that an evaluation of Afanas'ev's use of Ignatius must largely turn.

That the chief interest of Ignatius is the life of the various *local* churches to which he wrote can hardly be in doubt. Afanas'ev's belief that Ignatius was inspired by the Matthaean *logion* on the presence of Jesus in the assembly of two or three in his name may be well-founded, given the likely influence on Ignatius of the Matthaean tradition, whether in oral or written form.[25] The main message in Ignatius is the need for solidarity with the *proestōs* of each such gathering. The bishop is the president of the Church's assembly in each city, the leader of its 'choir', the head of the body, even though he may be assisted by other ministers, by presbyters and deacons. Around the bishop all must gather, uniting themselves to him in full obedience, doing nothing without him. To be with the bishop is to have a part in the Church, and so in Jesus Christ, and so in God. Whereas not to be with him, as the dissidents and false doctors are not with him, is to lack all these realities.[26]

Nevertheless, it may be questioned whether the ecclesiology of Ignatius is as wholly non-universalist as Afanas'ev believes. In the Letter to the Smyrnaeans, for instance, Ignatius speaks of Christ as, through his Resurrection, 'setting up an ensign', *arê sussêmon*, for all ages, for Jews and Gentiles alike, 'in the one body of his Church', *en heni sômati tês ekklêsias autou*.[27] Later, in the same letter, Ignatius appears to be working with an analogy which cuts across the Afanas'evan model of the Church: what the bishop is to the local church, Christ is to the Church universal.

> Wherever the bishop appears let the congregation be present; just as wherever Jesus Christ is, there is the Catholic Church.[28]

Most strikingly of all, in the Letter to the Magnesians, Christ is referred to by the title 'the bishop of all', *pantôn episkopos*.[29] The ontological link between the many churches and the one Church is not simply found in the 'intensive' catholicity of each's manifestation of the single mystery. Their interrelationship also possesses an 'extensive' dimension. It is possible that Afanas'ev misunderstood the term *agapê*, 'charity', at a vital point in the Ignatian corpus. The point concerns the ascription of 'priority' (to use Afanas'ev's language) to the Roman Church in the opening greeting of

Ignatius in his Letter to the Romans. The 'presidency in charity' of the Roman church in this passage is best translated as presidency *in the Church*. *Agapê* here is not a purely moral quality, the works of mercy and loving-kindness which some commentators have suggested.[30] As was pointed out as long ago as 1881, wherever the verb *prokathênai*, 'to preside', is used with a direct complement it is followed by a name indicating a place or a society.[31] *Agapê* here is in fact equivalent to *ekklêsia*. Ignatius has already used it to denote local churches.[32] Why should he not use it for the Church universal? Hence the Latin translation offered by F. X. Funk: *universo caritatis coetui praesidens*.[33] Though Afanas'ev was aware of the ecclesial force of Ignatius's *agapê* he proposed to protect the 'particularist' hypothesis by construing the phrase *prokathêmenê tês agapês* on the basis of the inscription of the Letter. There the Roman church is said to 'have the presidency in the country of the Romans': *prokathêtai en topô chôriou Rômaiôn*.[34] At the time of writing *Tserkov Dukha Sviatogo*, Afanas'ev believed that Rome's 'priority' was exercised, in the eyes of Ignatius, not in the universal *agapê* of Christendom at large but, rather, within the 'suburbicarian' local churches of central Italy, the foundation of the later Roman patriarchate. By the post-war years, however, Afanas'ev found in this text a twofold 'priority', both regional and worldwide, though he still insisted on interpreting the latter within the characteristic terms of eucharistic ecclesiology. But it is not certain that the mystery of co-inherence between the one Church and the many churches is exhausted for Ignatius by the local epiphany of the One in each of the Many. There may also be a sense in which the one Church is present in the many precisely as many. It is this further dimension, alluded to in the pregnant phrase 'the Charity' which Afanas'ev studiously ignores.

Nevertheless, he has captured the heart of Ignatian ecclesiology, which lies in the intensive presence of Christ's Church in the local community gathered around its bishop at the Eucharist. To that ecclesiology Afanas'ev himself wholeheartedly responded. One might think here, with Hans von Campenhausen, of the Ignatian sense of the contemporary Church as a living mystery, united in its totality to Christ.[35] (Ignatius is little interested in the possible historical derivation of the Church's particular structures from the apostolic group.) Or again, one cannot fail to note the Ignatian concept of unity as a union in sympathy, a harmony or fundamental agreement, something for which he favours musical images.[36] One could reflect on how little Ignatius is concerned with legal norms, focusing instead on the holy fellowship embodied in the conjunction of bishop, clergy and congregation.[37] Finally, one might consider what has justly been termed the 'cultic' character of the Ignatian ideal of Church office:

> Ignatius' total conception of the Church and of Christianity possesses a cultic character in this respect, namely that salvation becomes a reality only in unison with the activity of the visible congregation, performed both in the spirit and in the flesh; in this way the Church exhibits the divine world, and actualises it through its own way of life.[38]

One could hardly ask for a better summary of Afanas'ev's own teaching in *propria persona*. At root, this similarity derives from the shared ecclesiological conviction that the Church is a mystery of differentiated ministerial charity: it is in this sense, indeed, that Afanas'ev's fundamental doctrine of the Church is itself Ignatian.

Irenaeus

Afanas'ev's growing interest in the question of a 'church in priority', aroused by his study of Ignatius, and fostered by the *conjunctures* of his situation as an Orthodox exile in a Catholic culture at a time of accelerating ecumenical *rapproche-*

ment, inevitably directed his attention to Irenaeus, the author of the celebrated 'primacy text' of the *Adversus Haereses* ('Against the Heresies'):

> For with this church, which holds a leading position among the churches, it is right that every church – that is, the orthodox everywhere should agree, inasmuch as the apostolic tradition is always preserved by the orthodox who are everywhere.[39]

The context of this remarkable sentence is the context of the whole of the writings of Irenaeus: the defence of the orthodox faith against heretical Gnosis. As is well known, not least from his writings, a large part of the debate of the orthodox with the Gnostics turned on formal arguments of authority, appeals to public revelation on the side of the former, to esoteric revelation on the side of the latter. Since the discovery of an entire Egyptian Gnostic library at Nag Hammadi in 1946, it has been possible to control in some way the description by Irenaeus of his adversaries and the struggle with them.[40] The study of these fifty-one treatises very largely confirms the conclusions reached immediately after the Second World War by Père Sagnard.[41] The account of Irenaeus, if unimaginative, is reliable and fair – as we might expect from the hints he gives of how careful he has been to get acquainted with his opponents' arguments.[42] In terms of doctrinal content, Irenaeus directed his opposition to Gnostic dualism, to the notion that there are two worlds, one of which has its temporary outposts, eventually to be readmitted, in another which is otherwise alien to it. Against this, Irenaeus proposes that there is a single world, a world full of God's glory, and one God who contains it all and governs its history by his providence. Irenaeus substitutes for the Gnostic 'redemption-physics' a Christian 'redemption-history'. The Gnostics had seen their salvation, that is, as being by nature and from history; Irenaeus sees salvation, rather, as being by history, in nature. The starting-point of Irenaeus, therefore, is

what God has done for his people; centrally and most constitutively, what he has done in Christ.[43]

It follows from this that *formally* an accurate understanding of what Christ has done historically, and so publicly,
is vital. Thus the topic of the sources of revelation, *fontes
revelationis*, emerges for the first time as an explicit object of
theological reflection.[44] Irenaeus turns first to the Scriptures,
but the Gnostics disputed the orthodox interpretation of the
Scriptures in the light of their own occult tradition. They
took them in the light of their particular mythopoeic cosmology, rather than the other way round. Thus it was that
Irenaeus found himself obliged to appeal to

> that tradition which has come down to us from the apostles,
> guarded by successions of presbyters in the churches.[45]

If he wished, he could, he says, provide a list of all those who
have presided over the churches from the time of the apostles
onwards. But in fact he confines himself to giving the succession of these accredited witnesses to the apostolic tradition
as found in one local church, the church of Rome, which here
must stand for them all. When Christians disagree about the
true *gnôsis*, the content of Christian revelation, then their
practice is to have recourse to those communities that are
the most ancient among all the churches. The witness of the
churches where the apostles themselves taught stands for
the witness of all.

> Would it not be necessary to have recourse to the oldest
> churches, in which the apostles lived, and obtain from them
> some clear and definite ruling on the present subject of dis-
> pute?[46]

Here we have the clue to the appeal of Irenaeus to the faith of
the Roman church since in her these criteria of venerableness
and apostolicity are especially well evidenced. This church is

the greatest, most ancient and well-known church, founded by
the two most glorious apostles, Peter and Paul at Rome . . .[47]

We are now in a position to approach more closely the celebrated primacy text of the *Adversus Haereses* cited above.

Afanas'ev's discussion of this ecclesiologically momentous
text turns on the nature of the obligation involved in the
'recourse' to the Church founded on the *martyria* – at once
'martyrdom' and 'witness' – of Peter and Paul. What is the
ground and nature of this *necesse*, this 'must', which, according to the Latin translator of Irenaeus, obliges a church to
recurrere 'have recourse to', or *convenire*, 'turn to', the
Roman church for guidance? Afanas'ev suggests that *necesse*
in Irenaeus does not at all imply some kind of legal obligation. Instead, it is more like what may be called an ontological exigence. It springs from the very nature of the
Church. Where there is disagreement there will naturally (in
effect, *super*naturally) be recourse to the church with the
greatest authority. This church will bear her witness on
events in other churches, not sustaining this witness by force
of law, but by force of love. And so Afanas'ev can remark:

> If there has ever been a time in church history when the catch-
> word *Roma locuta est, causa finita* stood for something real, that
> time was before the church of Rome had any powers by law.[48]

What, then, is this 'greater authority', *potentior principalitas*,
with which Irenaeus credits the Roman church? Afanas'ev
admits that in the absence of the Greek original, the text is
hard to interpret. The exhaustive analysis of the phrase in
Sagnard's edition of this book of the *Adversus Haereses*
amply confirms this judgment.[49] But he proposes that what is
at stake here is not *power*, thus not a canonical ('political')
primacy of legislation and administration but rather *auth-*

ority, and more especially, the authority which flows from apostolic foundation and constitution by Peter and Paul. To mark this distinction between power and authority, Afanas'ev decrees that to be faithful to what Irenaeus meant we should speak here not of *primacy* but of *priority*. The Roman church is the church with the 'greatest priority'.[50]

In fact, this is to some degree a matter of verbal stipulation on Afanas'ev's part. 'Primacy' does not seem to connote 'power' more than 'authority' in the four Western languages in which Afanas'ev's essay appeared, any more than 'priority' necessarily connotes 'authority' more than 'power'. More significant is Afanas'ev's conjecture about the Greek term underlying the crucial words *potentior principalitas*. The word *archaiotês* which he holds to be original conveys the idea of being connected to a source, to some ultimate founda-tion, *archê* – just as, originally, the word *auctoritas* did in Latin. Because of its source or foundation in the apostles Peter and Paul, the witness of the Roman church among the churches takes on a unique and exemplary character. Her authority is simply the authority of this unique and exemp-lary character of witness, as that witness is applied to any matter of doctrine or life in another church which may come to her attention. Her 'powers' are powers to receive or to not-receive the actions, credal or practical, of another church. But because she is the church in priority, then her non-recep-tion of the choices of a local church are not merely a break-down in good relations between the churches. They are not simply an empirical disorder, an eruption on the surface of the body politic of the Church. Rather, they are a placing of that other local church under the judgment of the Lord of the Church, who is, for Afanas'ev as for Irenaeus, the true Fount of the apostolic witness.

It is, of course, because of the intimate relation between the *Spirit* and the Church that this is so; and thus brings us to the celebrated text of *Adversus Haereses* III which may be de-scribed as the 'signature-tune' of Afanas'ev's ecclesiology:

> Where the Church is, there is the Spirit of God, and where the Spirit of God is, there is the Church and all grace.[51]

For Irenaeus, indeed, the activity of the Spirit, the mediation of the Spirit, and the Church form an unbreakable unity. With the giving of the Spirit, as the *Demonstration of the Apostolic Preaching* points out, the concrete, historical Church is created.[52] Thus, as Heinz-Joachim Jaschke has written, the Church is, for Irenaeus, the true 'addressee' of the Spirit's outpouring.[53] The Lord himself 'has given the Church the Spirit of God',[54] so that for all time she may enjoy 'the same gift of the Spirit'.[55] The Church is not, then, the ultimate giver of the spiritual treasures that are in her, but, rather, the sign of the Spirit who holds sway there. The celebrated passage cited by Afanas'ev on the co-terminous quality of Spirit and Church precisely by giving expression to the 'innermost ground of the Church', is necessarily, therefore:

> ... a pointer to her existence in relationship with Another. She [the Church] is not an autonomous reality, because to the truth that is in her man simply responds.[56]

The Spirit, whose presence is the Church's characteristic quality, shows his activity in a pre-eminent way by leading the Church into the truth, and preserving her in it. In the struggle with Gnosis, this theme was, evidently, of fundamental interest to Irenaeus.

Although Irenaeus is too attentive a student of Paul to miss the connexion between the Eucharist and our incorporation into the Church as the body of Christ, he hovers, merely, around the possible connexion between these ideas and the pneumatological approach to the Church which sees her mystery as that of the reality of the Spirit. Though two passages, not, apparently, noted by Afanas'ev come close to an explicit affirmation of this link, it remains essentially implicit in Irenaeus's thought.[57] The tendency of Afanas'ev's reading of Irenaeus is, however, to render eloquent what was simply tacit in the Church Father – the Church as the Lord's body is the Church in which the Holy Spirit lives. Given by Christ, the Spirit becomes palpable in his body, just as, seen from a pneumatological perspective, we can also say that the Spirit's activity consists in his building up Christ in the Church, and therewith in realising the salvation of creatures.[58]

Tertullian and Montanism

A phrase from Tertullian's Montanist period gives Afanas'ev the title of *Tserkov' Dukha Sviatogo*.[59] Afanas'ev's references to Tertullian are sympathetic and very far from a tendency in some modern Orthodox writing to make Tertullian the father of an alleged all-pervasive legalism in the Latin Church (a case made out in some Western writers also, notably the late Walter Ullmann).[60] But it may well be that Tertullian was not, in fact, a *jurisconsultus*; it is *prima facie* unlikely that a Christian would have exercised this profession under the Antonines, and the legal knowledge shown in Tertullian's writings would be explicable on the thesis that he had simply received a normal good education of the period.[61] In any case what attracts Afanas'ev is not, oddly enough, the Catholic Tertullian but Tertullian the Montanist. Afanas'ev wishes to 'save' Tertullian for the Church by arguing that his account of the Church's nature applies, despite appearances, to the Catholic Church itself. The Church is at the deepest level what Tertullian believed it had ceased to be, namely, the 'Church of the Holy Spirit', a body essentially charismatic, and withdrawn from the 'structural patterns' (above all, the power-relationships) of 'this age'.[62]

The sharp division between the Church and the world in Afanas'ev, the stress laid on the Church as an eschatological reality placed, against nature, here and now in the space and time of a fallen *aiôn*, is markedly reminiscent of the North

African tradition to which Tertullian belonged.[63] Contemporary historians suggest that Christianity arrived in Africa in the Antonine age, via the Jewish community of Carthage. Be this as it may, the Christian Church in Africa Proconsularis soon took on its keynote of uncompromising rejection of an alien world, a note already audible in the *Acts of the Scillitan Martyrs*, while reception of the *Passio Felicitatis et Perpetuae* ('Passion of Saint Felicity and Saint Perpetua') at Carthage (where in Augustine's day it was read in church and treated by some as on the same level as the canonical Scriptures) indicates that the African church, precisely because of its thoroughgoing eschatological posture, would in all probability be open to Montanist influence.[64] The message of this text is that acceptance of prophecies and visions gives the Christian the courage to face martyrdom – exactly the claim made by Tertullian for the New Prophecy in his *De Fuga* ('Flight in Time of Persecution').[65]

Montanus began to prophesy in the Roman province of Asia around the year 170.[66] The New Prophecy spread rapidly and to judge from one source nearly achieved the recognition of the Catholic episcopate.[67] But as the Carthaginian church (which was coming to enjoy a quasi-patriarchal authority in North Africa) moved steadily away from Montanism, Tertullian moved towards it. Tertullian's interest in Montanism seems to have sprung from a sense that the Church had suffered an over-heavy institutionalisation (though such language is, of course, hardly of the second century).

> The Church is the Church of the Spirit thanks to the spiritual man. It is not the number of bishops that makes her Church.[68]

In addition, however, we must allow a place to the intellectual dialectic Tertullian faced during the writing of his anti-Gnostic and anti-Marcionite works. It was during the composition of these books that he came to accept the New

Prophecy.[69] Over against the systems of thought just mentioned, he insisted that Christianity was a revealed religion (not a religion excogitated out of inner experience), and that it was a religion based on (though not restricted to) the Scriptures (and that meant, *vis-à-vis* Marcion, the entire biblical corpus). But had this revelation ceased, or did the Spirit still speak to men and women? This concern with the charismatic contemporaneity of the Spirit to the Church was matched in Tertullian's case with a dislike of practical innovations in Church discipline, innovations that could be held to blur the radicalism of life in the Spirit as that (arguably) had been practised in the apostolic age.[70] Essentially, this was the problem of the forgiveness of post-baptismal sin. It was these two features in combination (how is revelation actual now?; must not the pristine integrity of Christian practice be maintained?) which led Tertullian to the New Prophecy. The crucial test of obedience to the Paraclete's inspiration and demands lay in the willingness to follow where this movement led. The Paraclete gives direct counsel to every Christian; his promptings preserve doctrinal orthodoxy and they enable men and women to live lives fitting to those who may well have to die martyrs' deaths.[71]

It follows that, insofar as Afanas'ev is concerned to redeem the Montanist Tertullian, and insofar as, in dependence on Tertullian, he regards his own view of the Church as 'charismatic', this has little if anything to do with the 'neo-Pentecostal' spirituality which began to touch all mainstream Christian churches (including the Orthodox of North America) in the decade which saw Afanas'ev's death. As Jean Steinmann pointed out, Tertullian was not attracted by the more exotic aspects of the Phrygian 'charismatic renewal'.[72] His devotion to the New Prophecy lay in the fact that it seemed to bear out his own prior teaching on the Paraclete, as, for instance, he had expressed that in the *Ad Martyres* which can be described as an essay in practical pneumatology.[73]

Quite credible in historical context is Steinmann's suggestion that, in separating himself from the Church, Tertullian 'takes his distance, in advance, from Constantine'. Steinmann proposed that by their disassociation from the New Prophecy

> the hierarchy was preparing the union of the new religion with the old structures of the imperial civilisation . . .[74]

The idea might well have been congenial to Afanas'ev, as we shall see from a consideration later in this chapter of his attitude to Augustine. For the fact is that even after Constantine (and, more to the point, even after Theodosius), the great majority of the African church remained hostile to or suspicious of the imperial connexion. Even such an anti-Donatist as Augustine came, in the *De Civitate Dei*, to share many of their doubts.[75] What Afanas'ev takes from Tertullian's Montanism is, then, firstly, a stress on the Spirit as the continuing and thus contemporary source of the life of the Church in all its native manifestations ('ministries') and, secondly, the notion that because the Spirit is the Spirit of the Parousia (his presence now is proleptic, a 'first-fruits' of the Resurrection whose full virtue will only be gauged by the 'events' of the end of time), the Church of her nature is incompatible with the pattern, laws and values of the age where she is set.

> When Tertullian himself joined the heretical and schismatic Montanists, it was because he believed the Catholic churches were no longer properly respecting the boundary between Christian and non-Christian in the discipline they exercised over their congregations.[76]

We shall return to this aspect of the North African, and more specifically Tertullianic, heritage in a moment, when we come to consider the background to Cyprian, whose defective ecclesiology – as Afanas'ev had perceived it from the time of his essay, *Dve idei vselenskoi Tserkvi* ('Two Ideas of the Church Universal'), onwards – is the dark foil to the shining splendour of Ignatius. Meanwhile, we can note here that what Afanas'ev decidedly does *not* take from Tertullian is the latter's counterposing of the *homo spiritalis* (the 'spiritual man') to the *numerus episcoporum* ('sum total of the bishops'). Neither has Afanas'ev any sympathy for the fundamental presupposition of this contrast: Tertullian's assertion that the distinction between *plebs*, the faithful (and catechumens), and *ordo*, the ordained ministry, is simply an ecclesiastical device, something of purely human origin. Afanas'ev's aim is to resituate the Church's ministries — ministries regarded by him as an internal differentiation of the Church's nature *qua* 'royal priesthood', within a pneumatic ecclesiology indebted to the later Tertullian.

Afanas'ev has rightly seen that for Tertullian, the person of the Holy Spirit is particularly engaged in the sphere of the Church: the Church is born at Pentecost, the parousia of the Spirit.[77] Afanas'ev does not mention, however, the important motif of the Church as mother in Tertullian, *ecclesia mater*, which may well have underground pneumatological connexions. Writers at various points in the tradition, ranging from the Syriac fathers in the patristic East to Gerard Manley Hopkins in the nineteenth-century West, have associated the Spirit with 'feminine' aspects of the divine economy in creation and redemption.[78] According to one major contemporary study, the theme of the Church as mother is a controlling image in Tertullian's presentation of the mystery of the Church, and an essence-revealing image at that. Pointing out that for ancient thought the image is not simply an illustration of some reality but is 'reality itself in its immediate visualisation as expression and representation', Karl Delehaye regards the primary images of the Fathers, following in the wake of the biblical authors, as an 'historicised' version of such an ontology of images.[79] Tertullian's symbol of *mater ecclesia* should, therefore, be given a fully ontological weight in pondering his ecclesiology. However, the implications of the symbol once rendered in conceptual theological discourse might well carry one towards the more unitary and so universalist ecclesiology which Afanas'ev deplores.

Origen

It is time to move on to look at another negative figure in Afanas'ev's *galère*, and one who occupies a chronologically midway stage between the Didachist and Cyprian. Origen of Alexandria plays a somewhat dislocated role in Afanas'ev's work. For, on the one hand, his writings are called in evidence for the principle of the 'concelebration' of sacramental acts by *proestôs* and people,[80] and for the development of the *proestôs* into a pastor.[81] But on the other hand, Origen is held responsible for the paternity of two notions that cut across the fundamental Afanas'evan view of the Church as a Spirit-given eucharistic assembly. These notions are the idea that an unworthy bishop cannot celebrate the Eucharist for the people[82] and the concept of 'spiritual communion'.[83] The first of these, at any rate, may be linked to another feature of Origen's teaching pointed out by Afanas'ev, the attack on bishops for their *prepotenza* (arrogance).[84] But thirdly, and without further explanation, Afanas'ev claims that Origen 'forcefully advanced' the universalist ecclesiology already found in the *Didache*.[85]

As elsewhere, the most controversial statement here is the last. By way of contrast, we can refer to the comments of Gustave Bardy, whose own grasp of patristic ecclesiology was encyclopaedic. For him, in sharp contradistinction to Afanas'ev, 'the Alexandrian doctor talks more willingly about churches than about the Church'. Bardy continues by speaking of Origen in these terms:

> He is sensitive to the fact that, in his time Christianity took the external form of a federation.[86]

But if true, this judgment must entail that Origen has a significant doctrine of the local church to which a universalist doctrine of the Church has been conjoined. It may well be, therefore, that here, as – so we shall see in a moment – with Cyprian, the presence of a universalism complementing or deepening a eucharistic particularism has sufficed to make Afanas'ev see only the former. And most certainly the former does exist in Origen. He speaks of the churches throughout the world as constituting the 'single body' of the Church;[87] of the Church as the 'single house' outside of which the paschal Lamb should not be eaten;[88] as the ark of Noah which alone saves from the Flood;[89] and as the Bride of Christ.[90]

What then are the main features of this portrait of the one and manifold Church? Origen takes for granted a *laos* (or 'holy people') served by a three-fold ministry: bishops, presbyters and deacons enjoy the divinely given *dignitates, principatus* or *ministeria Ecclesiae* as the homilies on Isaiah insist.[91] Yet Origen's special interest lies in his depiction of a group who cut across the distinction of *klêros* (clergy) and *laos*, the 'teachers' or *didaskaloi*. For him, both office-bearing and charismatic teachers may be *diadochoi tôn apostolôn* ('successors of the apostles'), and, once the pre-eminent importance of intellectual and moral virtue in churchmen is conceded, it becomes the most distinctive mark of the apostolate itself. As H. G. Vogt puts it:

> That Origen speaks so much of insight (knowledge) and of perfection, in the case of the apostles, and so little of their authority, their leadership of the community and the like, has its indubitable ground in his personal interests.[92]

Among such 'apostolic' teachers, Afanas'ev remarks, Origen's own place is by no means the least.[93]

Afanas'ev is surely right in singling out this element in Origen as revelatory of his deepest concerns. Origen's interest in the *didaskaloi*, the 'teachers' or 'theologians', probably derives from two sources. First, there is his concern with doctrinal clarity as well as truth, something amply attested by the *Peri Archôn* ('On First Principles') which has been called the first essay in systematic theology in the Church's history. Secondly, his attentiveness to the contribution of 'teachers' reflects his concern with Christian *gnôsis*, that is, with the contemplative appropriation of the Gospel as a wisdom. It is this latter which gives Origen a certain tendency to relativise the importance of the sacramental life. For him, the sacramental signs of the liturgy are chiefly of interest as images of and means to the reception of the Logos by human minds. It will readily be seen that such a tendency fits ill with Afanas'ev's own sacramental realism and his insistence on the transcendent (and therefore intellectually always mysterious) presence of the Holy Spirit in his ecclesial gifts.

If the notion of 'spiritual communion' can be explained in terms of Origen's Logos-centred intellectual mysticism, his Donatist-sounding language about the unworthy bishop depends on another but related aspect of his thought. Von Campenhausen has brought out the curious combination in Origen of, on the one hand, a thorough acceptance of the received pattern of the Church's life with, on the other, a certain *insouciance* in treating that received pattern. There is a sense in which, for Origen, the Church is primarily a 'living, free cosmos of spiritual gifts in which every Christian can share without the help of official mediators'.[94] But, at the same time:

> The normal and desirable thing in his view is that the one who is endowed with spiritual gifts should also be appointed to the corresponding position in the Church, so that he may be able to work for the benefit of the whole.[95]

It is revealing that while for Origen all bishops should have the gifts of *didaskalia*, if they lack them, God will not leave his people uninstructed. The *didaskaloi* are not for him a parallel authority in the Church to the 'pastoral magisterium' of the bishops.[96] What is original and constitutive in Origen's account is not the place given to the *didaskaloi* as such but the adoption of the ideal of Christian gnostic perfection as a norm for all those engaged in ministerial activity. The problem was that this ascetical-intellectual ideal eluded the Church's ministers as a body in Origen's time, as no doubt it would in any historical period. Origen's solution to a problem largely of his own making was to argue that where a bishop does not fulfil his spiritual duties he stands spiritually among the laity whom he ought to lead.[97] Conversely, frequently enough the layman is a bishop in the eyes of God, even though he has never been made such by consecration.[98]

Curiously, this does not lead to a rejection of the traditional pattern of the ministry in Origen because he is clear that such situations are contradictions of the proper spiritual norm, to be corrected by better discernment of gifts in the selection of the Church's servants. Origen's reasons for thus holding fast to the apostolic ordering of the community are well expressed by von Campenhausen:

The hierarchical structure of the Church is by now something so long established that Origen would never dream of questioning it. It is for him a sacred datum based on divine revelation; but it also corresponds to a universal and necessary cosmic law of moral and religious growth. All spiritual natures on their way upward towards God are bound by the law of gradual development through various stages each of which brings them closer to their goal; in the course of this progression they are constantly in need of governance and guidance and the helpful co-operation of other beings already at a higher stage.[99]

In the end, then, the office-holder is worth to the Church at large simply what he as a man of the Spirit can bring to his task. But does not Origen here remove the Spirit as source of personal grace in intellectual wisdom and practical charity from the graciousness displayed in shared and structured symbolic activity in the liturgy of the Church? Yet all grace is from the same holy and life-giving Spirit, so one can hardly remain happy with such a 'solution'.[100] Afanas'ev understandably departs at this point from the teaching of the Alexandrian master: all ministry is charismatic, but not all charisms consist in the transformation of personal gifts. Ecclesial functions are themselves charismatic: were they not, the communitarian, public, incarnational nature of Christian salvation would be overthrown.

The elusive quality of Origen's portrait of the Church and ministry is of a piece with his world-view as a whole which may be described not unfairly as Existentialism *avant la lettre*. All things are in movement up or down a ladder (*anagôgô*) towards or away from the one God. Their *ousia* (being) depends on where they have reached on the ladder: the quality of a creature's *theôria* (contemplation) of the One bestows on it its 'nature'.[101] In this Middle Platonist ontology rendered Existentialist by marriage with a radical doctrine of freedom it is difficult to find a place for stable covenanted, institutional manifestations of grace. In this respect, Origen's picture is corrected by the work of Denys, whose language at first hearing resembles Origen's but whose underlying presuppositions are of an entirely different order. Nevertheless, an Origenistic sub-tradition in ecclesiology lived on within the Byzantine church. It is found most notably in Symeon the New Theologian, a figure who, on the one hand, appears fully at home within Byzantine Christianity in its developed mediaeval form, and yet who, on the other, shows a freedom *vis-à-vis* office and order, especially in the sacrament of penance, that in the West would be highly redolent of the Reformers' critique of Catholicism.[102] Yet is there not a touch of such Origenism about Afanas'ev's own opposition to the idea of an ontological sacramental 'character'? If ecclesial grace has ontological implications should we not expect that the ordering of the Church's ministries will have too?[103]

Cyprian

The evaluation of Afanas'ev's use of patristic materials has no more crucial locus than his characterisation of Cyprian. According to Afanas'ev, it was Cyprian who, over-influenced by the world-state aspirations of the Roman *imperium*, took the fateful step of re-making the 'traditional' ecclesiology in its image.[104] The 'universalist' model of the Church steps on to the stage, the local church receding to the status of a part within the whole. By a natural progression, therefore, Cyprian began to think (at first, unwillingly) of the Church as a monarchy of which the Roman bishop is the head.[105] Although elements of the universalist picture may be found in the *Didache* and in Origen, the first clear articulation of its principles was Cyprian's (fateful) achievement.[106] It remained for Augustine to consolidate this achievement and (we may suppose) to secure its victory in the West by dint of his own enormous influence on the subsequent theological activity of the Latin church. Afanas'ev does not indicate how he thinks the selfsame account of the Church came to be dominant in Orthodox manuals in the modern period; but in fact it is clear that however it emerged in the West, it did come to have a great (though not necessarily a preponderant) influence by the later Western Middle Ages (Gallicanism being the main pocket of resistance) and entered the ecclesiology of the Eastern churches through their use of Catholic textbooks in the age of the Counter-Reformation and beyond. The placing of Cyprian at the fountain-head of this 'unitary' ecclesiology must entail a claim of a far-reaching sort for his importance. It becomes especially vital, therefore, to determine to what extent Afanas'ev's reading of Cyprian is correct.

Before turning to the writings of Cyprian it may be well to

make one general *a priori* point at the outset. Cyprian's life-setting in the North African church, his profound veneration for Tertullian, and his experience of two major persecutions by the Roman state, that of Decius and then of Valerian, conspire to make it unlikely that he would have regarded the political structures of the Roman empire as a model for the life of the Church. What could be asserted plausibly of Eusebius of Caesarea in this regard, is *prima facie* implausible when ascribed to Cyprian.[107] The endemic dislike of the superficially Romanised Punic and Berber population of North Africa for the Roman imperial government played a major part in the later Donatist movement, but it may reasonably be supposed to have pre-existed that movement, being the corporate response of an imperfectly colonialised people.[108] The North African Christian tradition reflected this dislike in the sharpened form of hostility to a persecuting state. Veneration for the martyrs was a substantial feature of North African Catholicism, its excesses combatted with varying success by the episcopate.[109] When a North African ecclesiology emerges with Tertullian, its portrait of the Church is as little Eusebian as can be conceived. The Church for Tertullian is an eschatological reality, the community of sanctified men and women who are bound here and now to lead the life of Christ in expectation of Him who is to come.[110] In his *Exposition of the Lord's Prayer*, Tertullian offers a brief ecclesiology: significantly, on reaching the words *qui est in caelis* ('who art in heaven').[111] The concept of heaven in Tertullian includes both the Kingdom of God, soon to come in power, and the present citizenship of Christians in this Kingdom, i.e. the Church. It is because the Church is already a heavenly reality that Tertullian regards it as totally separate from secular society and can specify a whole range of activities and occupations unfitting to the citizens of a more-than-earthly society.[112] Given Cyprian's well-documented veneration for Tertullian, it seems *a priori* probable that these attitudes would have been communicated to Cyprian also.[113]

If so, they would surely have been hardened by Cyprian's experience of the Decian persecution, not to mention the further troubles in the reign of Valerian which cost him his life.

However, and still remaining in the territory of Cyprian's background, it should be noted that Afanas'ev's thesis is capable of reformulation in a way which makes greater sense for the historical time and place it concerns. Not because of *admiration* for the empire but because of *competitive hostility to its claims* the African church may have seen itself as an inverted, rather than mimetic, image of the Roman authority. There is some reason to think that this is so in Tertullian's case. Christ is for Tertullian the 'imperial commander' to whom the Christian soldier (i.e. the Church member) owes complete obedience. The Gospel is 'our own law' over against the law of the empire. This law makes the Christian *plebs* (people) into an *ordo*, an ordered society with due governmental forms. The *honor* or public office of the Christian ministry gives them *consensus*, the right to adjudicate matters affecting the life of the body; this is especially so with the *summus sacerdos*, the bishop, the one who presides at the *sacrificium* of the Eucharist. All of these Latin terms are drawn from Roman imperial administrative practice but their use in Tertullian is ironic rather than straightforwardly analogical. In this sense it is possible to speak of the Church of Tertullian's vision as a 'shadow empire' over against the Roman state.[114] Nevertheless, the Church of Tertullian is not envisaged on the universalist model, much less is his ideal a governmentally unitary body. The unity of the Church for Tertullian rests on the fact that all local churches accept the binding authority of the *regula fidei*, the rule of faith handed down by the apostles.[115] In every church where the faith of the apostles (expressed above all in the possession of the Scriptures) is received, there the Church in the fullest theological sense can be found.[116] The tradition of the *regula fidei* passes from the apostles, who are its original *auctores*, to a succession of monarchical bishops in every church of apostolic foundation. In other churches founded since the close of the apostolic age the same is true, since these churches were planted by the directly apostolic churches and agree with them in adhering to the same rule of faith. It will be seen that this ecclesiology is at base an ecclesiology of the whole present in the part, the whole Church in the local church, for each local church in possessing the *regula fidei* is as much 'church' ontologically as is the whole Church spread throughout the world. This is in fact an interesting example of a particularist or intensivist ecclesiology (where the local church is equivalent intensively to the whole Church) that is not based on appeal to the nature of the Eucharist as in Afanas'ev's theory.

We must turn now to Cyprian himself, in the expectation that he will fit in some way into this background, although it would be deterministic to assume from the outset that he cannot depart creatively from it. Cyprian took from Tertullian a number of features: a thoroughly eschatological vision of the Church; an exaltation of martyrdom; the Church as the inverted image of the idolatrous State; a use (partly analogical, partly ironic) of Roman law concepts to analyse the structure of the Church; and finally a *point de départ* in the idea of the local church. To this he added notions of his own: the retrenchment of the idea that the Church shares in the achieved holiness of the last times: admitting that, in the light of the numbers of *sacrificatores* and *libellatici* (those who had sacrificed to the emperor's image and handed over the books of Scripture to the pagans) during the Decian persecution, there are evidently 'tares' in the Church, and consequently resituating the Church's holiness in the ecclesial purity of the episcopate;[117] the expansion of Tertullian's notion of the episcopate to include not only 'ownership' of the right to interpret the Scriptures but a wider ecclesial authority since the bishops succeed to the apostles *vicaria ordinatione* (as their vicars or substitutes); and finally, the working out of a much fuller notion than Tertullian's of the communion of all local churches in the one Church.[118] It is because Cyprian has a much more pronounced interest in the Church's unity than his African predecessor that Afanas'ev has been led to believe that Cyprian's departure point is something other than the local church.

As Adrien Demoustier showed, it is Cyprian's notion of the episcopate which is the key to his creative transformation of the Tertullianic heritage, a transformation which enabled him to work out an account of the Church in which both the local church and the one Church present in the local church receive their full due.[119] His is, as should emerge, a highly satisfactory integration of particularist (or 'intensivist') and universalist (or 'extensivist') perspectives, deriving from, or perhaps issuing in, a subtle ontology of the Church's being.[120] We may come to grips with the primary problems of Cyprian's ecclesiology by asking two questions. First, is the centre of unity for Cyprian the local bishop in the local church, or is it, as Afanas'ev alleges, at first the *connexio* of the bishops and later the universal primacy of the Bishop of Rome? (It seems from Afanas'ev's account that he accepts the authenticity of *both* the *Textus Receptus* ('Received Text') of the *De unitate ecclesiae* ('On the Unity of the Church') *and* of the *Primatus Textus* ('Primary Text') with its more strongly papalist colouring.) Secondly, has Cyprian substituted a juridical 'unitarism' for a more ancient 'intensivist' and sacramental view of the Church? The difficulty in answering these questions lies, as so often in patristic theology, in the occasional nature of Cyprian's writing, but an answer may be attempted nevertheless.

Cyprian's view of the episcopate in the period before the rise of Novatianism can only be glimpsed from a passing reference in Letter 3.[121] It appears to have been as 'Ignatian' as Afanas'ev could desire. There is an obligation to obey the bishop because God himself has established him in the community as the link between the people and himself; to gather around another altar than the bishop's altar is to sin against the one God.[122] A little later, in the period of African Novatianism, Cyprian is found insisting that each church is a hierarchically ordered society founded on Peter, the first of the apostles. By divine institution there can only be one church, and thus one bishop in any given place.[123] When Novatianism spreads to Rome and claims the papal chair in the person of Novatian himself, Cyprian replies that communion can only be with Pope Cornelius as – since there *is* only one bishop and that by succession – the first elected candidate must be the true bishop.[124] But in this (third) period Cyprian is not concerned simply to affirm the unity of *episkopê*, ministerial oversight, in the local bishop. He points out that the Church does not exist in one place only but is the totality of all local churches. Her unity demands that each local bishop be in union with the rest. This 'inter-communion' founds the unicity of the episcopate, and this unicity, along with the unicity of episcopal activity in the local church, is a necessary condition for the unicity of the Church herself. By the choice that it imposes – to support Novatian or Cornelius – the Roman schism will divide the bishops and thus the churches and so call into question the unicity of the Church. The Roman crisis, then, made Cyprian define his doctrine of collegiality. It is not sufficient for a bishop to be legitimately elected in his local church for him to be a true bishop in the Petrine succession. If a legitimately elected bishop separates himself from his co-bishops, he separates himself from the unity of the Church. This is why Cyprian devoted so much anxious energy to convincing his African colleagues of the need to support Cornelius at all costs.[125]

Cyprian lacks two notes of the later 'developed' Western ecclesiology of conciliarity: he has no conciliar theory, though he has a regular *practice* of holding councils.[126] Nor does he think that the common episcopal office gives one local bishop a right and duty to care for other flocks not his own (and them a similar right and duty for his).[127] Nevertheless, he does hold that each bishop must respect the Church's unity in the way just described, and that, taken together, the bishops as a body have charge of the whole Church. The difference between Cyprian's view of the latter and that of the full-scale universalist picture outlined by Afanas'ev is that for Cyprian the bishops taken together, as a body, have nothing that the single bishop lacks. As the *De unitate ecclesiae* lapidarily puts it:

> The authority of the bishops forms a unity, of which each holds his part in its totality.[128]

Moving on to the latter part of Cyprian's life, the period of pacification after the collapse of Novatian's party and finally the controversy over baptism, we find Cyprian refining and developing the basic lines of these doctrines. Cyprian stresses more and more the importance of the union of all local churches, and connected with this, of the unicity of the Church – *Ecclesia una*, but *not* in such a way as to lose sight of his own starting-point in the life of the local church. The bishop unites each of his faithful to the total Church since as a successor of the single episcopate of Peter he has the capacity to realise the unity of the body. He must be united to the other bishops, but the episcopate he possesses is simply that which all share together. Here, one equals all. As before, Peter is the origin of the episcopate of each bishop in each place. Yet the local church is not now envisaged in an isolated way but in its rapport with the whole Church. Each church is the whole Church, in the sense that the one and entire Church of Christ is entirely present in each *as united to the rest*. By a Petrine and apostolic succession, each church is identical with the original Church, and for this reason all the churches taken together form one single reality, despite the fact that they are dispersed in space and time. The Many co-exist, therefore, in the One, and so Cyprian applies to the universal Church the Pauline image of the body which he has already used for both the local church united around the bishop as successor of Peter and the unity of the bishops as successors of the apostles. This is the burden of the formula of Letter 55 cited by Afanas'ev:

> There is one Church throughout the world divided by Christ into many members . . .[129]

It should be clear by now that, far from being the slogan of a thoroughly universalist ecclesiology, this formula is part of a polyvalent application of the body image to a reality which is one and many at different levels.

This becomes clearer still from a consideration of the (not easily dateable) letter *Ad Fortunatum* and the *De unitate Ecclesiae*.[130] In the former, unity is realised in the Church by the intercommunion of the particular churches on the condition that each remains in communion with its origin, the apostolic Church of Peter. Thus communion between local churches does not merely *signify* the unity of the Church; it positively realises it – which is what we would expect on a 'particularist ecclesiology'. Nevertheless, it does not realise the Church's unity *by itself*. Each Church must preserve its identity with the *common* origin of all, which it does through episcopal succession which is, therefore, the condition of possibility for this actually realised unity through intercommunion. The Church now, in other words, is both one and many. Turning to the *De unitate ecclesiae* it becomes clear that for Cyprian the Church always was. Both versions of chapter 4 agree on this assertion and in the same words:

> No doubt the others ['the other apostles'] were all that Peter was.

With this we may usefully compare a phrase of chapter 5:

The Church forms a unity, however far she spreads and multiplies by the progeny of her fecundity.

The one and the many are found in the original episcopal college, and so quite naturally they are found again in the later Church which draws its life from that 'fertile' source. Thus Demoustier could sum up Cyprian's picture in these words:

> From the beginning, the single episcopate is possessed in its entirety by each bishop, and by all together. The first bishops – the apostles – each possessed the fullness of the episcopate, and all of them shared in that same power whose unicity was founded on Peter. Remaining united in the exercise of this episcopate, they brought about the unity of the Church: they were this first and unique Church of Christ. The succession – at once Petrine and apostolic – perpetuates *both* this possession by each one of the fullness of power (*super Petrum*, i.e. based on Peter) *and* this intercommunion of all in the single episcopate (*per apostolos*, i.e. through the apostles). In each of the bishops is found the power of all. Thus, communion with one bishop is communion with all; in communicating with his own pastor, the faithful of one church communicates with all the faithful of all the other churches: belonging to the body of one church is belonging to the total body.[131]

The conclusion must be that all the local churches are, by succession and mutual union, identical with the original Church. Those churches realise now what was already there at the beginning: the intercommunion in the unity of a single body of numerous parts each of which is identical with the whole. So, in relation to the first part of our first query about Cyprian: there is no need to choose between regarding the local bishop as centre of unity of the Church, and seeing the *connexio* of the episcopate at large as that centre of unity. For Cyprian, *pace* Afanas'ev, the second does not displace the first but rather qualifies it in a way which enriches it, while removing nothing of its significance.

What then of the second possibility mentioned by Afanas'ev in connexion with the status of the local church in Cyprian, that of the 'monarchical' tendency in Cyprian's portrait of the Roman bishop and his role in the scheme of things? This obliges us to come to some decision about the standing of the variant form of the *De unitate ecclesiae* known as the 'primatial text'. Given that Cyprian did not substitute for an Ignatian vision of the local church-with-its-bishop a purely corporatist system of general episcopacy to which the local church and bishop are tributary: nevertheless, at some stage did he not re-conceive the Church along the 'monarchical' lines of a society governed by the Roman bishop, what Afanas'ev calls a 'necessary concomitant' to the theory of a universal episcopate – for a body must needs have a head.[132] There can be no doubt of the great importance attaching to the Roman see in Cyprian's eyes. Even the baptismal quarrel with Pope Stephen manifests the weight which Cyprian placed on relations between Carthage and Rome. Before the crisis, the seriousness with which he viewed Rome's position among the churches had already been demonstrated in his stand over Novatian's claims as anti-pope. In principle, it is possible that Cyprian's interest in Rome depended on Rome's civil position within the empire. Since so many local churches had dealings with Rome, a Roman schism would – purely empirically – divide the Church more successfully than any other. But it is also equally possible that Cyprian regarded Rome as occupying a theologically unique position within the intercommunion of episcopally ordered churches. Scholars confessionally or temperamentally hostile to 'Roman claims' have noted quite correctly that for Cyprian *every* local church is founded on Peter and has the same power as Rome.[133] But while this is true, Cyprian says of no other church that it is the *locus Petri* ('Peter's place') or the *cathedra Petri* ('Peter's chair').[134] The key to resolving the problem lies in what Cyprian has to say about the significance of Peter *vis-à-vis* the other apostles.

Peter has the same power as the other apostles, yet they received theirs after him. His chronological priority over the college is the foundation of its unicity: it makes it numerically a single college. The apostles are one college because, while being in solidarity with each other, they are also in solidarity with the first to whom apostleship was given: Peter. The best explanation for a number of Roman references in the *Letters* (leaving aside for the moment the *De unitate*) seems to be that for Cyprian the Roman church preserves or represents this chronological priority and so authority of Peter in unifying the other churches in communion with her.

> They dare to sail ... to the chair of Peter and to the principal church whence sacerdotal unity has sprung.[135]

It is for this reason that Cyprian can call the Roman church the 'root' or 'mother' of the churches.[136] While other churches are founded on Peter, no other (as far as Cyprian is concerned) has been founded on Peter by Peter himself. As the *primus*, Peter's rôle is to manifest (*ostendere*) the origin of the unity of the apostles – for Christ did not found as many churches as there were apostles.[137] Just as the apostles received the single episcopate by entering into solidarity with Peter who had received it first, so the bishops of the churches retain their due episcopate by entering into, or remaining in, communion with that church whose foundation is the most ancient. The Roman church inherits the one rôle which is Peter's alone (in contradistinction to the other apostles), namely, to manifest the unicity of the Church. Rome is thus the sign of the presence of the 'root' (Peter as unifier) in the communion of the bishops. Although the unity of the bishops (and through them the unity of the churches) is not achieved through communion with Rome (but through fraternal intercommunion and the direct succession of each from the common source), nevertheless, it is only by communion with the Roman church that the bishops know and can demonstrate that they *are* united amongst themselves, and that this unity is the same as that which Peter himself signified at the beginning. Rome is thus for Cyprian the necessary centre of unity because it is the necessary sign of this primordial unity.

This interpretation of Cyprian's view of the Roman see, drawn from his *Letters*, enables us to say that *both* versions of the *De unitate* may be authentic. Both versions are compatible with Cyprian's doctrine as thus expounded. The one piece of external evidence we have about the book from Cyprian's pen, in Letter 54, implies that there may well have been two editions: the work, having been 'read' at Carthage was later dispatched, Cyprian tells us, to Rome. The thesis of Dom John Chapman that the *Textus Receptus* is the Carthaginian edition of the book, and the *Primatus Textus* a later Roman edition takes on a certain plausibility from these two premises.[138] The differences between the two editions may be explained by postulating two different audiences. The Carthaginian version envisages a divided episcopate, and is addressed to bishops; the Roman version envisages a divided flock and is addressed to the laity.

Finally, we must turn, but more briefly, to the second major question which Afanas'ev's presentation of Cyprian raises in an acute form. Did Cyprian's concern with authority lead him to replace a sacramental by a juridical conception of the Church? Has he an ontology in terms of law and power? The great Cyprianic images for the Church – mother, body, house of God – should alert us to the fact that there is something here deeper than the merely juridical and institutional. For Cyprian, the Church belongs to that peculiarly privileged reality which he terms *sacramentum*: in his thought, that term indicates the activity of Christ presenting itself through some reality perceivable by us. According to Cyprian, the Church is made by the sacraments of baptism and the Eucharist which are not simply liturgical rites but actions of God himself in and through the symbolic gestures

performed by the Church. Thus Demoustier can write, citing
De dominica oratione ('On the Lord's Prayer'), 4:

> The Church is not, therefore, solely the sociological reality
> which the episcopal hierarchy organises in juridical fashion. The
> Church addressed by Cyprian the pastor is primarily the euchar-
> istic assembly formed 'when we come together as one with the
> brethren and celebrate the divine sacrifice with God's priest'.[139]

In this regard the bishop's importance lies in his being the
ministerial condition for the baptismal and eucharistic life;
the connexion bishop-Eucharist is ever allusively present in
Cyprian's writing. Because of the need to discern where the
Eucharist is truly celebrated – that is, where it is celebrated
within the unity of Christ's seamless garment, episcopal intercommunion has a vital rôle to play *vis-à-vis* the Eucharistic
life.

At a deeper level of analysis still, the ultimate foundation
of the Church's unity in Cyprian's eyes is the unity of the
triune Lord of the Church. Cyprian transposes to the level of
ecclesiology the images of the tree, the spring and the sun
used by his master Tertullian to express the Father's hyposta-
tic particularity as source of the Son and Holy Spirit and in
this sense unifier of the Godhead.[140] The Church as mother
received from Christ as Bridegroom the ability to bring forth
new sons and daughters; she is *radix, fons, sol* ('root', 'fount',
'sun'), just as at the level of the divine processions the Father
is the inexhaustibly fertile source of Son and Spirit. While the
generative power of the Church is established first of all in
baptism it comes to its fruition in the Eucharist. There the
Trinitarian unity founds a human unity, the *vinculum con-
cordiae* ('bond of concord') of the Eucharist celebrated by
those in communion with the bishop. The articles of Adrien
Demoustier on Cyprian's ecclesiology which have been
largely followed here might well be, though they are not, a

deliberate response to Afanas'ev's hesitations about Cyprian. If, for Cyprian, the Eucharist as *sacramentum* signifies that it is Christ who realises the divine unity of the local assembly, the bishop is the guarantee that this assembly, gathered as it is here and now, is the self-same as that of the Last Supper, and all those which depend on that Supper through succession in time. How then can Cyprian be credited – or, rather, discredited – with the abandonment of the eucharistic ecclesiology of the ancient Church? Such a claim is implausible: for though Cyprian founds the Church's unity on that of the Trinity communicated in Christ, it is the Eucharist which permits of the passage between the merely sociological phenomenon of the gathering and this transcendent ground:

> Through the Eucharist, the Trinitarian unity, in the person of the Son who makes himself present, renders the symbol real – giving its own reality to what the assembly could no more than represent. The cultic assembly gives to the sociological assembly its reality as figure of the divine unity in Christ. The Trinitarian unity gives to the figure the reality which in itself the figure could no more than configure.[141]

In this masterly passage there is perhaps a certain tendency to 'read into' Cyprian the Augustinian and Thomist analysis of sacramental reality, *sacramentum et res* (sign and reality). Nevertheless, Cyprian's writings do contain the seeds of the developed Scholastic flower: the ultimate reality of the Eucharist, that for which it exists, is the unity of the Church. In the public world, to which both rite and concord, both liturgy and society, belong, the Eucharist needs its episcopal guardians. The mystery requires the institution and even the law. These serve a unity which at the deepest level is created by *the* Dominical sacrament *par excellence*. The episcopal intercommunion cannot create that unity; nevertheless, in a world where concord is never secure, the bonds it fashions serve a unity which is in the last resort eschatological and divine.

Augustine

Considering the richness of Augustine's writing on the Church (essentially divisible into three periods: first, apologetic writings, especially *vis-à-vis* Manichaeans and philosophically-minded pagans; secondly, the polemical treatises against the Donatists; thirdly, in the context of a theology of history), it is surprising that Afanas'ev did not extend his interests in African ecclesiology beyond Cyprian to Augustine. It seems that he was content to note, in an early essay, that Augustine had continued Cyprian's 'universalism' in ecclesiology, and to leave it at that. Except, that is, for one point but the point is a major one, both in Afanas'ev's work and in Augustine's. From Afanas'ev's earliest writing, in his Serbian phase, the theme had appeared of the essential difference between a polity based on law and a polity based on grace. Afanas'ev held that in the course of the Church's history, which despite the Spirit's presence is a history subject to the vagaries of process and contingency in this world, the ethics of law and the ethics of grace or charity had become confused. The *de facto* development of canon law was an instance of this confusion between two diverse realms. So was the phenomenon of State churches, the direction of churches by temporal rulers of the kind which the Church in Russia had suffered until the February Revolution of 1917. Afanas'ev could not but find Augustine's doctrine of the two cities congenial in this context. There is, therefore, in *Tserkov' Dukha Sviatogo* a remarkably positive assessment of Augustine, which contrasts sharply with the bleak presentation of him found in a number of modern Orthodox writers.[142]

Afanas'ev does not offer a very full account of Augustine's two cities. His principal concern is to show that by means of the doctrine of the *civitas terrena*, with its inner law of self-love and its will to power, over against the *civitas Dei* with its inner law of charity and *humilitas*, Augustine distanced himself in the clearest way imaginable from the 'imperial theology' which so marked the patristic Church after the conversion of Constantine. There can be little doubt that Afanas'ev is correct in isolating the figure of Augustine here as representing the fullest counter-statement in the patristic age to the theology of empire produced by, above all, Eusebius of Caesarea. The background of the imperial theology lies, as Francis Dvornik amply demonstrated, in attitudes to the figure of the emperor in the Hellenistic world.[143] In a sophisticated, Hellenised version of the theocratic concept of kingship in the ancient Near East, the emperor as sovereign was held to be the 'animate law' and the empire a mirror of the divine realm.[144] The Alexandrian Christian tradition stressed, following a hint in the Pauline letters, that the *pax augusta* (the civil peace wrought by the emperors) was a Providential condition of the Incarnation and the spread of the Church. Clement in particular espoused Philo's idea that the emperor, as the icon of the divine Steersman of the universe, could be regarded as participating in a special way in the powers of the Logos.[145] But the full working out of the theme had to await the conversion of the emperors to Christianity. For Eusebius, the emperor is the special friend of the Logos. His task is to bring the knowledge of the Logos incarnate to the ends of the earth. Aside from this missionary dimension, the emperor also has a role within the Church, namely to secure its peace and unity.[146] Although the author of the *De laudibus Constantini* and the *Vita Constantini* was to some extent working out his own personal notions here, it must be recognised that this imperial theology was also a reflection of the actual historical events. The early Councils *were* in some sense an imperial creation: probably they were technically in civil law meetings of the imperial Senate in its ecclesiastical aspect.[147] The decision to construct as

Constantine's mausoleum a 'church of the Twelve Apostles', symbolically reinforcing the Eusebian concept of the emperor as *isapostolos,* the 'equal of the apostles', may have aroused opposition, however, reflected in later interpolated versions of the *Vita Constantini* which considerably toned down the original 'high' language.[148] But the liturgical privileges of the emperor, which continued in East Roman practice until 1453 and are the subject of unfavourable notice by Afanas'ev went unchallenged in the Christian East.[149] Even before Augustine the opposition shown to them by Ambrose of Milan is notable and, of course, Western.[150]

While it is unlikely that Augustine ever accepted the imperial theology in anything like its full form, he does seem to have had a concept of *tempora christiana* (the Christian age in world history) in which the advent of the Christian emperors was seen as a decisive fact, in some sense a prolongation of the biblical history of salvation.[151] But by the time he began writing the *De Civitate Dei* Augustine had abandoned this notion for a more restrained and nuanced picture. Essentially, Augustine brings together various elements from his tradition and his own reflection and weaves them into a whole which can be called the first really satisfactory patristic theology of history. These elements are, the (partly biblical, partly Manichaean) imagery of two cities or kingdoms, the members of which declare their citizenship through a life devoted to good or to evil as the case may be;[152] the picture of the Church formed by reflection on the *corpus mixtum* of a pastor's flock, and particularly fully worked out in the wake of the Donatist crisis;[153] the continuing influence of the North African eschatological ecclesiology of Tertullian and Cyprian,[154] and the theory of biblical (and prophetic) inspiration which Augustine had formulated through his meditations on the nature of the authority of Scripture.[155] So, taking these elements in that order, we may say that for Augustine the Church is to be defined in relation to the City of God, whose way of life, *amor Dei, amor proximi* – the love of God and the love of neighbour – she represents on earth. She contains, however, wheat and 'tares', those in whom her faith and sacraments are not efficacious because in their own deepest orientation they belong to the other, and competing, city, the *civitas terrena*. Nevertheless, she will one day be purified, at the eschaton, and stand forth as the spotless Bride of Christ. Until then though every member of the Church can and must use what discernment is given him, there is no final judgment on any man, or any group, or any inner-historical event concerning the Church since the Spirit of prophecy spoke in Scripture and only there. Between the apostolic age and the Parousia we can have no new revelation, and so no direct access to the divine view of this-worldly events.

Augustine's view of the earthly city, and so of the empire, is implied by his description of the heavenly city, and thereby of the Church. Augustine no more identifies the empire with the *civitas terrena* (in a 'non-dialectical' way) than he identifies the Church with the *civitas Dei*. Nonetheless, just as the Church is directly related to the *civitas Dei* (not least through the Eucharist where the 'prince' of the City of God stands as Mediator in her midst),[156] so the empire is directly related to the *civitas terrena*. Powered by the *libido dominandi* (the drive to dominate), the empire is of its essence incapable of Christianisation except in some formal sense. The compacts and covenants made by rulers may in fact bring about the realisation of some values – often enough through prudence rather than authentic charity, as honour among thieves; but the nature and finality of power after the Fall precludes for Augustine its transformation by grace. It is indeed the antithesis of grace, its anti-type: to see what grace is not, we may look at power. Augustine is far from resurrecting the ferocious anti-imperialism of early Christian apocalyptic; still, it is inconceivable for him that the *imperium*, the *res publica* as such should become Church. Individual officers within it may be and act as members of the Church, the emperor Theodosius amongst them. But this for the mature Augustine is a world away from the imperial theology of a Eusebius. As Professor R. A. Markus has written:

> The earthly city has its own, unifying, social bond, located some-where among the perverse, self-centred and temporal purposes aimed at by its members. Their common allegiance to such fleet-ing values, even though it be, in the end, divisive, suffices in Augustine's eyes to constitute them a genuine society. But it is a society which, again like its heavenly counterpart, does not appear visibly as a society until the last judgement at the end of time ... Rome can only be called the earthly city in a secondary or derivative sense, in so far as the Empire is a society organised around loyalties with no positive relation to God. To accomplish this identification Augustine dwells on the idolatry of pagan Rome, on the lust for power and the quest for human glory and renown ... But Augustine was also acutely conscious of the limits of rhetoric ... 'What is Rome but the Romans (*Sermons* 81, 9)?' ... When 'our night whelms, whelms, and will end us', then the two cities will at last be disentangled from their inter-woven existence in the *saeculum*.[157]

Augustine's contrast of the cities, and with them Church and empire, is not explicitly related to the Pauline contrast of grace and law. It is remarkable that a mind so steeped in Paul's doctrine of the gracious predestining initiative of God did not articulate this relation. That it did not may be tenta-tively related to Augustine's pastoral realism. All men begin life as children, with childish ways, and by education they are drawn out to affirm for themselves the values originally imposed on them in the form of external norms and laws. The Augustinian 'Rule' is clear evidence that for Augustine the typical or mature Christian lives by the inner law of grace; nevertheless, it is equally clear from Augustine's epis-copal practice that he regarded canons, conciliar decrees, official sanctions of many kinds as appropriate instruments for moulding the common life of the Church.

It follows from this that while Afanas'ev has correctly grasped the principal lines of Augustine's distinction between the two cities, and the fact that this distinction challenges the Eusebian tradition in Christian historiography at its most central point, he has also added an element which is not found in the historical Augustine. The contrast of law and grace in the inner life and motivation of the individual believer is not in fact extrapolated to the corporate plane of the Church's life as a community in the way Afanas'ev seems to think. He departs from Augustine to offer a view of his own, a further extension of Augustinianism whose aim is the outlawing of all concept of legal norm and sanction in the Church. Afanas'ev's fundamentally favourable idea of canon law, and 'high' doctrine thereof, in the essays of 1933–36 was abandoned by him during the Second World War as he brooded more and more on the insight into the eucharistic nature of the Church that came to him in the winter of 1932–33. Given that both the Orthodox Church, to which Afanas'ev belonged, and the Catholic Church, which inherited the mainstream Augustinian tradition, know nothing of such an outright hostility to the very notion of canons for the ecclesial community, one is tempted to look instead, insofar as sources external to the author must be postulated, to a line of scholarship which insists that the institutional element in Christianity is alien to its original impulse. In order to explain the increasingly 'institutional' tone of Acts, the Pastoral Epistles and much early Christian writing outside the New Testament canon, the spectre of *Frühkatholizismus* ('Incipient Catholicism') began to stalk the land. What Afanas'ev deemed to be wrong with the evolution of the patristic Church was its 'juridicisation' of the Gospel community – hence his negative attitude to the Byzantine canonical tradition.[158]

Denys

For our last soloist in Afanas'ev's less than concordant *sumphonia* of patristic voices, we should consider his approach to the ecclesiology of Denys, certainly one of the most unusual to reach us from the patristic age, chiefly because of its author's insistence on clothing his writing in an idiom drawn from the Neo-Platonist writer Proclus.[159] As Fr Edward Booth has written of Denys's thought:

> Theological in the fullest Christian as well as Proclean sense, his structure discards some of Proclus's theses, but reincorporates others with a modification or different emphasis, for he found that many of the facilities created by Proclus had a usefulness in describing the action, creative and mysteric, of the Christian God, as well as its human response.[160]

Thus it transpires that, for example, Denys's account of evil and of providence is highly Proclean; his angelology, with its central idea of the Word of God reaching man via the mediations of successive angelic orders also has a neo-Platonist colouring. His mystical theology, too, is indebted to the neo-Platonic corpus in its depiction of the divine unity from which all things flow and to which they return. His theory of the three ways in prayer – purgative, illuminative and unitive – rests on a Platonic tradition with roots in Plato himself. The doctrine of *ecstasis* as giving perfected souls even in this world an intuitive (though not comprehensive) vision of God would be at least highly welcome to the disciples of Proclus. His language about the sacraments as a 'theurgical' *anagôgê*, 'rising up', to the Divinity shows every sign of deriving from one such disciple, Iamblichus, though how far his *doctrine* of the sacraments is Iamblichan may be doubted.[161] Denys's ecclesiology, essentially – like that of Afanas'ev – a meditation on sacramental practice, is of a piece with his theology as a whole in this regard. He wove a Neo-Platonic natural theology into the texture of Christian believing.[162] On the other hand, the main effect of this, linguistically so dramatic, importation, is to confer a distinctive cast on materials themselves drawn from Scripture and the liturgical tradition.[163]

The pivot of Denys's theology, and so of his ecclesiology, is the union of man with God by deification. From this fontal idea of his flows his principal organising category, that of the hierarchies, both angelic and ecclesiastical, the latter modelled on the former. Each is destined to bring us to *theôsis* ('divinisation') by *henôsis* ('union') with God.[164] In Denys's account, the law of graduation reigns everywhere, in heaven as in the Christian community, in the world of *nous* (mind) as well as in the world of *sôma* (body). (There is a point of contact here with Origen.) The angelic hierarchy Denys divides into nine choirs (three groups of three) which transmit the divine Light to each other on a descending scale of closeness to the uncreated Source. Similarly, in the ecclesiastical hierarchy, there are three successive degrees of ministry, those of bishop, priest and deacon. These orders are differentiated by their differing rôles in relation to the sacraments, for it is by the sacraments or 'mysteries' that our deification is begun, continues and is brought to its completion. Baptism is its opening and foundation, and the Eucharist (which Denys ascribes, Afanas'ev-like, to the ministry of the bishop, the principal *proestôs*) is the means of its achievement.

Afanas'ev's interest in Denys lies chiefly in the latter's account of baptism.[165] The baptised are for Denys *within* the ecclesiastical hierarchy: it is to them that the phrase 'the hierarchy' refers. As yet the 'sword', as Afanas'ev terms it, of the doctrine of consecration by the sacrament of Order (leaving the royal and universal priesthood in some sense in the world of the profane) has not yet cut off the *plebs sancta Dei* ('holy people of God') from their presidents in the Lord. Denys does indeed stress in the *De hierarchia ecclesiastica* that the reality of the Church 'comprises one and the same power across all its hierarchical functions'.[166] The gift of the divine self-communication, received by the angels in a single and utterly simple fashion, the tradition of Scripture has transmitted to men in a way better adapted to our humanity, namely, 'in the manifold variety of diverse symbols'.[167] The apostles received from the triune God the fullness of the 'holy gift' of saving grace and were charged with spreading it to others. This they did by communicating the single mystery through a multiplicity of signs, a manner of proceeding as well suited to the human order as it would be out of place in the order of the angels.

> In the human hierarchy we shall, by contrast, see multiply, in accordance with our human nature, that variety of those sensuous symbols which raise us up, in a hierarchical manner, to the very unity of deification – inasmuch as that can be reached by us.[168]

Far from entailing a sacramental materialism, Denys's teaching stresses the need to dispose ourselves properly for receiving these signs of grace: a demand which he equates with the command to 'keep my words' of the Johannine Christ. That teaching might best be described, indeed, as 'sacramental intellectualism'. For Denys, the sacraments present everything that is truly intelligible, life-giving food for thought, in the Christian economy. Yet, as Dr Andrew Louth has stressed, sacramental efficacy is not, for Denys, solely a matter of intelligibility.[169] The 'common term' of all hierarchy, whether human or angelic, is 'continuous love for God and what is God's',[170] and this *koinônia* (communion) with the Holy Trinity involves friendship with God in both soul *and body*.[171]

In the *De hierarchia ecclesiastica* II we have Denys's account of the liturgy of baptism which Afanas'ev draws on for his statement about the 'establishment' of the royal priesthood by that sacrament. The 'mystery of illumination' constitutes Christian initiation, and founds the 'mystery of communion', that is, the Eucharist. Denys's sense that these two principal sacraments structure an entire economy of grace in the Church, and bestow on each person who receives them a new dignity, and, through the entire symbolic structure which undergirds them and surrounds them, a new vision of God and the world in their interrelation (*theôria*), is very close to Afanas'ev, even though the conceptual and literary idiom could scarcely be more different.

Afanas'ev's patristic ressourcement: a conclusion

Afanas'ev can hardly serve as a full or even a balanced introduction to the patristic writers whom he cites. But it is not his intention to write a history of patristic ecclesiology. He has his own portrait to paint, even though in painting it he is indebted to the images of others for much of his own iconography. The elements of various patristic writers are reassembled and juxtaposed in an *ensemble* which is not meant to be simply a kaleidoscopic impression of the early Church but also to suggest how it might be appropriate to see the pattern of life of the contemporary Church. Afanas'ev sought a Church which would be Ignatian in its respect for the local church and the bishop, Irenaean in its concern for the witness of the church in priority, Tertullianic in its conviction that the Church is inbreathed by the Holy Spirit. Such a Church should be Dionysian in the intensity of its sacramental living, and Augustinian in its refusal to marry the Church to the world. For the Didachist, Origen and Cyprian, Afanas'ev has less time. This division into two camps is not based on any corporate judgment by the Church (as an 'ecclesiastical writer' rather than, strictly speaking, a 'father', the later Tertullian is at least as vulnerable on this criterion as is Origen). It is based rather on the relation of these two galleries of figures to the universalist ecclesiology which Afanas'ev so strenuously opposes. We have found reason to think that the two 'models' of eucharistic and universalist ecclesiology coexist side-by-side in these authors rather more than Afanas'ev would like to think. At the same time, this judgment, if correct, calls into question the idea that an adequate ecclesiology could be created on one of those models, the eucharistic – or, as we have also termed it, particularist or intensivist – alone.

In conclusion, an attempt may be made to specify the nature of Afanas'ev's patristic *ressourcement*. What place do the Fathers hold among the *loci theologici* (theological sources and authorities) of his work? Perhaps the best description of Afanas'ev's attitude to the patristic witness occurs in an essay of Père Yves Congar.[172] The Fathers for Afanas'ev are privileged, but not infallible, guides to the tradition of Christianity whose own primary expression is found in Scripture. There is no doctrine of the *consensus patrum* ('agreement of the Fathers') in Afanas'ev; nor is there an appeal to later Church teaching as a way of sifting the good from the bad (or the less good) in their theology. They are approached as sources of illumination, but they are also judged in the light of principles deriving (Afanas'ev holds) from Scripture itself. The chief idea in debate is the notion that the Church of the Holy Spirit is the local church celebrating the Eucharist around the figure of its *proestôs*, a notion which Afanas'ev considers to be fully warranted by the New Testament evidence.

It will be seen at once that in terms of fundamental theology, or of what constitutes theological authority, there is a certain ambiguity in his position. For what could be said to one who simply disagreed, on the basis of reading the same New Testament Scriptures, that the structure of the Church in apostolic times was as Afanas'ev describes it? Let us suppose that all participants in the resultant conversation would agree that the witness of the Fathers is a subordinate standard of faith compared with the witness of the Scriptures. Nevertheless, do not the Fathers have a super-ordinate rôle in terms of the discernment of the Scriptures *vis-à-vis* the individual believer, either as simple reader of the Scriptures or as exegete? The common consent of the Orthodox (and Catholic) tradition here has been to answer, 'Yes'. But if they have such a rôle, by what principle does Afanas'ev choose to privilege

certain Fathers (above all, Ignatius of Antioch) and to disen-
franchise others (the author of the *Didache*, Origen as ecclesiologist, Cyprian).[173] If Afanas'ev be taken to withdraw
himself from the common tradition so far as to say that the
Fathers do not have a super-ordinate rôle *vis-à-vis* the individual churchman or scholar, then his appeal to the patristic
age becomes a purely historicist one. That is, its 'authority' is
simply the authority of a principle arrived at exclusively from
within historical science itself, namely that the closer people
are to some historical phenomenon (in this case, the origins
of Christianity) the more acceptable is their account of it.

A moment's reflection will show that this principle is in
itself highly debatable. Investigation of the hermeneutical
process suggests that in certain respects the opposite of the
principle is likely to be true. The passing of time opens up a
space for reflection in which the significance of an historical
event can display itself.[174] The tradition of responding to the
event is inseparable in interpretation from the event itself.
This is part of what is meant by saying that the event belongs
to the human (and not simply the physical) world. In this
sense, the Incarnation, by involving God in accepting all the
conditions of entering the human world, including hermeneu-
tically-relevant conditions, entailed a divine decision that the
significance of what was done in the humanisation of the
Word would only be fully understood in retrospect. But what
is true of the Incarnation will be true of all the actions of the
Word Incarnate, both in his historical ministry and in his
glorified, Spirit-filled, state. It will be true then, of the foundation of the Church.

The uncertain way in which the principle of appeal to the
Fathers operates in Afanas'ev's writing is both cause and
effect of his central, possibly obsessive, concern with one
idea, an idea whose importance to him is bound up with the
history of Russian Orthodoxy and so is partly autobiographical. At the back of Afanas'ev's mind is the notion that a State-
territorial church must be avoided at all costs. But any

'extrinsically universalist' account of the Church might lend itself to territorialisation and Erastianism since a 'part' of the 'whole' Church could conceivably be organised in separation from the rest. Therefore, any tendency towards extrinsic universality in the picture of the Church offered by the Fathers must be played down. In the early centuries, the term 'Catholic Church' must be regarded, wherever possible, as attached exclusively to the local church in which the mystical reality of Christ's body, flowing as this does from the celebration of the Eucharistic body, appears on this earth. Afanas'ev set out to trace the outlines of an Orthodox ecclesiology of a (theologically) new kind. Insofar as this ecclesiology could not be described as simply a reflection of the common teaching of the Fathers, but is an evaluation of that teaching in which some ancient writers speak more clearly than others, Afanas'ev could not appeal purely to the *consensus patrum* as the authoritative ground of his reading of Scripture. To express his evaluation Afanas'ev turned to patristic studies as an ancillary discipline in Church history. This was a subject which had attained considerable maturity in the Russia of the late-nineteenth century, and which was even more flourishing in the German- and French-speaking West of the interwar years.[175] But at the level of Church history, the *theologoumenon* (theological thesis) Afanas'ev wished to propose to dogmatic theologians became simply a hypothesis about the mentality of the early Church. And, notoriously, there is a fine line in scholarship between holding an imaginative hypothesis leading to the illumination of the data, on the one hand, and thraldom to an *idée fixe* on the other. In attempting to identify the *sanior pars* ('wiser part') of the Fathers dogmatically considered with the mainstream tradition of the Fathers positively or historically conceived, Afanas'ev risked, and risks, pleasing nobody. Nevertheless, the intrinsic interest and importance of his thesis about the patristic Church is such that profit may be gained even from its exaggerations.

VII
The Dogma of the Image at Nicaea II

The dogmatic definition (*horos*) of the Second Council of Nicaea is perhaps best thought of as a selective summary of the Iconophile theologies of the previous decades, a summary placed at the service of a fundamental doctrinal affirmation: namely, that it is legitimate to make, and to venerate, Christian images. I say 'Iconophile theologies', in the plural, because the defenders of the images, on both Byzantine and Arab soil, by no means presented a monolithic bloc of arguments. On the one hand, we have a John Damascene with his multiple, if analogically related, concepts of the image, all situated within a world-view at once Neo-Platonist and incarnational.[1] On the other hand, we have in the rather earlier Cypriot writer Leontius of Neapolis an Iconophile *avant la lettre* whose defence of the veneration of images, *vis-à-vis* Jewish critics, is based on appeal to the Old Testament theme of man as 'the icon of God in the temple of the world', with a subsidiary appeal to the evidence of miracles performed through the icons.[2]

And, indeed, behind this plurality of Iconodule theologies there is also the wider pluralism of patristic theology on which they drew. This wider world of patristic sources includes not only the occasional references of the Fathers to the value of visual images for Christian teaching and devotion, but also the much more considerable corpus of reflection conveniently referred to as 'patristic image theology', for the word *eikôn* was liable to appear in what would later be regarded as quite diverse areas of dogmatic thought. Thus, in the Fathers' use of biblical and Hellenistic sources, we find the cosmos itself regarded as the extended image of God.[3] We also find man portrayed – more particularly – as God's living image.[4] Finally, we find that the figure of Jesus Christ is accorded a quite unique role in such 'image theology' as the supreme, and absolutely definitive, divine icon.[5]

The *horos* of Nicaea II must certainly be interpreted against this background of theological aesthetics, cosmology, anthropology and Christology, which is its necessary foil. And yet the definition itself is not just another contribution to the theology of the image, merely one more brick added to a building. It is also, as its ecumenical reception indicates, in some sense a climax and a summation. Nevertheless, the *horos* summarises or crowns the earlier developments precisely by selecting from among them. It chooses to highlight certain elements in the body of Iconophile thought, and that of relevant patristic theology at large, whilst leaving others in shadow. Thus for instance, the drafters of the definition show a certain intellectual chastity in leaving on one side the Iconophile argument from miraculous images, or from the artworks commanded by the God of Israel in the Pentateuch, and, perhaps more surprisingly, the sophisticated Christological argument founded on the notion of *perigraphê*, 'circumscription', introduced into the debate by the lay theological efforts of the Iconoclast Emperor Constantine V. Yet all of these types of argument had played a major part in the Council's discussions. A contemporary theological reappropriation of the conciliar *horos* must take as its first task, therefore, the identification of the salient points. What dishes did the Council Fathers choose from a menu which offered something of an *embarras de richesses*? I propose to answer this question by commenting on the stages of the *horos* as they unfold.

The definition opens with a lengthy prologue setting forth, in polemical style, the fundamental issue of the Iconoclast crisis.[6] In this prologue, the work of Christ is described in both positive and negative terms. Positively, it is illumination, for he shed abroad *phôs tês autou epignôseôs*, the 'light of the knowledge of himself'. Here, not for the first time in the patristic period, Christian salvation is described in the beautiful metaphor of light inaugurated by Paul in 2 Corinthians.[7] Negatively, the work of Christ is liberation from the 'darkness of idolatrous folly', *skotos tês eidôlikês manias*. Here the members of the Council are found stealing the thunder of the opponents of the images. They accept an account of the redemption, namely, the freeing of man from domination by idols, which had figured prominently in anti-Iconophile writing, and most notably in the *horos* of the Iconoclast council of Hiereia of 754, to whose refutation Nicaea II had devoted its sixth session.[8]

The prologue goes on to locate the ultimate origin of Iconoclasm in a failure of Christian discrimination. The Iconoclasts had failed to distinguish 'between the holy and the profane', *meson hagiou kai bebêlou*, calling the image of the Lord and his saints 'like unto the statues of diabolic idols', *homoiōs tois zoanois tôn satanikôn eidôlôn*. The *horos* regards this failure as a falling away at once from right reason and from tradition. The Iconoclasts committed, then, a twofold apostasy, from *both* philosophical rationality *and* their specifically Christian inheritance of texts and customs. Philosophically, they did not appreciate that the understanding of the relation between the created and the uncreated in the cult of images was markedly different from that found in pagan idolatry. Theologically, this led them to misinterpret both the anti-idolatrous texts of Scripture and early Fathers, and the iconic practices of their own contemporary fellow Christians. However, the emphasis of the *horos* lies quite decidedly on the second, theological aspect.[9] The Iconoclasts ignored the ecclesiological significance of the Church's tacit consent to the rise of a Christian art. They ignored the fact that, with a reference to the Letter to the Ephesians,[10] Christ had taken the Church to himself as his immaculate Bride, and that, moreover, and this time with a concealed citation of the closing verse of the Gospel of Matthew, he had promised to conserve her in the truth until the end of the world.[11] The Iconoclast bishops are compared to the unworthy shepherds of the book of Jeremiah where, in a poetic oracle placed on the lips of the God of Israel, bad pastors are said to have 'destroyed my vineyard, . . . trampled down my portion'.[12]

The *horos* then proceeds, in what by the late-eighth century was required fashion, to reaffirm the Creed of Nicaea-Constantinople, following this up with an explicit repudiation of the more egregious Trinitarian and Christological heresies of the period of the first six Councils.[13] Affirming in global terms the authenticity of the entire Tradition of the Church, whether written or unwritten, the Council Fathers now turn to address the question of the hour, namely, that particular aspect of Tradition which is *eikonikês anazô-graphêseôs ektupôsis*, 'the formation of representative images'. The phrase is broad enough. And in fact, before moving into the act of dogmatic definition strictly so called, the *horos* pauses to identify more clearly the kind of images it has in mind.[14] Those images are, firstly, artworks which concord with the *historia* – a difficult term – of the Gospel proclamation. Secondly, they are such as serve to confirm the reality of the Incarnation. Thirdly, they are those images which are profitable, or practically valuable, for believers. In these three clauses, the Council is at one and the same time determining *which* images it proposes to defend, and indicating arguments in their support. Each clause will repay, therefore, closer attention.

The first clause informs us that the images favoured by the bishops constitute a pictorial equivalent of the Gospel narrative. The term *historia* seems to have caused translators some trouble. Marie-France Auzepy provided the version 'the letter of the message of the Gospel'.[15] It is true that the largest number of entries for the term in Lampe's *Patristic Greek Lexikon* do translate as 'letter': that is, the literal sense of Scripture, as contrasted with the spiritual sense, either in itself or in one of its particular forms, such as anagogy or allegory.[16] However, the concentration of the Lampe lexicon on this meaning is perhaps to be explained by its compilers' awareness of their readers' likely interest in the issue of exegetical method in patristic Bible study. But, as the Lampe entry itself admits, this sense of *historia* is only a sub-division of a more general meaning: 'narrative' or 'history'. Naturally enough, these two meanings are interrelated: frequently, the literal sense of Scripture will indeed be a narrative, a story embedded in facticity. Hence I. Mendham translates *historia* as 'history'.[17] Nevertheless, a third possible sense of the word offered by Lampe is highly pertinent as well, and this is the meaning 'picture' or 'representation' as found in a letter ascribed in the manuscript tradition to the fifth-century ascetic writer Nilus of Ancyra.[18] In this letter, whose authenticity is not fully certain, the author speaks of *historiai*, 'pictures ... of the Old and New Testaments which churches may contain for the sake of the illiterate'. The *Acta* of the Council are familiar with this letter, which they quote.[19] Moreover, two references to images in the letter of Pope Adrian I to the co-emperors Constantine and Irene which precede the *Acta* have been translated by the term *historia*, one by way of transliteration – for the pope had referred to the *divinae historiae scripturarum* ('divine histories of the Scriptures') which, as he put it, for the 'sake of devotion and teaching' we depict in our churches.[20] Indeed, in the Latin-speaking area of Mediterranean Christendom, the great sequences of narrative art found in the basilicas of Rome and Ravenna were themselves termed *historiae*.[21] Nor would the Eastern bishops of Nicaea II have been unfamiliar with such art, whose purpose may be stated as the proclamation of the Gospel through its embodying in a series of narrative scenes which echo the characteristic mode of communication of the four evangelists themselves, as also of the Old Testament Law and prophets, among whom a considerable portion of the historical books of the Hebrew Bible were originally numbered. The miniatures of the Rossano Gospels, and the Vienna Genesis, probably of Syrian provenance, and those of the Sinope Gospels, located to Asia Minor, show a marked narrative realism, and if we may follow the cue of the historian of Byzantine art, Ernst Kitzinger, by the late-sixth century this interest in narrative iconography was well established in the Byzantine capital itself, from which it was communicated to the outposts of East Rome in the Western sphere.[22] The miniatures of the Macedonian renaissance will later show precisely this marriage of visualised Gospel scene and Gospel text: *Bild und Botschaft* ('Image and Message').[23] More monumentally, the *historiae* of Rome and Ravenna may have had their counterparts in such Byzantine churches as St Sophia, the church of the Holy Apostles and the Chrysotriklinium under Justin II and Tiberius II.[24] My suggestion is, then, that the *historia* of the *horos* of Nicaea II carries three connotations: the letter of Scripture; a letter which is frequently biblical story or narrative; a narrative which is itself often pictorial in literary mode. Granted that the form of the Gospel proclamation is already that of a story consisting in dramatic set-pieces, from the Lucan Annunciation scene to those of the Passion, the Resurrection appearances and the outpouring of the Spirit at Pentecost, it seemed reasonable to the bishops of Nicaea II to allow that such verbal vignettes might also have their visual counterparts: counterparts which would *sunadein*, 'agree with', or, as the use of the word in Clement of Alexandria and Methodius of Olympus might suggest, 'concelebrate' the events of the Gospel story.[25] Such images would be exercises in what today is termed 'narrative theology'.[26]

I shall deal rather more briefly with the other two clauses. The second makes the point that those images the Council has in mind are such as confirm the reality, the 'non-phantastic' character of the Incarnation *hê alêthinês kai ou kata phantasian tou Theou Logou enanthrôpêsis* ('the true and not imaginary humanisation of God the Word'). In the previous century, the Council *in Trullo* of 692[27] had seen the image in analogous terms, perhaps as a challenge to Christological heretics. Its value lay in its power to make palpable the Incarnation of the Logos in Christ. Thus, for instance, in the legend cycle which surrounds the Cappadocian image of Christ known as the *Camuliana*, the image is presented as a new Incarnation, *nea Bêtleem*, 'a new Bethlehem'.[28] As at Bethlehem the Word of God was manifested for the first time by his birth from the Virgin, so at Kamoulia, runs a seventh-century homily ascribed to one of the Cappadocian Gregories, he 'has deigned to be venerated today in his mortal body'. And the unknown homilist praises the appearance of the image, which is of the kind known as *acheiropoiêtoi* ('not made by hands'), because it is the vehicle of a renewed 'condescension of the Lord, lover of men, towards his servants'.[29] George Pisides, in the more martial context of his *De expeditione persica* ('The Persian Expedition') will echo this exalted language.[30] In the *Acta* of Nicaea II, the synodal letter of Theodore of Jerusalem gives particularly striking expression to this notion of a special relationship between Incarnation and icon. Though Christ 'was God and invisible', nevertheless

> he appeared, on earth, and was seen by men, being brought up together with them; and he laboured, hungered and thirsted according to the law of our nature which he had taken upon himself. We worship, therefore, the image of Christ – that is, of the personal appearance which was seen among men.[31]

Canon 82 of the Trullan Council will, indeed, be explicitly appealed to at the Council of 787, for example by Elias, archpresbyter of the church of the Blachernae, during the

fourth session.[32] What we have in such references is, I
believe, the notion that the painterly image of Christ is an
enacted metaphor of the Incarnation itself.[33] For in both a
transcendent meaning is presented through a sensuous
medium.

Thirdly, the Council characterises the images whose legit-
imacy it wishes to define as those which are serviceable to the
Christian life – they procure for us *homoia lusiteleia*, a 'like
profit', that is – a benefit commensurate with the goal of the
Incarnation itself, and thus indeed, as in the translation
offered by Bishop Christoph von Schönborn 'a *great*
profit'.[34] This may be described as an experiential or even a
pragmatic argument, an appeal to what might nowadays be
termed Christian *praxis*. Such appeals to the proven practical
value of visual images had already been made in some earlier
references to the presence of artworks within the Church.
These might be couched in didactic terms of the usefulness of
images for teaching, as, in the East, with Basil of Caesarea's
Oration on the Martyr Barlaam[35] or, in the West, in Paulinus
of Nola[36] and Gregory the Great.[37]

Alternatively, or additionally, they could be presented in
terms of the devotional utility of images for the deepening of
prayerful relationship with the holy figures depicted in them.
Thus we find Gregory of Nyssa offering an illustration of this
in his comments on an image of the Sacrifice of Isaac known
to him.[38] And as Bishop Theodore of Catana had pointed
out, not unreasonably, in the Council's fourth session:

> If the holy Gregory, ever watchful in divine contemplation (*ho
> hagios Grêgorios, ho grêgorôn* . . .) wept on seeing the picture of
> Abraham, how much more ought the image of the incarnate
> dispensation of our Lord Jesus Christ, who for our sake became
> man, to cause edifying tears to flow forth from all who behold
> it?[39]

In similar fashion, the fifth-century historian Philostorgius remarks that in the man who lingers with joy over an image of Christ we see a demonstration of love for the figure portrayed.[40] And there is also, finally, a splendid dialogue in much these terms in the *Questiones ad Antiochum ducem* where an unknown early Christian author defends the veneration of images by saying:

> We make an obeisance to express the attitude and love of our souls for those represented in the icon ... to show our longing for them, just as we do in greeting our fathers and our friends.[41]

We can note with Kitzinger that, as both cause and symptom of this devotional attitude, images had been changing their form and location in the years since the reign of Justinian.[42] The figures in both paintings and mosaics had become more physically accessible. They were placed lower down on the church walls as at St Demetrios in Salonika, or in the frescoes provided by Pope John VII at Sta Maria Antiqua.[43] They were increasingly associated with the areas where the most intense liturgical activity took place: these years see the beginnings of the rise of the iconostasis, as panel icons are attached to chancel rails or pillars,[44] the clearest evidence coming, curiously enough, from the far West of the Christian world, in Benedict Biscop's Northumbria[45] and the Irish monastic church of Kildare.[46] Above all, there were the portable icons, which any of the faithful might place in their homes or find in the everyday world of the city street. As Kitzinger puts it:

> Released from the serried ranks of a narrative cycle or of a pictorial litany or calendar, and no longer part of a universal scheme, an objective, supra-personal order, the sacred representation may become the object of a more intimate rapport, a more personal relationship.[47]

We shall return to this topic in a moment, when considering the dogmatic definition, *sensu stricto*.

Moving on then to the doctrinal definition proper, we may note first, that the definition is introduced by the statement that the holy images are to be given the same status as the sign of the 'honourable and lifegiving Cross', *ho timios kai zōopios stauros*. Here the Council shows for the second time something of an eirenic intention, despite the strength of its language against the Iconoclast bishops. The special place given to the Cross in Iconoclast teaching, what Prof Stephen Gerö has called the Iconoclast *theologia crucis*,[48] is not denied: rather is it insisted that it must be widened to include the images, whether of Christ, of his mother or of the angels and saints.

But why? The *horos* in the narrow sense offers only one reason, namely that by means of the iconic *anatupôsis* or 'impression', those who look at such images are led towards 'the memory and desire of their prototypes' (*pros tên tôn prôtotupôn mnêmên kai epipothêsin*), and that, correspondingly, the honour done to the image whether by a kiss, by *timêtikê proskunêsis* ('a worshipful prostration'), or by the bringing of incense and lights is in fact 'given to the prototype' (*epi to prôtotupon diabainei*),[49] with a reference to Basil the Great's celebrated simile in the *De Spiritu Sancto*[50] – what Père Gervais Dumeige has called 'this frequently appealed to text'.[51] Thus the one who prostrates himself before the icon prostrates himself before the *hypostasis* (person) who is there *engraphomenos* ('graphically depicted'). Here we have what appears at first sight to be the argument from devotional practice discussed a moment ago, but the inflexion of the text is changed by the introduction of a term from classical Christology, *hypostasis*, which introduces a further, metaphysical dimension. It is this new dimension which the Iconophile doctors of the second Iconoclast period, Nicephorus of Constantinople and Theodore of Studios,[52] will take up in their own work, and whose changing fortunes, from the First Council of Nicaea to the Second have been so admirably described by von Schönborn.[53] Once again, the art historian can enlighten the historical theologian here, for though the more impressionistic, three-dimensional and mobile figures of the Hellenistic current in Byzantine art could perfectly well be the objects of devotion, it is the more abstract current, with its conceptual rendering of the human form, and symmetric display of fully facing figures which is the more easily associated with the expectations aroused by the *horos* in its climatic affirmation. The serial portraits, removed from their dramatic, narrative contexts, become the portrait icons.[54] The Madonna of Sta Francesca Romana, the Christ with St Menas of Bawit, the St Peter of St Catherine's, Mount Sinai: these are the perfect illustrations of the central iconological idea of the *horos* of Nicaea II.[55]

One final thought may be in order. It was pointed out as long ago as 1956[56] that here, where *hypostasis* finds itself equated with *prôtotupos*, the use of the former term is not strictly that of the customary 'philosophical-dogmatic concept' of post-Chalcedonian Christology for which, as the *Acta* of Nicaea II themselves indicate, it means the bearer of a nature, *phusis*.[57] When used as, effectively, a synonym for *prôtotupos*, it introduced, or so Ernst Hammerschmitt believed, a disconcerting vagueness into the theology of the icon, which the subsequent Eastern tradition had failed to dispel.[58] I believe that the clue to a solution is found in the mediating notion of *prosôpon*, understood in one of its most ancient but by no means wholly discarded senses, namely, 'face'. The image discloses the face, and the face is the visible self-presentation of the *hypostasis*,[59] which may therefore be described as the prototype of the image.

A contemporary theological appropriation of this teaching might well draw here on the notion of face – *le visage* – found in the work of the present-day French philosopher Emmanuel Levinas, for whom relation with the face of the other is the means whereby the Infinite breaks in on the closed world of the individual self, with its tendency to reduce all reality to what is commensurate with its own constructed view of being, what Levinas terms *identité*. By means of the face, true otherness, *altérité*, breaks through, calling upon us for a self-abnegating response.[60] It thus effectively launches us into that life of communion, *koinônia*, with other persons, divine and human, which is the goal of the saving economy.

As a contemporary Orthodox theologian of the icon, Paul Evdokimov, wrote of the image of Christ:

> Truly, it is not the human individuality but the Hypostasis of Christ which reveals itself to each iconographer in a unique manner, at once ecclesial and personal, just as the Resurrection appearances have multiple aspects. The Church preserves in her memory the unique Holy Face 'not made by human hands', and there exist as many Holy Faces as there are iconographers'.[61]

In such a recovery of the central doctrinal insight of the *horos* of Nicaea II we may see fulfilled a thought of T. S. Eliot's: 'The purpose of re-ascending to origins is that we should be able to return, with greater spiritual knowledge, to our situation.'[62]

VIII
St Thomas Aquinas on the Passion of Christ

In June 1272, a General Chapter of the Order of Preachers met in Florence. Among other things, it decided that a new theological study house, open to the general public (a *studium generale*) should be established in Italy, under the auspices of the Roman Province. That Province, accordingly, entrusted the project to brother Thomas d'Aquino. The choice of site was left, with, perhaps, a certain disregard for administrative propriety, entirely to him. For various reasons, not least among them the support of the Neapolitan crown, he selected Naples. Development was sufficiently fast for him to begin lecturing there that same September. Forty-six years old (probably), he had somewhat over a year left to live. He was ending his career as he had begun it: entrusted with the formation of young theologians.[1] What better opportunity to finish his great unfinished work, the *Summa Theologiae*, described in what has been called Thomas's only recorded joke (but the remark was seriously meant) as an introduction to the subject for beginners.[2] Having dealt already with man's sovereign Good, and with the general pattern of his return to God, as suggested by the dynamic structures of human nature, it remained for Thomas to consider how, in the concrete, this return to God might come about. As he wrote in the prologue to the *Tertia Pars* (the work's 'Third Part'):

Our Saviour, the Lord Jesus Christ, as he was, according to the

Angels' witness, saving his people from their sins, showed in his own Person that path of truth which, in rising again, we can follow to the blessedness of eternal life. This means that, after our study of the final goal of human life, and of the virtues and vices, we must bring the entire theological discourse to completion by considering the Saviour himself, and his benefits to the human race.[3]

As is well known, the method of the *Summa Theologiae* consists in asking questions. The question or *quaestio* form had a long history, starting with the exegetical problems of the Church Fathers, as they grappled with the biblical text.[4] But in Thomas's case, it expressed, additionally, the whole set or tendency of an enquiring mind. As a boy at the monastic school of Monte Cassino, he had asked, seriously and with persistence, 'What is God?'[5] It should not surprise us that he opens his account of the Passion by asking, 'Was it really necessary?'[6]

Was it actually necessary for Christ to suffer? Thomas approaches an answer to his own question by distinguishing between two kinds of necessity. Something may be necessary because it follows absolutely from the nature of reality. By an inbuilt necessity God must be good. By a similar necessity I must live in society. In this absolute sense, Christ did not have to suffer his Passion: suffering is not built into the very idea of God made man. But there is also a second kind of necessity which follows on the selection of a goal.[7] If I decide to go to London I must take steps to get there, by train, car, or shanks' pony. X is necessary if without it some objective cannot be attained, or, at least, cannot be attained so *convenienter*, so 'fittingly', so well. Given that the Son of God, in assuming human nature, took as his 'goal', *finis, liberatio hominis*, our 'liberation', then the Passion was a necessity. But does this mean, then, Thomas asks, that God could have freed man in no other way than by Christ's Passion?[8] No; when Christ says that the Son of Man must suffer, he means: given that God foreknows and pre-ordains that *this* will be the way for human liberation to come about. In principle, God could have freed man from sin without proposing any compensation from the human side, any *satisfactio*, any 'making-up'; for human evil. Unlike a human judge, God is not different from the justice which he executes. God is the measure or criterion of justice, being in himself what Thomas calls the 'supreme and common good of the whole universe', the goodness that all justice reflects.[9] But, in decreeing that man would make compensation for sin in the Person of the Incarnate Word, God showed the world greater mercy than had he forgiven us through a simple declaration of reconciliation.[10]

The reasons for this emerge when Thomas asks whether there could be a *better* way to free man than through the Passion of Christ.[11] Granted that there could be other ways, could there be more fitting ways? How do we determine fittingness when choosing between different means, all of which are capable of taking us to the same end? Basically, so Thomas suggests, we look at the number of factors helpfully relevant to the projected end in any given means.[12] He points out in this connexion that liberation from sin is not the whole of human salvation. Negatively, salvation is liberation from sin, but positively, it is gracious reunion with God. That positive dimension is, clearly, highly pertinent to liberation from sin, since, without the new life of grace, the sources of sin within us would be as effective as ever. Thomas gives five reasons why, in choosing the Passion as the means of our liberation, God ensured that the *fructus humanae salutis*, the 'fruitfulness of our salvation' would possess a maximal richness.

First, the Passion of Christ, as distinct from some other means of liberating man, enabled us to see how much God loves us, and thus aroused us to love God back. In such love for God, Thomas remarks, the *perfectio*, 'making perfect', of human salvation precisely consists.[13] Secondly, in the way he underwent his Passion, Christ gave us an example of the virtues that we too must practise if we are to appropriate our salvation in a definitive manner – through such qualities as obedience, humility, constancy.[14] Thirdly, as a result of the Passion, man feels a greater obligation to keep himself free from sin.[15] Fourthly, through the fact that it was by *human* suffering that our salvation came about, a greater dignity accrues to man. It was man himself who overcame evil.[16] Thomas presents each of these points, be it noted, as exegesis of the New Testament letters, and his choice of texts is overwhelmingly Pauline in character. Behind the 'systematic theologian' created by modern theological historiography, we hear, in the construction of this case, the accents of the historical Thomas's self-understanding: that of a commentator on the *sacra pagina*, the (biblical) Word of God. Finally, Thomas points out that, in his Passion, Christ not only made satisfaction for sin but also merited for us grace and glory.[17] That means: through the obedient love which his suffering expressed, Christ, as man, won the moral right to God's friendship. The aim of his Passion is not only the liberation of the sinful but also the exaltation of his own humanity as that of the unique innocent one. As the Letter to the Hebrews put it:

> For the joy that was set before him, he embraced the Cross, endured the pain of it, and now sits at God's right hand.[18]

But this is not simply of relevance to Christ as a human individual. He suffers, not as an individual in isolation, but as the *caput*, 'head', of a new humanity – what Paul terms the 'new' or 'second' Adam. Between Christ and all those who will form holy Church there is a mysterious but real identity. Through God's predestining grace, Christ is the head and we are the members, united so closely as to form what Thomas calls 'one mystical person', *una mystica persona*.[19] The moral unity of this mystical corporate personality is such that, Thomas insists, what Christ merits for himself he also merits for his members, just as if each of them were his own self. Through the Passion, we enjoy the right to share in Christ's exaltation. By the grace of justification, we begin to live here and now with Christ's own righteousness, his holy existence, and this grace, planting within us the Spirit of Christ as the principle of our sanctification, prepares us for the beatitude, or happiness, that will be ours in the life of glory.[20] For all these reasons, Christ's Passion was a most fitting way for God to achieve our liberation, and a fuller manifestation of his mercy than the mere declaration of our forgiveness.

But granted that Christ's Passion was, in the sense explained, both necessary and highly appropriate, why a cross?[21] Why that particular form of suffering, rather than some other? Citing Augustine, Thomas points out that crucifixion was a particularly horrifying death – 'most execrable and formidable' – and in this sense it showed that the good man ought not to fear any type of dying.[22] But his answer turns principally on the *symbolism* of the Cross. Here he brings into play his considerable knowledge of the patristic, and early mediaeval, tradition, where symbol and image enjoyed a greater rôle in the construction of theology than they did for the Scholastics.[23] So (for example) Thomas can cite the fourth-century Greek father Gregory of Nyssa on how the very shape of the Cross corresponds to the universality of the salvation wrought upon it. For Gregory had written:

> The form of the Cross radiates out from the centre in four different directions, thus denoting the universal diffusion of the power and providence of him who hung upon it.[24]

Such symbolism may be, as in this case, cosmic, natural symbolism, but it may also be, alternatively, a matter of symbolic correspondences between particular narratives within Scripture. Thus (for instance) Thomas regards it as highly suitable that original sin, which came about through taking the fruit of a tree, should find its remedy in a nailing to the tree of the Cross. As the rhetoric of the Roman liturgy has it on the feast of the Exaltation of the Cross:

> The tree of man's defeat became his tree of victory; where life was lost, there life has been restored.[25]

In what sense are such considerations genuinely *argument*, however – argument in favour of the claim that the Crucifixion was the most fitting way for the Word to suffer in his human nature? Insofar as, both cosmically and biblically, the human mind finds the symbolism of the Cross imaginatively satisfying, to that extent it was especially appropriate that the Cross should be the means of our salvation. It is part of Thomas's account of what it is to be human that, for us, nothing can be really known unless it is mediated in some way by sense appearance.[26]

Yet the suffering involved in the Passion was not limited, of course, to the actual Crucifixion itself. Thomas considers that, in one sense, Christ's Passion includes every principal category of suffering that there is.[27] Of course, Christ did not endure every particular type, *species*, of suffering. Some of these are, in any case, mutually exclusive: if one is going to die by fire one cannot also die by drowning. Yet *secundum genus*, in terms of broader categories, the Passion was representative of all those things *in quibus homo potest pati*, 'in which man can suffer'. Christ suffered in his friends as they deserted him; in his good name when he was blasphemed; in his honour from the mockery of others; in his possessions when his garments were torn from him; in his soul when he knew sadness, weariness and fear; in his body by wounds and blows. This range of suffering is reflected in the variety of people who induced it: pagans, Jews, men, women (like the maidservant who occasioned Peter's denial), princes and servants, enemies and friends. All this was greatly *conveniens* to someone whose Passion was to be of universal significance.

And this is true even though *una minima passio Christi*, 'the very least of Christ's sufferings', would have sufficed to redeem mankind from all its sins, a conclusion expressed more lyrically in the *Adoro devote*, a hymn on the Eucharist as memorial of the Passion ascribed (but by no means with total security) to Thomas himself:

> *Pie pellicane, Jesu Domine,*
> *me immundum munda tuo sanguine:*
> *Cujus una stilla salvum facere*
> *totum mundum quit ab omni scelere*[28]

In Hopkins's translation:

> Bring the tender tale true of the pelican;
> Bathe me, Jesu Lord, in what thy bosom ran –
> Blood that but one drop of has the power to win
> all the world forgiveness of its world of sin.[29]

In mediaeval legend, the pelican tore its own breast in order to nourish its young with its blood. The legend's message is that of *pietas*, love for one's kindred. Thomas holds that the *dolor*, 'pain', attached to Christ's suffering exceeded that of all other human pains,[30] excepting only those of the damned which exceed all negative experiences in this world as much as the saints' enjoyment of glory exceeds all positive. For, first of all, there is in crucifixion a severe bodily pain: a *mors acerbissima* ('most bitter death'), Thomas calls it, giving quite concrete physiological details. The nails pierce the hands and feet where the highly sensitive nerve-endings are located. The weight of the hanging body constantly increases the pain. Thomas notes that, physically, Jesus must have been particularly sensitive to experience. Since his body was formed miraculously in Mary's womb, it must have been *optime compleximatus*, 'exceptionally well put together', and hence unusually receptive to sensation. Thomas reminds us in this connexion of the miraculous wine of the Marriage Feast at

Cana. Since that wine was the direct work of the Creator, it shared his excellence in its own mode. As the steward of the feast discovered, it was, so to say, the Palestinian equivalent of *Nuits Saint-Georges*, far removed from *vin de table*.[31] But Christ also suffered *inner* pain: the 'sadness', *tristitia*, which results from awareness of some *nocementum*, some 'hurt'. Christ's inner suffering derived from his awareness of the sins of all mankind, which sins, indeed, he quasi-ascribed to himself.[32] Because all his inner powers were rendered more acute by the union of his human nature with the divine Word, Christ would have perceived this, and other causes of his sadness, with the greatest possible clarity.

It followed from Thomas's philosophical conviction that the soul is the form of the human body, being found whole in that body, and in any part of it, that Christ, in suffering in the body, suffered in the essence of his soul.[33] In this sense, for Thomas, physical suffering *is* spiritual suffering. Insofar as all the powers of the soul – and notably intellect and will – are rooted in the soul's essence, they too were affected by the physicality of the Passion. Yet in what Thomas terms the highest part of the soul, comparable, perhaps, to the *apex animae* of the Christian mystical tradition, where the soul has its point of contact with its divine Source, Christ continued to find God not a source of grief but of delight and joy: *delectatio et gaudium*.[34] Thomas was aware that there was here a *prima facie* contradiction. Owing to the unity of man, the hammering in of the nails must have affected even the highest part of Christ's soul. Yet by appeal to the same unity, the 'joy of enjoying God', *gaudium fruitionis*, would still qualify the very essence of Christ's human individuality. Without trying to evoke what this might be like psychologically, Thomas confines himself to remarking that it is not, at any rate, formally contradictory.

There is nothing to prevent contrary things co-existing in the same subject if they are there under different formalities. Thus the joy of fruition can pertain to the superior part of Christ's reason by its own proper act, but the pain of the Passion by reason of the subject (that is, the fact that Christ has only one soul, which is the subject of all his powers). The pain of the Passion pertains to the essence of the soul, because of the body which it informs, but the joy of fruition is there by reason of the faculty, which the soul contains as subject.[35]

From the heights of philosophical psychology, and how they might help us to understand the pain of One who was God, Thomas now descends to consider the relevance to the Passion of the well-known adage that there is a time and a place for everything. Did Christ die at the right time,[36] and at the right place?[37] Thomas reflects on the argument that Christ would more appropriately have died on the feast of Passover proper, since, as our Redeemer, he is our Passover lamb. And yet, if we follow the gospels, with the exception of St John, we discover that he died a day too late. Thomas discusses the relative merits of the Synoptic and Johannine dating of the Passion, and finishes, like most modern students, fairly inconclusively. He mentions, without explicitly accepting, John Chrysostom's opinion that the term 'Passover' could have a broad connotation: the seven days surrounding the feast itself. As Chrysostom was well informed about Jewish life in the Levant in his own day, this hint of a solution may not be without value.[38] In other respects, however, Thomas has no doubt that Jesus did indeed die at a *tempus conveniens*. Following an anonymous Latin patristic text, the *Quaestiones Novi et Veteri Testamenti*, it was fitting that Christ should die at the spring equinox. Citing his source:

The Lord wished to redeem and refashion the world at the equinox, when he created it. At that time of the year, the days grow longer than the nights, as we, through the Saviour's Passion, are led out of darkness into the light.[39]

In the same way, so Thomas believed, Jesus had taught in the parable of the Fig Tree that the Parousia would take place just as summer is arriving. The 'perfect illumination' of our minds that will follow the Second Coming takes place, very properly, as the summer light starts to fill the sky. It is also important to Thomas that Christ died as a young man. To draw attention to his love, Christ went to death at the height of his vital powers. It would have been quite unsuitable for him to have died of old age or of disease, *cum sit vita*, 'since he is life itself'.[40]

What then of the place? Aptly, he died at the centre of the inhabited world, the *omphalos* or navel, Jerusalem. It fitted his humanity that he should die a shameful death in such a celebrated city. Rightly, he died not in the Temple, where the ritual sacrifices were being offered in their hundreds and thousands as the events of the Passion unfolded, but outside the City gates. This, Thomas thought, was to discourage the supposition that his death was for the sole benefit of the Jewish people, gathered in their liturgical capital. On the contrary, it was to benefit the whole earth. Similar considerations suggest why he died appropriately between thieves.[41] If we look at this from the viewpoint of his Jewish opponents, it was to degrade him. *Sed non ita evenit*: 'but things turned out differently'. And here Thomas cites, in somewhat impressionistic form, words of his exegete of predilection, Chrysostom:

No one speaks of them now, but his Cross is honoured everywhere. Kings, setting aside their diadems, wear the Cross. Throughout the whole world, on purple robes, diadems and swords, and on the Holy Table, the Cross shines forth in splendour.[42]

To understand how the best laid schemes of Christ's enemies thus went agley, we need to look at the rôle of the two thieves from the viewpoint of God's *ordinatio*, his ordering of things.

Christ died *noxius inter noxios*, 'a criminal among criminals', so as to show that no human being lies beyond the range of the redemption.

This is almost the end of Thomas's *questio de passione Christi*, and one might have thought that he could hardly do better than to end on such a note. But he has yet to tell us why, at the most fundamental level, all of this should matter to us.[43] During his years of work in the *Latium* (central Italy to the west of the Apennines) Thomas's tracks had crossed with those of the Roman Curia, then something of a mobile university in its own right. As now, it possessed a valuable archive, the forerunner of the present 'Vatican Archives'. The archive included a collection of Church-historical documents, Conciliar texts in particular, unique for completeness in the Western Christendom of the day. Probably there, but just possibly in some monastic holding, Thomas uncovered the Acts of the Council of Ephesus. He thus had access to the original terms in which – on soteriological grounds centering on the Passion – the mystery of Christ's being was affirmed to be that of a single divine Person who had assumed a human nature without any diminution of his Godhead.[44] Thomas, despite his realistic Aristotelean concreteness where Jesus' human powers were concerned, became an enthusiast for Ephesus, and, more especially, for Cyril. Godhood and manhood are united in the single Person of the Lord in such a way that – citing Cyril's celebrated, or notorious, twelfth anathema in the third letter to Nestorius – 'any man who does not confess that the Word of God suffered in the flesh, and was crucified in the flesh' deserves condemnation[45] (even though anathemas are not Thomas's style). The death of Christ was, thanks to the personal union, *tanquam mors Dei*, 'as it were the death of God'.[46]

Thomas's theology of the Passion is a curious blend of rationality and symbolism, with no sense of discontinuity between where the first ends and the second begins. But this is only to say that he was a mediaeval. It is also remarkable that, whereas, conventionally, he is thought of as a theological rationaliser, who tried to deduce a set of systematically interrelated truths from the articles of the Creed, the great majority of his reflections on the Passion of Christ are explorations of the *convenientia* (suitability), or, in his preferred word, *congruentia* (congruence), of that redeeming death, both in itself and in its circumstances. While such arguments from fittingness must be handled carefully, they are in themselves perfectly legitimate. Given what we know of the world by natural means, and of the Christian God by the light of divine faith, we try to exhibit the coherence of his saving plan.[47]

And of course Thomas's interest in the Passion was not primarily in an aspect of a belief system: it was an affair of a relationship with One who was personal. As Bernard Gui, one of his earliest biographers, has it:

> Thomas' hold on divine things resembled that Apostle (Thomas Didymus) in entering the abyss of the side of Christ ... as one invited, and therein searching out and expressing the mysteries contained there ...[48]

According to a second early biographer, William of Tocco, it was when the *Tertia Pars* was being composed that Thomas had his 'auditory vision' before a crucifix in the priory church at Naples. There he heard Christ say to him, 'You have written well of me, Thomas. What do you desire as a reward for your labours?' And we are told that Thomas replied, 'Lord, only yourself.'[49] At Mass there on Passion Sunday it was as if he had been admitted to a share in the sufferings of Christ. For a long while he remained as in a trance, his face bathed in tears. At last some of the brethren came up and touched him, and brought him back to himself, and he went on with the Mass. But afterwards, when asked by them, and by some knights who were his friends, what had happened to him during the trance he refused to tell them.[50] Here, in other words, we leave the realm of theological enquiry and formulation, and enter that mysterious place where the realities of God and man actually touch and greet each other.[51]

IX
Homage to Scheeben

The centenary of the death of the Rhineland theologian Matthias Joseph Scheeben (1835–88) was celebrated with symposia in both Germany and Rome. A disciple of St Thomas, but with wider enthusiasms in both mediaeval theology (notably Richard of Saint Victor) and the Fathers (especially Cyril of Alexandria), Scheeben was a product of the Roman theology of the 1850s.[1] He was formed by a series of German-language Roman Jesuits – Joseph Kleutgen, Clemens Schraader, Johann Baptist Franzelin – who provided the main theological impetus for the two Dogmatic Constitutions of the First Vatican Council as well as for such major documents of the succeeding pontificate as Leo XIII's letter on biblical inspiration, *Providentissimus Deus* ('Most Provident God'). Since it is often assumed that the theological culture of this period was moribund and sterile – with honourable 'unofficial' exceptions like John Henry Newman and the writers of the Catholic Tübingen school – it is at first surprising to see how such an Ultramontane author has not ceased to arouse sympathetic interest in the German-speaking world.[2]

For Ultramontane Scheeben certainly was, indeed a typical Ultramontane populist of his period, a period dominated by memories of the 'year of revolutions', 1848, with its spectre of an alliance between the bourgeois intelligentsia and a 'Febronian' higher clergy suspicious of Rome and desirous of a national church under a German metropolitan. In his essays on the 'Vatican Decrees', Scheeben appealed, shrewdly enough, over the heads of liberals, whether political or ecclesiastical, to the inarticulate masses of the 'poor and the weak'.[3] They will find, he predicts, a 'mighty helper' not in the self-appointed 'tribunes of the people' or 'people's friends', but in a universally primatial and doctrinally infallible visible head of the earthly Church. By the latter's proclamation of an everlasting law of ethics, and of the Last Judgment, the equal dignity of all men, despite their outward inequality, will be brought home to human minds, and in no other way.

However, Scheeben's articles in defence of *Pastor aeternus* ('Eternal Shepherd', the Constitution of the First Vatican Council on the Petrine ministry) were essentially occasional pieces, unrepresentative of the general tenor of his theological work. If any public controversy in the Church lay behind that work, it was not the quarrel over the interrelation of the papacy and local churches (and governments), but the earlier dispute over theological rationalism which had stirred passions both in the North German Confederation and in Austria. For the followers of Georg Hermes and Anton Günther, impressed by the philosophical mileage which German (Protestant) Idealists like Hegel and Schelling had been able to extract from the revealed doctrines of the Trinity and the Incarnation, hoped to commend Catholic dogma by presenting it as *only contingently* mysterious and supernatural.[4] Though these truths, in point of historical fact, had entered human minds from without, by direct divine intervention, once lodged there they were capable of rational demonstration. Otherwise, such theological rationalists held, the act of faith could not be termed reasonable, nor the theological exploration of its content scientific. It was because these ideas were lapped up so eagerly by his fellow-countrymen, consonant as they pre-eminently were with the culture of the age, that Scheeben embarked on an ambitious project of theological writing whose key terms are *Mysterium*, 'mystery', and *übernatürlich*, 'supernatural'.

The context of Scheeben's work was the archdiocesan seminary of Cologne, where he taught from 1860, the year after his ordination, until his premature death in 1888. But from the outset of his teaching, he refused to let his perspectives be limited by the sole needs of priestly formation. He addressed his writings at one and the same time to professional theologians and to a wider audience of the faithful. As he wrote:

> I cherish the deep conviction that speculative theology is of supreme importance for the truest and highest formation of mind and heart, and that under the guidance of the great doctors of the Church, secure roads must be built, reaching to the very summits of divine truth, roads that can be travelled without excessive hardship not only by a few privileged spirits, but by anyone who combines courage and energy with a sufficiently sound education.[5]

If his first major work, *Natur und Gnade* ('Nature and Grace')[6] was directed more towards trained theologians, his *Die Herrlichkeiten der göttlichen Gnade* ('The Splendours of Divine Grace')[7] was meant chiefly for a lay audience, despite its sometimes difficult language. Not that he was incapable of writing in a more popular style, as his directly devotional works show. These range from lives of contemporary saints through a Marian anthology to the making of a Catholic prayer book. But Scheeben's masterpiece was undoubtedly his *Die Mysterien des Christentums* ('The Mysteries of Christianity'), a revised edition of which, solicited by his friend the publisher Benjamin Herder, he was preparing at the time of his death. Scrupulously reconstructed from his notes, it was eventually published in 1941, and translated into English five years later.[8] Finally, once the controversies of the *Konzilskrieg* (the 'War over the Council') had died down, he created the comprehensive trilogy *Handbuch der katholischen Dogmatik* ('Handbook of Catholic Dogmatics'), one of the finest manuals of the modern period.[9]

'Mystery' and 'Supernatural'

Let us return to what I have called Scheeben's 'key-terms':
'mystery' and 'supernatural'. In the preface to the commem-
orative volume published in Scheeben's honour by the
Roman Academy of St Thomas, Cardinal Ratzinger attempts
to draw out their significance.[10] Whereas, since Aristotle,
scientific understanding has been largely regarded as a matter
of evaluating the particular in terms of more general principles, a tendency which contemporary historical-critical
tools of biblical study have inherited, Christian faith is concerned with a new, and 'non-derivable' beginning in history.
Scheeben expresses the distinction of levels which this element of novelty requires by his term 'mystery'. As Scheeben
puts it:

> The greater, the more sublime, and the more divine Christianity
> is, the more inexhaustible, inscrutable, unfathomable, and mys-
> terious its subject matter must be. If its teaching is worthy of the
> only-begotten Son of God, if the Son of God had to descend
> from the bosom of his Father to initiate us into this teaching,
> could we expect anything else than the revelation of the deepest
> mysteries locked up in God's heart?[11]

And in the aesthetic vocabulary which is all-pervasive in his
writing he goes on:

> A truth that is easily discovered and quickly grasped can neither
> enchant nor hold. To enchant and hold us it must surprise us by
> its novelty, it must overpower us with its magnificence; its
> wealth and profundity must exhibit ever new splendours, ever
> deeper abysses to the exploring eye.[12]

For the Swiss theologian Hans Urs von Balthasar, it is
Scheeben's concept of mystery which makes him a vital figure
in Balthasar's own recovery of a 'theological aesthetics',
based on the glory or beauty of God.[13] Situated as he is at the
opposite pole from a merely apologetic theology, Scheeben

regards the most important criterion of the truth of faith as the *inner splendour* of the realities that faith grasps. He offered a total overview of the Christian mysteries, aimed at showing the organic interrelatedness of the revealed truths, their wonderful harmony both with each other and with the truths of the natural order to which they are linked, as well as their value for human living, their capacity to satisfy the needs of the human heart. This was not anti-intellectualist: to Scheeben, it was the absence of all shadow of contradiction between the revealed truths, and the ability of each to gather, concentrate and reflect all the rest, and to complete the truths of nature, that constituted the evidence for their truth claims.[14] In a sense, therefore, the writing of dogmatics becomes itself, in his work, the defence, and the proclamation, of the faith.

The other key term, 'supernatural' also has a relevance for the present situation of Catholic theology. As Ratzinger points out in the essay already mentioned, the debates over that word, occasioned by Henri de Lubac's pioneering investigations into its historical background, led to a certain wariness in its use.[15] It was, for example, avoided by the Fathers of the Second Vatican Council. However, de Lubac's intention was not to suppress the supernatural, but, on the contrary, to expand it. Originally, the refusal of a dualism of natural and supernatural was meant to favour the supernatural: each and every reality, it was said, must be interpreted christologically. But with the anthropocentric turn of, first, transcendental Thomism, and then political theology, the rejection of dualism was made to serve naturalistic ends, with christology reduced by stages to a category of human existence, and, finally, to the level of political messianism. In the wake of this development, Ratzinger argues, human nature itself grows smaller. The 'interior' and the 'higher' are spurned in the name of everyday realism, and into the resulting experiential vacuum there moves 'Asiatic monism', the religions of India and China. Scheeben, so Ratzinger believes, would have taxed contemporary theology, above all, for its neglect of the doctrine of the indwelling of the Holy Spirit, whereby God touches the person as Person, and is with his creature 'really as God, and not just through mediations'.[16]

It is true that, for Scheeben, one can only do justice to the being of the world by allowing Christian thinking to retain its radically theocentric character.[17] The creature has its being from the living God and towards him. Man and the world are only finally intelligible in the light of the divine economy: in the light, that is, of theology's proper material object which is God himself as midpoint of the supernatural order, the principle and goal of the mediation of his own divine nature. It is in this way that theology is (with a side-swipe at Kant) the 'true transcendental knowledge' which enables us to gain a discernment of our own powers, of the world around us, and of how the two are to be co-related.[18]

The Redemptive Order

What Ratzinger's essay does not succeed in underlining, however, is Scheeben's sharp focus, not on the general pattern of the supernatural order, but on the redemption as its crowning. The leitmotif of his account of the supernatural is, unconsciously, announced by the angelic chorus in Newman's *Dream of Gerontius*.

> And that *a higher gift than grace* should flesh and blood refine:
> God's presence and his very self and essence all-divine.[19]

From its beginnings, the creation was situated within a supernatural order of grace. Thus enriched by grace, the created world has ever been the greatest expression of God's glory, with the glorification of God its first and chief purpose. Because, precisely, of the preciousness of the graced creation, it was, with the advent of sin, fitting and, as Scheeben remarks, 'more than fitting', that the Creator should not leave the divine ordering of the world compromised or obscured, but, on the contrary, should confirm it *through establishing an even higher order*. This higher order is that of the Son of God made man, whose incarnation and saving work bring not only the natural order but the *supernatural order itself* to a new and unsurpassable state of realisation. As Scheeben insists again and again in *Die Mysterien des Christentums*, Christ's work cannot be restricted to the reconciliation of a sinful world with the good God. Additionally, that work entails the 'conclusion of an inexpressibly intimate covenant between God and mankind'.[20]

Scheeben presents the God-man Jesus Christ as the most concrete realisation of both the divinely given order of grace and the humanly offered glorification of God. He has no 'separate Christology'. Although he offers the interested reader a refined account of Christ's ontological make-up, this is meant to be read and meditated upon *within* the circumambient soteriology. Vital to Scheeben are those principles and elements in our Lord's total being which determine his relation with fallen humanity and with the whole creation, and render comprehensible the extension of the effect of the redemption to humanity at large – and beyond. Scheeben's central thought here is the primacy of the God-man *vis-à-vis* creation. The human Christ, because of his uncreated divine and personal principle (his divine nature and hypostasis) 'shares in that highest supremacy which belongs to the Creator of all things'.[21] All humanity forms an organism, or body, in relation to Christ who is, for that humanity, the source of a new quality of supernatural life.

Moving from an account of the Incarnation to the Atonement, Scheeben sees the Cross of Christ as, above all, a sacrifice of praise and thanksgiving. Only by virtue of this 'latreutic' character (essential to the salvation and transfiguration of a world made for the glory of God) is Christ's death a matter of expiation and reconciliation for sinful humanity.[22] As Scheeben explains it, the moment of expiation is brought about by the reflection on humankind of the perfect sacrifice of praise. Nor does he separate the Atonement, as glorification of God, from the sacrificial ethos of the whole life of Jesus. Good Friday and Easter cannot be sundered from Christmas and the Annunciation. In all these events, a work undertaken in history is taking effect in the universe. Despite his stress on the intimacy of the divine covenant relationship, Scheeben's theological imagination is cosmic in scope. Through the Incarnation, the material world is irrevocably destined to the service of spirit, and to spiritualisation as its ultimate goal, while, at the other end of the cosmic spectrum, the angels experience an increase and consolidation of their beatitude through this extraordinary union of the Creator with the creature.

Mary and the Church

The scattering of the seeds of glory, as the tree of the Cross is shaken by the wind of the Spirit, was possible because, as we have seen, the God-man, in the specific structure of his being, can relate the world to God in a new fashion. Scheeben finds a similar causal efficacy to that of the Logos on the world, as mediated by the human freedom of Jesus, in the relation between the Spirit and the Church, mediated by the consent of Mary. Scheeben's Mariology turns on the idea of our Lady's 'sponsal motherhood'.[23] Her consent to the Angel is related to the very nature of a motherhood inseparable from the act whereby God became man. Taking his cue from John Damascene's *On the Orthodox Faith*, Scheeben sees Mary as sponsally united to the Logos, and so both daughter of the Father and sanctuary of the Spirit.[24] Mary's person is willed with the Incarnation: she is *for* the Son in his incarnate condition. At the same time, she also enjoys a special relation with the Spirit, which Scheeben associates with the symbolism of the New Eve. Indeed, while the Man in our salvation represents the Logos, the Woman reflects the Spirit. As the

Spirit's sanctuary, it is in Mary that the Church is both born and, in its first member, fully realised. Moreover, the *perichôrêsis* or mutual exchange between Mary and the Church is so close that 'one can be fully understood only in the other'.[25] The Church is our Mother because Mary's motherhood is included within the Church and remains active within it, energising and sustaining, by the Spirit's action, the creature's response to the Father in Christ. How remarkably Scheebenesque is the poem by Gerard Manley Hopkins comparing the Blessed Virgin Mary to 'the air we breathe': that grace of God's mothering Spirit, embodied in Mary, which is not simply 'the supernatural' *tout court*, but our sharing in the 'higher gift' of the Incarnation:[26]

> . . . I say that we are wound
> With mercy round and round
> As if with air: the same
> Is Mary, more by name.
> She, wild web, wondrous robe,
> Mantles the guilty globe,
> Since God has let dispense
> Her prayers his providence:
> Nay, more than almoner,
> The sweet alms' self is her
> And men are meant to share
> Her life as life does air.
>   If I have understood,
> She holds high motherhood
> Towards all our ghostly good
> And plays in grace her part
> About man's beating heart,
> Laying, like air's fine flood,
> The deathdance in his blood; . . .

Scheeben's theology is that extraordinary thing, a *lyrical Scholasticism*, in which the mind in love, while abandoning nothing of its rigour in thinking, does not fear to end its activity in adoration and praise. This is our 'reasonable worship':[27] it was for this that the mind of man was made.

Notes

Prelude: A Dominican's Story

1. R. Otto, *The Idea of the Holy* (Et: Oxford 1958).
2. A. Nichols, O.P. (ed.), *Geoffrey Preston, O.P., God's Way to be Man: Meditations on Following Christ through Scripture and Sacrament* (London 1978).
3. A. Nichols, O.P. (ed.), *Geoffrey Preston, O.P., Hallowing the Time: Meditations on the Cycle of the Christian Liturgy* (London 1980).
4. Congregation for the Doctrine of the Faith, *Instruction on Certain Aspects of the Theology of Liberation* (Vatican City 1984); *Instruction on Christian Freedom and Liberation* (Vatican City 1986).
5. The text of Kaiser Karl's 'Völkermanifesto' can be found in E. Feigl, *Kaiserin Zita von Österreich, nach Österreich* (Vienna 1986⁴), p. 385.
6. A. Nichols, O.P., *Theology in the Russian Diaspora: Church, Fathers, Eucharist in Nikolai Afanas'ev, 1893–1966* (Cambridge 1989).
7. A. Nichols, O.P., *Rome and the Eastern Churches: A Study in Schism* (Edinburgh 1991).
8. A. Nichols, O.P., *The Art of God Incarnate: Theology and Image in Christian Tradition* (London 1981).
9. S. Undset, *Kristin Lavransdatter* (Et: London 1930).
10. A. Nichols, O.P., *Yves Congar* (London 1989).
11. A. Nichols, O.P., *A Grammar of Consent: The Existence of God in Christian Tradition* (Notre Dame, Ind., 1991).
12. A. Nichols, O.P., *The Theology of Joseph Ratzinger: An Introductory Study* (Edinburgh 1988).
13. A. Nichols, O.P., *Holy Order: The Apostolic Ministry from the New Testament to the Second Vatican Council* (Dublin 1990); *The Holy Eucharist: From the New Testament to Pope John Paul II* (Dublin 1991).
14. A. Nichols, O.P., *The Shape of Catholic Theology: An Intro-*

duction to its Sources, Principles and History (Collegeville, Minn., 1991).

15. A. Nichols, O.P., *From Newman to Congar: The Idea of Doctrinal Development from the Victorians to the Second Vatican Council* (Edinburgh 1990).
16. O. Chadwick, *From Bossuet to Newman. The Idea of Doctrinal Development* (Cambridge 1957).

Chapter I: Intelligent Conservatism as an Ecclesial Stance

1. Mt 13:52.

Chapter II: François Dreyfus on Scripture Read in Tradition

1. F. Dreyfus, *Jésus, savait-il qu'il était Dieu?* (Paris 1984).
2. F. Dreyfus, 'Exégèse en Sorbonne, exégèse en Eglise', *Revue Biblique* 82, 3 (July 1975), pp. 321–59.
3. W. Wink, *The Bible in Human Transformation* (Philadelphia, Pa., 1973), pp. 1–2.
4. M. Noth, K. Elliger, *et al.* (eds), *Biblischer Kommentar zum Alten Testament* (Neukirchen 1955).
5. A. Wikenhauser and O. Kuss (eds), *Herders theologischer Kommentar zum Neuen Testament* (Freiburg 1964²).
6. G. A. Buttrick *et al.* (eds), *The Interpreter's Bible: The Holy Scripture in the King James and Revised Standard Versions with General Articles and Introduction, Exegesis, Exposition for Each Book of the Bible* (Nashville, Tenn., 1952–57). To this enterprise under Episcopalian auspices one could add a reference also to the *Proclamation Commentaries*, produced by the Lutheran publishing house Fortress Press, Philadelphia, Pa., from 1975 onwards.
7. T. Maertens and J. Frisque, *Assemblées du Seigneur* (Paris 1970²) (Et: *Guide for the Christian Assembly: A Background Book of the Mass Day by Day*, London 1977). A one volume work by an Anglophone author in the same *genre* is R. C. Fuller, *Preaching the New Lectionary. The Word of God for the Church Today* (Collegeville, Minn., 1974). For a survey of such liturgically-oriented exegesis, see E. Achtemeier, 'Aids and Resources for the Interpretation of Lectionary Texts', *Interpretation* 31 (1977), pp. 154–64.
8. F. Dreyfus, 'Exégèse en Sorbonne, exégèse en Eglise', *Revue Biblique* 82, 3 (July 1975), pp. 326–7.

9. *Dei verbum* 11.
10. F. Dreyfus, 'Exégèse en Sorbonne, exégèse en Eglise', *Revue Biblique* 82, 3 (July 1975), p. 329.
11. W. Richter, *Exegese als Literaturwissenschaft* (Göttingen 1971). The sub-title translates as: 'A Sketch for an Old Testament Literary Theory and Methodology'.
12. H. Gunkel, 'Ziele und Methoden der Erklärung des Alten Testaments'. Republished as *Reden und Aufsätze* (Göttingen 1913), pp. 11–20.
13. D. Barthélemy, *Dieu et son image* (Paris 1963).
14. F. Dreyfus, 'Exégèse en Sorbonne, exégèse en Eglise', *Revue Biblique* 82, 3 (July 1975), pp. 334–6.
15. Ibid., pp. 337–8.
16. Mt 11:25.
17. F. Dreyfus, 'Exégèse en Sorbonne, exégèse en Eglise', *Revue Biblique* 82, 3 (July 1975), pp. 339–46.
18. H. Gunkel, 'Ziele und Methoden der Erklärung des Alten Testaments'. Republished as *Reden und Aufsätze* (Göttingen 1913), p. 12.
19. R. Lapointe, *Les trois dimensions de l'herméneutique* (Paris 1967), pp. 36ff.
20. F. Dreyfus, 'L'actualisation à l'intérieur de la Bible', *Revue Biblique* 83, 2 (April 1976), pp. 161–203.
21. 1 Cor 7:24.
22. F. Dreyfus, 'L'actualisation à l'intérieur de la Bible', *Revue Biblique* 83, 2 (April 1976), pp. 164–5.
23. H. W. Robinson, 'The Hebrew Conception of Corporate Personality', in *Werden und Wesen des Alten Testaments* (Berlin 1936), pp. 49–62.
24. F. Dreyfus, 'L'actualisation à l'intérieur de la Bible', *Revue Biblique* 83, 2 (April 1976), pp. 165–6.
25. Esdras 9:6–15; Neh 9:33; Dan 9:5.
26. Gal 3:23; Eph 1:11; Rom 11:30.
27. *Tractate on the Passover*, 10, 5, with an internal citation of Ex 13:8.
28. F. Dreyfus, 'L'actualisation à l'intérieur de la Bible', *Revue Biblique* 83, 2 (April 1976), p. 171.
29. C. Westermann, *Tausend Jahre und ein Tag. Unsere Zeit im Alten Testament* (Stuttgart 1965²).
30. J. L. Vesco, 'Abraham, actualisation et relectures', *Revue des Sciences Philosophiques et Théologiques* 55 (1971), p. 45.
31. Jn 19:5.

32. F. Asensio, 'Entrecruce de simbolos y realidades en el Salmo 23', *Biblica* 40 (1959), pp. 237–47.
33. Ps 51:9.
34. Hos 14:3.
35. Jer 9:24.
36. Joel 2:13.
37. F. Dreyfus, 'L'actualisation à l'intérieur de la Bible', *Revue Biblique* 83, 2 (April 1976), p. 176.
38. Ibid., pp. 177–86.
39. Eph 6:2.
40. F. Dreyfus, 'L'actualisation à l'intérieur de la Bible', *Revue Biblique* 83, 2 (April 1976), p. 184.
41. Ibid., pp. 194–7.
42. *Dei verbum* 19.
43. F. Dreyfus, 'L'actualisation à l'intérieur de la Bible', *Revue Biblique* 83, 2 (April 1976), p. 197.
44. F. Dreyfus, 'L'actualisation de l'Ecriture'. I. 'Du texte à la vie', *Revue Biblique* 86, 1 (January 1979), pp. 5–58.
45. Ibid., pp. 9–11.
46. Ibid., p. 11.
47. Ibid., p. 13.
48. Ibid., pp. 18–20.
49. *Sacrosanctum Concilium* 2; 5–8; 10; 47; 61; 83–7; 102.
50. F. Dreyfus, 'L'actualisation de l'Ecriture'. I. 'Du texte à la vie', *Revue Biblique* 86, 1 (January 1979), p. 23.
51. Ibid., p. 25.
52. It appeared in 1709, five years after the author's death.
53. C. Westermann, *Tausend Jahre und ein Tag. Unsere Zeit im Alten Testament* (Stuttgart 1965²).
54. F. Dreyfus, 'L'actualisation de l'Ecriture'. I. 'Du texte à la vie', *Revue Biblique* 86, 1 (January 1979), pp. 27–8.
55. M. Noth, 'Die Vergegenwärtigung des Alten Testaments in der Verkündigung', *Evangelische Theologie* 12 (1952–53), pp. 6–17.
56. F. Dreyfus, 'L'actualisation de l'Ecriture'. I. 'Du texte à la vie', *Revue Biblique* 86, 1 (January 1979), pp. 31–2.
57. Ibid., pp. 33–6.
58. Mt 5:31–7.
59. F. Dreyfus, 'L'actualisation de l'Ecriture'. I. 'Du texte à la vie', *Revue Biblique* 86, 1 (January 1979), pp. 36–57.
60. *Gaudium et spes* 58.
61. Rom 13:1–5.

62. *Homilia super Canticum Canticorum* 37, 3; see on this P. Dumontier, *Saint Bernard et la Bible* (Paris 1953). Also, C. Bodard, 'La Bible, expression d'une expérience religieuse chez S. Bernard', in *S. Bernard, théologien* (Rome 1955²), pp. 24ff.
63. F. Dreyfus, 'L'actualisation de l'Ecriture'. II. 'L'action de l'Esprit', *Revue Biblique* 86, 2 (April 1979), pp. 161–93; idem., III. 'La lace de la Tradition', ibid., 3 (July 1979), pp. 321–84.
64. Lk 24:45.
65. 2 Pet 1:20.
66. 2 Cor 3:14–16.
67. 1 Cor 2:10–16.
68. Jerome, *In Micham* 1, 10.
69. John Chrysostom, *Homilia super Genesim*, 21.
70. Gregory the Great, *In Ezechielam* I., *homilia* 7.
71. William of Saint Thierry, *Epistola aurea* I, 10, 31.
72. Thomas Aquinas, *In Epistolam ad Romanos* 12, 2; *Quaestiones quodlibetales* 12, 17.
73. Robert Bellarmine, *De controversiis* I. 1, 3.
74. F. Dreyfus, 'L'actualisation de l'Ecriture'. II. 'L'action de l'Esprit', *Revue Biblique* 86, 2 (April 1979), p. 166.
75. H. Cazelles, *Ecriture, Parole et Espirit. Trois aspects de l'herméneutique biblique* (Paris 1971), p. 91.
76. F. Dreyfus, 'L'actualisation de l'Ecriture'. II. 'L'action de l'Esprit', *Revue Biblique* 86, 2 (April 1979), pp. 167–8.
77. *Dei verbum* 10.
78. F. Dreyfus, 'L'actualisation de l'Ecriture'. II. 'L'action de l'Esprit', *Revue Biblique* 86, 2 (April 1979), pp. 172–82.
79. F. Dreyfus, 'L'actualisation de l'Ecriture'. III. 'La place de la Tradition', *Revue Biblique* 86 (July 1979), pp. 322–9.
80. H. I. Marrou, *De la connaissance historique* (Paris 1975, 7th ed.), pp. 26–63.
81. F. Dreyfus, 'L'actualisation de l'Ecriture'. III. 'La place de la Tradition', *Revue Biblique* 86, 3 (July 1979), pp. 330–2.
82. Ibid., pp. 334–7.
83. Ibid., pp. 337–8.
84. Jn 16:12.
85. F. Dreyfus, 'L'actualisation de l'Ecriture'. III. 'La place de la Tradition', *Revue Biblique* 86, 3 (July 1979), pp. 340–3.
86. *Dei verbum* 43.
87. John Chrysostom, *Homilia super Genesim* 17, 1.
88. F. Dreyfus, 'L'actualisation de l'Ecriture'. III. 'La place de la Tradition', *Revue Biblique* 86, 3 (July 1979), pp. 345–6.

89. Ibid., pp. 347–8. There is a marked resemblance of thought here between Dreyfus and that of his fellow-countryman, Maurice Blondel. See on the latter, A. Nichols, O.P., *From Newman to Congar. The Idea of Doctrinal Development from the Victorians to the Second Vatican Council* (Edinburgh 1990), ch. 5.
90. Ibid., pp. 348–51.
91. Ibid., p. 371.

Chapter III: T. S. Eliot and Yves Congar on the Nature of Tradition

1. E. Lobb, *T. S. Eliot and the Romantic Critical Tradition* (London 1981), p. 11.
2. T. S. Eliot, 'Tradition and the Individual Talent', in *The Sacred Wood: Essays on Poetry and Criticism* (London 1920).
3. Ibid., p. 48.
4. Ibid., p. 49.
5. See G. Smith, *T. S. Eliot's Poems and Plays: A Study in Sources and Meaning* (Chicago, Ill., 1960), p. 255.
6. T. S. Eliot, *The Sacred Wood: Essays on Poetry and Criticism* (London 1920), p. 51.
7. Ibid., p. 52.
8. Ibid., p. 56.
9. T. S. Eliot, *Selected Essays* (London 1961 3), p. 203.
10. T. S. Eliot, *The Use of Poetry and the Use of Criticism* (London 1964²), pp. 137ff., where Eliot especially commends the Abbé Henri Brémond's *Prayer and Poetry* for its attempts to 'establish the likeness, and the difference of kind and degree, between poetry and mysticism'.
11. See S. Prickett, *Romanticism and Religion. The Tradition of Coleridge and Wordsworth in the Victorian Church* (Cambridge 1976).
12. H. U. von Balthasar, *Herrlichkeit. Eine Theologische ästhetik* (Einsiedeln 1961), II, 2, pp. 720–1.
13. J. H. Newman, *Essay in Aid of a Grammar of Assent* (London 1870; 1895), p. 119.
14. See H. Blamires, *Word Unheard: A Guide through Eliot's Four Quartets* (London 1969).
15. For an account of this in terms of verbal images, see A. Farrer, *The Glass of Vision* (London 1948), and in terms of visual images, A. Nichols, O.P., *The Art of God Incarnate: Theology and Image in Christian Tradition* (London 1980).

16. Y. M.-J. Congar, *La Tradition et les traditions* (Paris 1960–3) (Et: *Tradition and Traditions*, London 1966).
17. Ibid., pp. 237ff.
18. Ibid., p. 239, with a glance at St Thomas's opening article in the *Summa Theologiae* which Congar explores further in 'Traditio und Sacra Doctrina bei Thomas von Aquin', in *Kirche und Überlieferung* (Festgabe J. Geiselmann) (Freiburg 1960), pp. 170–210.
19. Y. M.-J. Congar, *Tradition and Traditions* (London 1966), pp. 240–1.
20. Ibid., pp. 14–15.
21. Ibid., p. 243.
22. Ibid., pp. 338–46.
23. Ibid., pp. 287–91.
24. Ibid., pp. 156–69 where Congar follows particularly the studies of E. Ortigues, 'Ecritures et Traditions apostoliques au concile de Trente', in *Recherches de Science Religieuse* 36 (1949), and J. R. Geiselmann, 'Das Konzil von Trient über das Verhältnis der Heiligen Schrift und der nicht geschriebenen Traditionen', in M. Schmaus (ed.) *Die mündliche Überlieferung* (Munich 1957).
25. How much should be 'read into' this is still disputed; Congar comments: 'Doubtless the Fathers of Trent did not see, in the option they took, what we see', *Tradition and Traditions* (London 1966), p. 166.
26. See, e.g., G. Tavard, *Holy Writ or Holy Church?* (London 1966), pp. 3–21.
27. Y. M.-J. Congar, *Tradition and Traditions* (London 1966), pp. 14–15.
28. Ibid., pp. 427–58.
29. Ibid. See pp. 193–6 for Congar's sympathetic reading of Möhler's *Die Einheit in der Kirche* (1825) and *Symbolik* (1832). The combination of admiration for Möhler and acceptance of Geiselmann's thesis on Trent is not fortuitous: both were Tübingen theologians with the characteristic organic, holistic sense of Tradition learnt partly from German Romanticism.
30. T. S. Eliot, *The Sacred Wood: Essays on Poetry and Criticism* (London 1920), p. 57.
31. Ibid.
32. The 'Word and Image': if a statement of the transcendent Subject of tradition requires a pneumatology, then surely a statement of its transcendent Object requires a Christology. The

Father is alluded to, in an appropriately apophatic way, as Origin and Goal of these two economies.

33. For the notion of an 'ecclesiological *a priori*' theology, see C. Ernst, *Multiple Echo. Explorations in Theology* (London 1979), p. 139.
34. It is the great merit of H. G. Gadamer's, *Truth and Method* (London 1975) to suggest how this can be so.
35. H. Küng, *On Being a Christian* (New York 1976), pp. 126–33.
36. H. Hesse, *The Glass Bead Game* (London 1970; Harmondsworth 1972), p. 16.

Chapter IV: The Roman Primacy in the Ancient Irish and Anglo-Celtic Church

1. J. M. C. Toynbee, 'Christianity in Roman Britain', *Journal of the British Archaeological Association* 16 (1953), pp. 1–24. See also, W. H. C. Frend, 'The Christianising of Britain', in M. W. Barley and R. P. C. Hanson (eds), *Christianity in Britain 300–700* (London 1968), pp. 37–49.
2. Bede, *Ecclesiastical History of the English People*, I. 7.
3. Evidence considered in W. Bright, *Chapters of Early English Church History* (Oxford 1878), pp. 9–12. Athanasius appears to claim that British bishops attended Sardica, *Apologia contra Arianos* 1; *Historia Arianorum* 28. The founder of modern scholarly study of early Christianity in the British Isles, the Catholic priest John Lingard (1771–1851), followed Athanasius here in his *History and Antiquities of the Anglo-Saxon Church* (London 1845²), I., pp. 6–7. But the shorter list given in the encyclical letter sent by the Western assembly to the Alexandrian Church, which lacks a mention of British bishops, is now more generally followed: thus L. W. Barnard, *The Council of Serdica, 343 A.D.* (Sofia 1983), pp. 56–7.
4. K. H. Jackson, *Language and History in Early Britain* (Edinburgh 1953), ch. 5.
5. K. Hughes, 'The Celtic Church and the Papacy', in C. H. Lawrence (ed.), *The English Church and the Papacy in the Middle Ages* (London 1965), p. 4. This article remains the classic *resumé* of its subject.
6. Bede, *Ecclesiastical History of the English People*, I. 4. Birtha was the citadel of an Edessan king, Lucius. See, on Eleutherius and the origins of the British Church, A. H. Thompson, *Bede, his Life, Times and Writings* (Oxford 1935), p. 135.

7. Prosper of Aquitaine, *Chronicon*, 51, cols. 594–5.

8. K. Hughes, 'The Celtic Church and the Papacy', in C. H. Lawrence (ed.), *The English Church and the Papacy in the Middle Ages* (London 1965), p. 5. See also, M. Sheehy, 'The Relics of the Apostles and Early Martyrs in the Mission of St Patrick', *Irish Ecclesiastical Record* (June 1961), pp. 372–6.

9. G. S. M. Walker (ed.), *Sancti Columbani Opera Scriptores Latini Hiberniae* II (Dublin 1957), pp. 38–9, *Epistola* V. 3.

10. L. Bieler, 'Patriciology: Reflections on the Present State of Patrician Studies', in T. Ó Fiaich (ed.), *Seanchas Ardmhacha: The Patrician Year 1961–1962* (Armagh 1962), p. 16.

11. E. G. Bowen, *The Settlements of the Celtic Saints in Wales* (London 1956), pp. 36ff. See also: N. K. Chadwick, 'Intellectual Life in West Wales in the Last Days of the Celtic Church', in N. K. Chadwick (ed.), *Studies in the Early British Church* (Cambridge 1958), p. 145; C. Brooke, 'The Archbishops of St David's, Llandaff and Caerleon-on-Usk', in ibid., pp. 203–4; G. H. Doble, *St Dubricius* (Guildford 1943).

12. Bede, *Ecclesiastical History of the English People*, III. 4; on Ninian, see J. MacQueen, *St Nynia* (Edinburgh and London 1961); C. Thomas, *Britain and Ireland in Early Christian Times, A.D. 400–800* (London 1971), pp. 78–80.

13. H. Mayr-Harting, *The Coming of Christianity to Anglo-Saxon England* (London 1971), p. 38.

14. L. Bieler, *St Patrick and the Coming of Christianity* (Dublin 1967), pp. 24–7; 61–7.

15. A. O. Anderson, and M. O. Anderson, *Adomnàn's Life of Columba* (London 1961).

16. K. Hughes, 'The Celtic Church and the Papacy', in C. H. Lawrence (ed.), *The English Church and the Papacy in the Middle Ages* (London 1965), pp. 5–6.

17. P. Hunter-Blair, *An Introduction to Anglo-Saxon England* (Cambridge 1962), pp. 1–49. See also, P. Hunter-Blair, *Roman Britain and Early England 55 B.C.–871 A.D.* (London 1975), pp. 161–77.

18. H. Mayr-Harting, *The Coming of Christianity to Anglo-Saxon England* (London 1971), p. 35. See also: L. Alcock, 'Wales in the Fifth to Seventh Centuries A.D.: Archaeological Evidence', in I. L. Foster and G. Daniel, *Prehistoric and Early Wales* (London 1905); V. E. Nash-Williams, *Early Christian Monuments of Wales* (Cardiff 1950).

19. Gildas, *De excidio Britanniae* 109. See also: M. Winterbottom

(ed.), *Gildas: The 'Ruin of Britain' and Other Documents* (London 1978), pp. 78–9.

20. K. Hughes, 'The Celtic Church and the Papacy', in C. H. Lawrence (ed.), *The English Church and the Papacy in the Middle Ages* (London 1965), p. 9.
21. On the complex issue of the variety of Easter tables on offer in the patristic Church, see the introduction by C. W. Jones to his *Bedae Opera de Temporibus* (Cambridge, Mass., 1943); and by the same author in *Speculum* 9 (1934), pp. 408–21. For the issue in the Celtic sphere, see L. Gougaud, *Christianity in Celtic Lands* (Et: London 1932, pp. 185–201). See also: P. Grosjean, 'Recherches sur les débuts de la controverse pascale chez les Celts', *Analecta Bollandiana* LXIV (1946), pp. 200–44; ibid., LXXVIII (1960), pp. 233–74.
22. Bede, *Ecclesiastical History of the English People*, II. 2.
23. H. Mayr-Harting, *The Coming of Christianity to Anglo-Saxon England* (London 1971), p. 72, with a reference to *Regula Pastoralis* II. 6.
24. K. Hughes, 'The Celtic Church and the Papacy', in C. H. Lawrence (ed.), *The English Church and the Papacy in the Middle Ages* (London 1965), p. 12.
25. R. Ehrwald (ed.), *Aldhelmi Opera Monumenta Germaniae Historia, Auctores Antiqui* (Berlin 1918), p. 484.
26. K. Hughes, 'The Celtic Church and the Papacy', in C. H. Lawrence (ed.), *The English Church and the Papacy in the Middle Ages* (London 1965), p. 12.
27. Ibid. See reference in pp. 21–2 and the citation from Meilyr, p. 28. For the latter, the earliest-known Welsh court poet, fl. 1100–1137, see M. Dillon and N. K. Chadwick, *The Celtic Realms* (London 1972²), p. 264.
28. K. Hughes, 'The Celtic Church and the Papacy', in C. H. Lawrence (ed.), *The English Church and the Papacy in the Middle Ages* (London 1965), p. 27.
29. D. A. Binchy, 'St Patrick and his Biographers, Ancient and Modern', *Studia Hibernica* II (1962), pp. 7–173, offers the fullest survey of the sources and 'solutions'.
30. C. Mohrmann, *The Latin of St Patrick* (Dublin 1961).
31. Cited in L. Bieler, *St Patrick and the Coming of Christianity* (Dublin 1967), pp. 11–12 from the source: namely, a prefix to the *Collections* of Tirechàn, in A. Gwynn (ed.) *The Book of Armagh*, = *Liber Ardmachanus* (Dublin 1913).
32. *Peregrinatio Egeriae* 14, 5; J. Jungmann, *Missarum Solemnia*

(Freiburg 1962⁵), I., p. 440.

33. L. Bieler, *St Patrick and the Coming of Christianity* (Dublin 1967), p. 14.

34. W. M. Hennessy and B. McCarthy (eds), *The Annals of Ulster* (Dublin 1887–1901), *sub anno* 441.

35. T. Ò Fiaich, 'St Patrick and Armagh' in T. Ò Fiaich (ed.), *Seanchas Ardmhacha: The Patrician Year 1961–1962* (Armagh 1962), p. 125.

36. Cited by K. Hughes, 'The Celtic Church and the Papacy', in C. H. Lawrence (ed.), *The English Church and the Papacy in the Middle Ages* (London 1965), p. 20.

37. H. Wasserschleben (ed.), *Collectio Canonum Hibernensis* (Leipzig 1885), p. 61.

38. For dates regarding Columbanus, see G. S. M. Walker (ed.), *Sancti Columbani Opera Scriptores Latini Hiberniae* II (Dublin 1957), pp. 38–9, *Epistola* V. 3, pp. ix–xxxi.

39. Ibid., pp. 6–7, *Epistola* I. 4.

40. Ibid., pp. 8–9, *Epistola* I. 5.

41. Ibid., pp. 24–5, *Epistola* III. 2.

42. K. Hughes, 'The Celtic Church and the Papacy', in C. H. Lawrence (ed.), *The English Church and the Papacy in the Middle Ages* (London 1965), p. 15.

43. G. S. M. Walker (ed.), *Sancti Columbani Opera Scriptores Latini Hiberniae* II (Dublin 1957), pp. 38–9 *Epistola* V. 3, pp. 36–7, *Epistola* V. 1.

44. Ibid., pp. 38–9, *Epistola* V. 3.

45. Ibid., pp. 42–6, *Epistola* V. 7.

46. Ibid., pp. 50–1, *Epistola* V. 12.

47. Cited by K. Hughes, 'The Celtic Church and the Papacy', in C. H. Lawrence (ed.), *The English Church and the Papacy in the Middle Ages* (London 1965), p. 18. For this synod, see C. de Smedt and J. de Backer (eds), *Acta Sanctorum Hiberniae ex Codice Salmanticensi* (Edinburgh 1888), col. 411.

48. K. Hughes, 'The Celtic Church and the Papacy', in C. H. Lawrence (ed.), *The English Church and the Papacy in the Middle Ages* (London 1965), p. 18.

49. *Patrologia Latina* 87, cols. 969ff.

50. Cited by K. Hughes, 'The Celtic Church and the Papacy', in C. H. Lawrence (ed.), *The English Church and the Papacy in the Middle Ages* (London 1965), p. 19.

51. K. Hughes, *The Church in Early Irish Society* (London 1966), pp. 77–8.

52. G. S. M. Walker (ed.), *Sancti Columbani Opera Scriptores Latini Hiberniae* II (Dublin 1957), pp. 38–9, *Epistola* V. 3, pp. 36–7, *Epistola* V. 1, p. xiii.
53. K. Hughes, *The Church in Early Irish Society* (London 1966), pp. 21–3.
54. H. Mayr-Harting, *The Coming of Christianity to Anglo-Saxon England* (London 1971), p. 8.
55. Bede, *Ecclesiastical History of the English People*, III. 25.
56. Cited by K. Hughes, 'The Celtic Church and the Papacy', in C. H. Lawrence (ed.), *The English Church and the Papacy in the Middle Ages* (London 1965), p. 18.
57. Cited from M. T. A. Carroll, *The Venerable Bede. His Spiritual Teachings* (Washington, D.C., 1946), pp. 86–7.
58. H. Mayr-Harting, *The Coming of Christianity to Anglo-Saxon England* (London 1971), p. 43.
59. Bede, *Ecclesiastical History of the English People*, II. 25.
60. Ibid., 26–7.
61. M. Deanesley, 'The Anglo-Saxon Church and the Papacy', in C. H. Lawrence (ed.), *The English Church and the Papacy in the Middle Ages* (London 1965), pp. 43–4. 'Bretwalda' 'Ruler of Britain'.
62. Bede, *Ecclesiastical History of the English People*, IV. 2.
63. M. Deanesley, 'The Anglo-Saxon Church and the Papacy', in C. H. Lawrence (ed.), *The English Church and the Papacy in the Middle Ages* (London 1965), pp. 45–53.
64. W. Levison, *England and the Continent in the Eighth Century* (Oxford 1946); sources, in translation, in C. H. Talbot, *The Anglo-Saxon Missionaries in Germany* (London and New York 1954).

Chapter V: St Augustine in the Byzantine-Slav Tradition

1. J. D. Zizioulas, 'Ecclesiological Issues Inherent in the Relations between Eastern Chalcedonian and Oriental Non-Chalcedonian Churches', *The Greek Orthodox Theological Review* 16 (1971), pp. 144–62. This article was reprinted in P. Gregorios *et al.* (eds), *Does Chalcedon Divide or Unite?* (Geneva 1981). For an actual historical example, drawn from Catholic-Syrian Jacobite relations, see C. A. Frazee, *Catholics and Sultans. The Church and the Ottoman Empire 1453–1923* (Cambridge 1983), p. 75.

2. A. Schmemann, *Russian Theology 1920–1965* (Richmond, Va., 1969), p. 19.

3. P. Deseille, 'L'Eglise Orthodoxe et l'Occident', *Le Messager Orthodoxe* 100 (1985), p. 19.

4. *The Greek Orthodox Theological Review* 28 (1983), pp. 382–4.

5. S. Rose, *The Place of Blessed Augustine in the Orthodox Church* (Etna, Calif., 1982).

6. Eph 120:10.

7. B. Altaner, 'Augustinus in der griechischen Kirche bis auf Photius', in G. Glockmann (ed.), *Kleine Patristische Schriften* (Berlin 1967), pp. 59–98, 60. What follows is indebted to this ground-breaking study.

8. Cf. H. Reuter, *Augustinische Studien* (Gotha 1887), pp. 156–61.

9. B. Altaner, 'Augustinus in der griechischen Kirche bis auf Photius', in G. Glockmann (ed.), *Kleine Patristische Schriften* (Berlin 1967), p. 62.

10. Eph 179.

11. W. H. C. Frend, *The Rise of Christianity* (London 1984; 1986), p. 678. These letters are published as Letters IV and VI in J. Divjak (ed.), *Corpus Scriptorum Ecclesiasticorum Latinorum* 88 (Vienna 1981).

12. B. Altaner, 'Augustinus in der griechischen Kirche bis auf Photius', in G. Glockmann (ed.), *Kleine Patristische Schriften* (Berlin 1967), p. 66.

13. Ibid., pp. 66–7.

14. *Patrologia Latina* 53, 845ff.

15. See Eph 117 and 118.

16. Possidius, *Vita Augustini* 11.

17. The work in question quotes Augustine in his 'Discourses to Aurelius, pope of Carthage'. See B. Altaner, 'Augustinus in der griechischen Kirche bis auf Photius', in G. Glockmann (ed.), *Kleine Patristische Schriften* (Berlin 1967), pp. 74–5.

18. Ibid., p. 76, with reference to L. Hahn, 'Zum Sprachenkampf in römischen Reich bis auf die Zeit Justinians', *Philologus* Suppl. Vol. X (1907), pp. 675–718.

19. B. Altaner, 'Augustinus in der griechischen Kirche bis auf Photius', in G. Glockmann (ed.), *Kleine Patristische Schriften* (Berlin 1967), pp. 77–8.

20. Ibid., p. 79; citations from Eph 137 *ad Volusianum*, 9; *Tract. in Joh. ev.* 78, 2.

21. As described in J. Reuss, *Matthaeus-, Markus- und Johannes-Katenen nach den handschriften Quellen untersucht* (Münster 1941). The citation is from *En in Ps.* 93, 19.
22. The letter refers to *De Trin.* II., 9, 16 and *Enchiridion* 38, 12.
23. B. Altaner, 'Augustinus in der griechischen Kirche bis auf Photius', in G. Glockmann (ed.), *Kleine Patristische Schriften* (Berlin 1967), pp. 84–5.
24. Ibid., pp. 85–7.
25. Ibid., p. 88.
26. Mansi, *Concilia* XII, 1965f. At least, Altaner confesses himself unable to trace the reference, 'Augustinus in der griechischen Kirche bis auf Photius', in G. Glockmann (ed.), *Kleine patristische Schriften* (Berlin 1967), pp. 94–5.
27. Ibid., p. 96.
28. Ibid., p. 98.
29. M. Rackl, 'Die griechische Augustinusuebersetzungen', *Miscellanea Fr. Ehrle* I. (Rome 1924), pp. 1–38, 4. I am most grateful to Fr Leonard Boyle, O.P., Prefect of the Apostolic Vatican Library, for kindly providing me with a copy of this article.
30. Mansi, *Concilia* XIV, 128f. Cf. J. Quétif-Echard, *Scriptores Ordinis Praedicatorum* (Paris 1719–21), I., p. 146. See also: B. Birckmann, *Die vermeintliche und die wirkliche Reformschrift des Dominikanergenerals Humbert de Romains* (Berlin 1916).
31. M. Rackl, 'Die griechische Augustinusuebersetzungen', *Miscellanea Fr. Ehrle* I. (Rome 1924), p. 6.
32. For Bessarion's laudatory remarks, see *Patrologia Graeca* 161, col. 317.
33. M. Rackl, 'Die griechische Augustinusuebersetzungen', *Miscellanea Fr. Ehrle* I. (Rome 1924), pp. 12–17. See also: S. Valoriani, 'Massimo Planude traduttore di s. Agostino', in S. G. Mercati (ed.), *Atti dell'VIII Congresso Internazionale di Studi Bizantini* (Rome 1953), p. 234.
34. M. Rackl, 'Die griechische Augustinusuebersetzungen', *Miscellanea Fr. Ehrle* I. (Rome 1924), p. 12. Cf. W. O. Schmitt, 'Lateinische Literatur in Byzanz. Die Uebersetzung des Maximus Planudes und die moderne Forschung', *Jahrbuch der österreichischen Byzantinischen Gesellschaft* XVII (1968), pp. 127–47.
35. For the Kydones brothers, and notably Demetrios, see D. M. Nicol, *Church and Society in the Last Centuries of Byzantium* (Cambridge 1979), pp. 78–84.
36. Cited by M. Rackl, 'Die griechische Augustinusuebersetzun-

gen', *Miscellanea Fr. Ehrle* I. (Rome 1924), p. 20, from Cod. Vat. gr. 1103, fol. 36r–36v; Vat. gr. 614, fol. 121v–122r.

37. A. Ebert, *Allgemeine Geschichte der Literatur des Mittelalters im Abendlande* I (Leipzig 1889), p. 366. Cf. A. Hamman, 'Prospero d'Aquitania', *Dizionario patristico e di antichità cristiane* (Casale Monferrato 1983), II., cols. 2928–9.

38. J. Turmel, *Histoire de la théologie positive depuis l'origine jusqu'au concile de Trents* (Paris 1904), p. xxiii. Cf. M. Simonetti, 'Fulgenzio di Ruspe', *Dizionario patristico e di antichità cristiane* (Casale Monferrato 1983), I., cols. 1407–9.

39. M. Rackl, 'Die griechische Augustinusuebersetzungen', *Miscellanea Fr. Ehrle* I. (Rome 1924), pp. 23–8.

40. Ibid., pp. 29–31.

41. Ibid., pp. 31–2.

42. Ibid., pp. 32–3.

43. Ibid. A copy exists in the library of the Greek College in Rome as BXXVIII 5/12. I must thank Fr George Mifsud, of the Congregation for the Eastern Churches, for permitting me to see it.

44. [*Hierou Augoustinou*], *Hê Politeia tou Theou* (Athens 1954). Even here, only Books I–V were included.

45. See 'Le Synaxaire de Sirmond', *Analecta Bollandiana* XIV (1895), pp. 404–7; 'Catalogus codicum hagiographicum graecorum bibliothecae nationalis Neapolitanae', ibid., XXI (1902), pp. 393–5.

46. S. Salaville, 'Une mention de s. Augustin dans les diptiques de la liturgie grècque de S. Jacques', *Année théologique augustinienne* 11 (1950), pp. 52–6.

47. M. Rackl, 'Die griechische Augustinusuebersetzungen', *Miscellanea Fr. Ehrle* I. (Rome 1924), pp. 37–8. Boulgaris produced an anthology of extracts from Augustine (Leipzig 1864), as did another pro-Augustinian Greek hierarch slightly later, N. Kephalas, whose selections were published in Athens in 1910.

48. D. S. Balanos, 'Augoustinos Avrelios', in *Megalê Hellênikê Enkyklopideia* VI (Athens 1928), pp. 177–80. Two general surveys of patrology, both published in 1930 by professors in the University of Athens (K. I. Logothêtês and D. S. Balanos) were also highly favourable according to S. Salaville, 'S. Augustin et L'Orient', *Angelicum* VIII (1931), pp. 3–25.

49. At least one major monograph has been produced: E. Theodorou, *Ho Hagios Augoustinos kai hê Philosophia tês Thrêskeias* (Athens 1955).

50. C. Kern, *Traductions russes des textes patristiques. Guide bib-*

liographique (Chevetogne 1957), pp. 11–14. See also: M. Jugie, 'S. Augustin dans la littérature théologique de l'Eglise russe', *Echos d'Orient* 33 (1930), pp. 389–90.

51. M. Jugie, 'S. Augustin dans la littérature théologique de l'Eglise russe', *Echos d'Orient* 33 (1930), pp. 390–1. The Latin text used was the Benedictine edition found in J. P. Migne's *Patrologia Latina*.

52. C. Kern, *Traductions russes des textes patristiques. Guide bibliographique* (Chevetogne 1957), pp. 390–4.

53. A. Nichols, O.P., *Theology in the Russian Diaspora. Church, Fathers, Eucharist in Nikolai Afanas'ev, 1893–1966* (Cambridge 1989).

54. N. N. Afanas'ev, *L'Eglise du Saint-Esprit* (Paris 1975), pp. 351, 364.

55. S. N. Bulgakos, *Le Paraclet* (Paris 1946), pp. 67–8, 74.

56. V. N. Lossky, 'Les éléments de Théologie négative dans la pensee de s. Augustin', *Augustinus Magister* I (Paris 1954), pp. 575–81. For Lossky, the Western tradition had to await the Latin translations of Denys, as also John Scotus Eriugena, and the later revival of the Plotinian themes of Marius Victorinus in the *Porretani*, together with 'd'autres influences encore' before the elements of negative theology in Augustine's work could receive 'la sombre lueur de l'apophase mystique'. For the other (more fully positive) judgment cited, see V. N. Lossky, *The Mystical Theology of the Eastern Church* (London 1957), p. 12.

57. G. Florovsky, *Collected Works* (Belmont, Mass., 1972), I. p. 41; III. pp. 128–9.

58. J. S. Romanides, *Franks, Romans, Feudalism and Doctrine. An Interplay of Theology and Society* (Brookline, Mass., 1982). This study is based on the same author's *Rômeosunê, Romania, Roumelê* (Thessalonica 1975).

59. J. S. Romanides, *Franks, Romans, Feudalism and Doctrine. An Interplay of Theology and Society* (Brookline, Mass., 1982), p. 63.

60. In a letter (1 September 1985) to the author.

61. See, e.g., W. S. Perry, *A History of the American Episcopal Church 1587–1883* (Boston, Mass., 1885), I. pp. 147–56, 561–76; II. pp. 606–7. The central figure is Samuel Johnson of Guildford, Conn., on whom see D. F. M. Gerardi, 'Samuel Johnson and the Yale "Apostasy" of 1772: the Challenge of Anglican Sacramentalism to the New England Way', *Historical Magazine of the Protestant Episcopal Church* XLVII.2 (1978),

pp. 153–75. Though Johnson's combination of patristic interests, Arminian sympathies and devotion to the Caroline divines renders Every's suggestion likely, the *Works* need investigation for explicit anti-Augustinianism.

62. Words spoken at an address to students at Lincoln Theological College (England) just before the Second World War, as reported by E. L. Mascall, in 'George Florovsky (1893–1979)', *Sobornost* N.S. 2:1, pp. 69–70. I am indebted for this reference to the kindness of Fr George Lawless, O.S.A.

63. Not till then will the claims of recent popes for Augustine's universality ring wholly true: for Paul VI, see 'Allocution aux membres de l'Ordre de S. Augustin à l'occasion de l'inauguration de l'Institut patristique *Augustinianum*' (4 May 1970), *Documentation Catholique*, No. 1566 (1970), pp. 608–9; for John Paul II, see 'Lettre apostolique *Augustinum Hipponensis*', ibid., No. 1925 (1986), pp. 835–6.

Chapter VI: The Appeal to the Fathers in the Ecclesiology of Nikolai Afanas'ev

1. For a full account of the background, life and work of Afanas'ev, see A. Nichols, O.P., *Theology in the Russian Diaspora. Church, Fathers, Eucharist in Nikolai Afanas'ev, 1893–1966* (Cambridge 1989).

2. C. Bigg, *The Doctrine of the Twelve Apostles* (London 1898), p. 21.

3. F. E. Vokes, *The Riddle of the Didache* (London 1938). Vokes re-expressed in fuller form the hypothesis about the origins of the *Didache* suggested by Dom R. H. Connolly, in 'The *Didache* and Montanism', *Downside Review* LV (1937), pp. 339–47.

4. F. E. Vokes, *The Riddle of the Didache* (London 1938), p. 7.

5. For Harnack's estimate, see A. Harnack, *Die Lehre der zwölf Apostel* (Leipzig 1884). A comment on p. 94 of this latter work amply bears out those strictures expressed by Vokes on the exaggerations of its first students: 'The *Didache* has brought us endless light.' For Sabatier's study, see P. Sabatier, *La Didache ou L'Enseignement des douze apôtres* (Paris 1885).

6. F. E. Vokes, *The Riddle of the Didache* (London 1938), p. 220.

7. Ibid., p. xiii. See also N. Afanas'ev, *Tserkov' Dukha Sviatogo* (Paris 1971), p. 67.

8. Ibid., pp. 131–4.

9. F. E. Vokes, *The Riddle of the Didache* (London 1938), p. 135.

10. J. Daniélou, *The Development of Christian Doctrine up to the Council of Nicaea* (London 1964). Compare Daniélou's division of this work, volume I being entitled 'The Theology of Jewish Christianity', while volumes II and III are devoted to the Hellenistic and Latin cultural worlds respectively.
11. C. H. Dodd, 'Christian Beginnings. A reply to Dr Barnes's *The Rise of Christianity*', *London and Holborn Quarterly Review* (July 1947), p. 8.
12. J.-P. Audet, *La Didache. Instructions des apôtres* (Paris 1958).
13. Ibid., pp. 91–103.
14. Ibid., pp. 121–86.
15. Ibid., pp. 187–210.
16. See J. M. Ford, 'Was Montanism a Jewish-Christian heresy?', *Journal of Ecclesial History* 17 (1966), pp. 145–58.
17. Judging by his citations, Afanas'ev accepts the 'middle recension' of the letters of Ignatius argued for by T. Zahn, *Ignatius von Antiochen* (Gotha 1873) and J. B. Lightfoot, *The Apostolic Fathers* (London 1885). For a discussion of modern attempts to undermine the scholarly consensus after Zahn and Lightfoot, see W. R. Schroedel, 'Are the Letters of Ignatius of Antioch authentic?', *Religious Studies Review* 6 (1980), pp. 196–201.
18. Ignatius, *Ad Smyrn* 8,2; N. Afanas'ev, *Tserkov' Dukha Sviatogo* (Paris 1971), p. 39, pp. 96–7, 232, 245–6.
19. Ignatius, *Ad Eph* 4,2; N. Afanas'ev, *Tserkov' Dukha Sviatogo* (Paris 1971), p. 66.
20. Ignatius, *Ad Smyrn* 8,1; *Ad Magn* 6,1; *Ad Trall* 1; N. Afanas'ev, *Tserkov' Dukha Sviatogo* (Paris 1971), pp. 232–4.
21. Ignatius, *Ad Magn* 4.
22. N. Afanas'ev, *Tserkov' Dukha Sviatogo* (Paris 1971), pp. 246–62. On the presbyters of the church of Ignatius, see A. Vilela, 'Le Presbyterium selon saint Ignace d'Antioche', *Bulletin de Littérature chrétienne* 74 (1973), pp. 161–86. On the bishop, see especially E. Kauser, 'Tritt der Bischof an die Stelle Christi? Zur Frage nach der Stellung des Bischofs in der Theologie des heiligen Ignatius von Antiochen', in V. Flieder (ed.), *Festschrift Franz Loidl zum 65. Geburtstag* (Vienna 1970), I, pp. 352–9.
23. N. Afanas'ev, *Tserkov' Dukha Sviatogo* (Paris 1971), pp. 253–8.
24. A hypothesis familiarised by W. Bauer's, *Rechtglaübigkeit und Ketzerei in ältesten Christentum* (Tübingen 1934). For a criti-

cism, see H. E. W. Turner, *The Pattern of Christian Truth* (London 1954), pp. 60–3.

25. E. Massaux, *Influence de l'évangile de Saint Matthieu sur la littérature chrétienne avant Saint Irénée* (Louvain 1950), pp. 94–135. See H. Koester, *Synoptische Überlieferung bei den Apostolischen Vätern* (Berlin 1957), pp. 26–61. See also Ignatius, *Ad Smyrn* 8,2 and *Ad Eph* 5,2.

26. Ignatius's apparently unprecedented stress on the authority of bishops can be related to his reaction to the 'Judaizers' of Philadelphia and the Docetists of Smyrna'. See, e.g., W. R. Schoedel, *Ignatius of Antioch* (Philadelphia, Pa., 1985), p. 12: 'If we are correct that it is Ignatius who polarised these situations, it is no doubt because he saw a threat (real or imagined) to the central significance of suffering (the Lord's and his own) for the Christian way, and because he sensed an independence of mind in his opponents that threatened the unity he regarded as essential to the success of his own martyrdom.'

27. Ignatius, *Ad Smyrn* 1,2.

28. Ibid., 8,2. But A. Garcia Diego, *Katholikê Ekklêsia: El significado de epíteto 'Catholica' aplicado a 'Iglesia' desde san Ignacio de Antioquía hasta Origenes* (Mexico City 1953), questions whether *katholikê* here has any immediate geographical reference, preferring to identify its meaning in terms of an idea of organic unity or completeness. W. R. Schoedel, *Ignatius of Antioch* (Philadelphia, Pa., 1985), p. 244, speaks of, not a denial of a geographical catholicity but an 'undifferentiated conception' out of which extensive catholicity will eventually emerge.

29. Ignatius, *Ad Magn*, 3,1.

30. Cf. G. Bareille, 'Ignace d'Antioche', DTC VII.A.col.709. The Letter to the Romans by Dionysius of Corinth (ap. Eusebius, *Historia ecclesiastica* IV, 23.10 Cf. I Clem 55:2) ascribes to the Roman church a long history of benefactions to the poor and those sent to the mines. This interpretation has recently been revived by W. R. Schoedel, *Ignatius of Antioch* (Philadelphia, Pa., 1985), p. 166.

31. F. X. Funk, *Opera Patrum apostolicorum* (Tübingen 1878–1881), I, p. 213.

32. See Ignatius, *Ad Trall* 13,1; *Ad Rom* 9.3; *Ad Philad* 11,2; *Ad Smyrn* 12,1.

33. F. X. Funk, *Opera Patrum apostolicorum* (Tübingen 1878–1881), I, p. 213.

34. Ignatius, *Ad Rom* Inscr.
35. H. von Campenhausen, *Ecclesiastical Authority and Spiritual Power in the Church of the First Three Centuries* (London 1969), p. 98.
36. Ignatius, *Ad Eph* 4; *Ad Philad* 1,2; *Ad Rom* Inscr. and 2,2. Later traditions accredited Ignatius with being a hymn-writer, and even the inventor of antiphonal singing: see M. Viller and K. Rahner, *Aszese und Mystik in der Väterzeit* (Freiburg 1939), p. 27. There is a congenial intuition here which may be contrasted with an 'architectural' metaphor at work in a monolithic view of the Church's unity.
37. E. van der Glotz, *Ignatius von Antiochen als Christ und Theologe* (Leipzig 1894), pp. 161ff.
38. H. von Campenhausen, *Ecclesiastical Authority and Spiritual Power in the Church of the First Three Centuries* (London 1969), p. 106.
39. Irenaeus, *Adversus Haereses* III. 3,1.
40. J. M. Robinson, 'The Coptic Gnostic Library Today', *New Testament Studies* XVI (1968), pp. 356–401.
41. F. Sagnard, *La Gnose Valentinienne et le témoignage de saint Irénée* (Paris 1947), pp. 99–103.
42. *Adversus Haereses* I. Praef. 2; IV. Praef. 1. For a less sanguine view of the merits of Irenaeus as a reporter, see K. Rudolph, *Gnosis. The Nature and History of an Ancient Religion* (Et: Edinburgh 1983, pp. 11–12). For the Nag Hammadi texts, as well as other Gnostic literature known earlier, see pp. 25–52 of Rudolph's work.
43. On this 'biblicism' of Irenaeus, see J. Lawson, *The Biblical Theology of Saint Irenaeus* (London 1948), pp. 140–98.
44. N. Brox, *Offenbarung, Gnosis und Gnostischer Mythos bei Irenaeus von Lyon* (Salzburg 1966), pp. 69–104, 133–68.
45. *Adversus Haereses* III. 2,2. See B. Reynders, '*Paradôsis*. Le progrès de l'idée de la tradition jusqu'à saint Irénée', *Recherches de théologie ancienne et mediévale* 5 (1933), pp. 151–91 for the concept of tradition in Irenaeus *vis-à-vis* his predecessors.
46. *Adversus Haereses* III. 4,1.
47. Ibid., 3,2.
48. N. Afanasieff, 'L'Eglise qui préside dans l'Amour', in N. Afanasieff *et al.*, *La primauté de Pierre dans L'Eglise Orthodoxe* (Neuchâtel 1960), p. 55.

49. F. M. Sagnard, *Irénéé de Lyons, Contre les Hérésies III. Sources Chrétiennes* 54 (Paris 1952), pp. 414ff.
50. N. Afanasieff, 'L'Eglise qui préside dans l'Amour', in N. Afanasieff *et al.*, *La primauté de Pierre dans L'Eglise Orthodoxe* (Neuchâtel 1960), p. 56.
51. *Adversus Haereses* III, 24, 1.
52. *Epideixis* 41.
53. H.-J. Jaschke, *Der Heilige Geist im Bekenntnis der Kirche. Eine Studie zur Pneumatologie des Irenäus von Lyon im Ausgang vom altchristlichen Glaubensbekenntnis* (Münster 1976), p. 226.
54. *Adversus Haereses* III. 17,3.
55. Ibid., V. 20,1.
56. H.-J. Jaschke, *Der Heilige Geist im Bekenntnis der Kirche. Eine Studie zur Pneumatologie des Irenäus von Lyon im Ausgang vom altchristlichen Glaubensbekenntnis* (Münster 1976), pp. 226–7.
57. *Epideixis* 57; *Adversus Haereses* IV. 38,1.
58. H.-J. Jaschke, *Der Heilige Geist im Bekenntnis der Kirche. Eine Studie zur Pneumatologie des Irenäus von Lyon im Ausgang vom altchristlichen Glaubensbekenntnis* (Münster 1976), p. 271.
59. Tertullian, *De pudicitia* 21,17: '*Ipsa ecclesia proprie et principaliter est Spiritus.*'
60. See W. Ullmann, *A History of Political Thought: the Middle Ages* (London 1965), pp. 20ff.
61. For the classic statement of Tertullian's profound legal learning, see A. Beck, *Römische Recht bei Tertullian und Cyprian* (Halle 1930; 1967), pp. 13–105. For the counter-case, see T. D. Barnes, *Tertullian, A Historical and Literary Study* (Oxford 1971), pp. 22–9.
62. N. Afanas'ev, *Tserkov' Dukha Sviatogo* (Paris 1971), pp. 1–3.
63. See R. F. Evans, *One and Holy. The Church in Latin Patristic Thought* (London 1971), pp. 5–20; cf. W. S. Babcock, 'Christian Culture and Christian Tradition in Roman North Africa', in P. Henry (ed.), *Schools of Thought in the Christian Tradition* (Philadelphia, Pa., 1984), pp. 31–48.
64. See H. Musurillo, *The Acts of the Christian Martyrs* (Oxford 1972), pp. 106–31; T. D. Barnes, *Tertullian, A Historical and Literary Study* (Oxford 1971), pp. 77–80.
65. *De fuga* 14,3. On the religious sensibility of the *Passio*, see E.

H. Dodds, *Pagan and Christian in an Age of Anxiety* (Cambridge 1965), pp. 47–53.

66. On Montanism in general, see P. de Labriolle, *La Crise Montaniste* (Paris 1913).

67. That is, according to Tertullian himself: *Adversus Praxean* 1,4.

68. *De pudicitia* 21,17.

69. In writing, for example, the *Adversus Hermogenem*, the *Adversus Marcionem* and the *De praescriptione haereticorum*, Tertullian's mind began to focus more on theological issues so that, in the words of T. D. Barnes, *Tertullian, A Historical and Literary Study* (Oxford 1971), p. 121, he was led on to 'a systematic exploration of theology'. Continuing (p. 129), Barnes considers that it was indeed 'during the composition of his vast disquisitions on problems raised by Gnosticism and by Marcion that he had come to accept the New Prophecy'.

70. In a group of late treatises, the *De ieiunia, De monogamia, De virginis velandis* and *De pudicitia*, Tertullian defended what he took to be the practice of the apostolic age against innovations introduced by those who would not accept the New Prophecy.

71. Cf. *De anima* 58,8: *De resurrectione mortuorum* 63, 7ff. *De fuga* 14,3.

72. J. Steinman, *Tertullien* (Paris 1967), p. 285.

73. *Ad martyres* 1; 3.

74. J. Steinmann, *Tertullien* (Paris 1967), p. 287.

75. See below, and, in general, R. A. Markus, *Saeculum. History and Society in the Theology of Saint Augustine* (Cambridge 1970).

76. W. S. Babcock, 'Christian Culture and Christian Tradition in Roman North Africa', in P. Henry (ed.), *Schools of Thought in the Christian Tradition* (Philadelphia, Pa., 1984), p. 39.

77. *De praescriptione haereticorum* 22. The peculiar stress of Tertullian on the Spirit in ecclesiology is noted by A. d'Alès, *La Théologie de Tertullien* (Paris 1905), p. 215.

78. For example, Aphraates, *De virginitate contra Judaeos* 18, 10; G. M. Hopkins, 'The Blessed Virgin compared to the Air we Breathe', in W. H. Gardner and N. H. Mackenzie (eds), *The Poems of Gerard Manley Hopkins* (London 1967[4]), pp. 93–7.

79. K. Delehaye, *Ecclesia Mater chez les Pères des trois premiers siècles* (Paris 1964), p. 19.

80. Origen, *In Levit.* IX.1; N. Afanas'ev, *Tserkov' Dukha Sviatogo* (Paris 1971), p. 40.
81. In *Josue* VII.2; N. Afanas'ev, *Tserkov' Dukha Sviatogo* (Paris 1971), p. 73.
82. In Mt 12:14; N. Afanas'ev, *Tserkov' Dukha Sviatogo* (Paris 1971), p. 41. Cf. Mt 24; N. Afanas'ev, *Tserkov' Dukha Sviatogo* (Paris 1971), p. 100; J. Daniélou, *Origène* (Paris 1948 2), p. 83.
83. In Mt 12:14; in Num 16:19; N. Afanas'ev, *Tserkov' Dukha Sviatogo* (Paris 1971), p. 59; J. Daniélou, *Origène* (Paris 1948 2), pp. 74f.
84. In Mt 16:8; N. Afanas'ev, *Tserkov' Dukha Sviatogo* (Paris 1971), p. 141.
85. N. Afanas'ev, *Tserkov' Dukha Sviatogo* (Paris 1971), p. 134.
86. G. Bardy, 'Origène', *Dictionnaire de Théologie Catholique* XI.B. col. 1553.
87. In Mt 13:24.
88. In Gen 12:3.
89. Ibid., 2:3–6.
90. In *Cant. Cant.* 1.7.
91. In Is Hom. VI.1.; cf. H. G. Vogt, *Das Kirchenverständnis des Origenes* (Cologne-Vienna 1974), p. 4.
92. Ibid., p. 20; cf. In Num. hom. xi.3.
93. N. Afanas'ev, *Tserkov' Dukha Sviatogo* (Paris 1971), p. 135.
94. H. von Campenhausen, *Ecclesiastical Authority and Spiritual Power in the Church of the First Three Centuries* (London 1969), p. 249.
95. Ibid., pp. 249–50.
96. Cf. G. W. Olsen, 'The theological and the magisterium. The ancient and mediaeval background of a contemporary controversy', *Communio* 7 (1980), pp. 292–319. On Origen's concept of the *didaskalos* see C. V. Harris, *Origen of Alexandria's Interpretation of the Teacher's Function in the Early Christian Hierarchy and Community* (New York, NY., 1966).
97. In Num 11:1; in Jer 11:3; in Luc 20.
98. In Mt 12; in Lev 6:5–6. Cf. H. G. Vogt, *Das Kirchenverständnis des Origenes* (Cologne and Vienna 1974), p. 31.
99. H. von Campenhausen, *Ecclesiastical Authority and Spiritual Power in the Church of the First Three Centuries* (London 1969), p. 254. See also, Hans Urs von Balthasar, *Origen: Spirit and Fire* (Washington, D.C., 1984), p. 20 where he writes:

'Church itself for Origen is so little a merely inner community that it was precisely the fundamental tension between ritual church and hierarchical church on the one hand and the corpus mysticum on the other that became for him a tragic experience. But he never gave a thought to striking his way out of this conflict by denying the first aspect of the Church.'

100. However, in an author of this period, one cannot wholly discount the possibility that the *disciplina arcani* may underlie Origen's disappointing silence here.

101. J. W. Trigg, *Origen. The Bible and Philosophy in the third-century Church* (London 1985), pp. 103–20.

102. H. G. Beck, *Kirche und theologische Literatur im byzantinischen Reich* (Munich 1959), pp. 360–1.

103. N. Afanas'ev, *Tserkov' Dukha Sviatogo* (Paris 1971), p. 19.

104. N. Afanasieff, 'L'Eglise qui préside dans l'Amour', in N. Afanasieff *et al.*, *La primauté de Pierre dans L'Eglise Orthodoxe* (Neuchâtel 1960), pp. 16–25.

105. N. Afanas'ev, 'Dve idei vselenskoi Tserkvi', *Put'* 45 (1934), pp. 17–19.

106. Ibid., p. 20.

107. See R. Faina, *L'Impero e l'imperatore cristiano in Eusebio di Caesarea. La prima teologia politica del cristianesimo* (Zürich 1966).

108. W. H. C. Frend, *The Donatist Church. A movement of protest in Roman North Africa* (Oxford 1952), pp. 106–10.

109. F. van der Meer, *Augustine the Bishop* (London 1961), pp. 471–92.

110. R. F. Evans, *One and Holy. The Church in Latin Patristic Thought* (London 1971), p. 9.

111. Tertullian, *De oratione* 2.

112. R. F. Evans, *One and Holy. The Church in Latin Patristic Thought* (London 1971), pp. 10–16.

113. Jerome, *Liber de viris illustribus* 53.

114. R. F. Evans, *One and Holy. The Church in Latin Patristic Thought* (London 1971), p. 19.

115. Ibid., pp. 24–6.

116. Cf. *De praescriptione haereticorum* 15; 20f.; 28, 32; 36f.

117. Cyprian, Eph 33,1; 68,2,3; 69,9; 76,3,6.

118. Thus, R. F. Evans, *One and Holy. The Church in Latin Patristic Thought* (London 1971), p. 48: 'The Church as an object of reflection attains a new kind of significance in Cyprian.' This could, but need not, be taken in an Afanas'evan way.

119. A. Demoustier, 'Episcopat et union à Rome selon saint Cyprien', in *Recherches de Science Religiense* 52 (1964), pp. 337–69.
120. A. Demoustier, 'L'ontologie de l'Eglise salon saint Cyprien', in *Recherches de Science Religiense* 52 (1964), pp. 554–88.
121. For the chronology of Cyprian's writings, see P. Monceaux, *Histoire littéraire de l'Afrique chrétienne* II (Paris 1902).
122. Eph 3.
123. Ibid., 33:43.
124. Ibid., 24:55.
125. A. Demoustier, 'Episcopat et union à Rome selon saint Cyprien', in *Recherches de Science Religiense* 52 (1964), pp. 343.
126. Ibid., p. 345.
127. Eph 72:3.
128. *De unitate ecclesiae* 5.
129. Eph 55:4; N. Afanas'ev, 'Dve idei vselenskoi Tserkvi', *Put'* 45 (1934), p. 19.
130. *Ad Fortunatum* 2; *De unitate Ecclesiae* 4; 5.
131. A. Demoustier, 'Episcopat et union à Rome selon saint Cyprien', in *Recherches de Science Religiense* 52 (1964), pp. 351–2.
132. 'Dve idei vselenskoi Tserkvi', *Put'* 45 (1934), pp. 19–20.
133. Cf. E. W. Benson, *Cyprian: his Life, Times and Work* (London 1897), pp. 180–97.
134. Eph 55:8; '*locus Petri*'.
135. Eph 59:14; '*cathedra Petri*'.
136. Eph 48:3: '*ecclesiae catholicae matricem et radicem agnoscerent et tenerent*'.
137. Eph 73.
138. J. Chapman, 'Les interpolations dans le traité de saint Cyprien sur l'unité de l'Eglise,' *Revue Bénédictine* 20 (1903), pp. 26–52.
139. A. Demoustier, 'L'ontologie de l'Eglise selon saint Cyprien', in *Recherches de Science Religieuse* 52 (1964), p. 5701. Cf. Cyprian Eph 63,13.
140. Thus *De unitate Ecclesiae* 5 picks up the imagery of Tertullian, *Adversus Praxean* 8.
141. A. Demoustier, 'L'ontologie de l'Eglise selon saint Cyprien', in *Recherches de Science Religiense* 52 (1964), pp. 587–8.
142. N. Afanas'ev, *Tserkov' Dukha Sviatogo* (Paris 1971), pp. 283–8. Cf. A. Nichols, O.P., 'The Reception of St Augustine

and his Work in the Byzantine-Slav Tradition', *Angelicum* LXIV (1987), pp. 437–52.

143. F. Dvornik, *Early Christian and Byzantine Political Philosophy* (Washington, D.C., 1966).

144. Ibid., p. 249.

145. On Philo: Dvornik remarks that he absorbed into his political scheme all the elements of the Hellenistic doctrine of kingship care deification itself: see, *De specialibus* IV. 187; *De vita Moysi* II.5. On Clement's Christianising of such notions, see F. Dvornik, *Early Christian and Byzantine Political Philosophy*, II (Washington, D.C., 1966), p. 600.

146. See especially Eusebius, *De laudibus Constantini* 2.

147. Cf. F. Dvornik, 'Emperors, popes and councils', *Dumbarton Oaks Papers* 6 (1951), pp. 1–23.

148. The Arian crisis, wherein Constantius frequently found himself on the 'wrong side', was also a major factor in the cooling of Eusebian-inspired ardour for the concept of the Christian *basileus:* cf. Athanasius, *Historia Arianorum* 44.

149. See G. Ostrogrosky, 'The Byzantine emperor and the hierarchical world order', *Slavonic and East European Review* 35 (1956–7), pp. 1–14.

150. F. H. Dudden, *The Life and Times of Saint Ambrose II* (London 1935), pp. 371–92.

151. Augustine, *De catechezandis rudibus* 27 (53). Cf. R. A. Markus, *Saeculum. History and Society in the Thought of Saint Augustine* (Cambridge 1970), pp. 32–3.

152. J. J. O'Meara, *The Young Augustine* (London 1954), pp. 61–91.

153. See, for example, Eph 140. Cf. G. G. Willis, *Saint Augustine and the Donatist Controversy* (London 1950).

154. R. F. Evans, *One and Holy. The Church in Latin Patristic Thought* (London 1971), p. 121.

155. R. A. Markus, *Saeculum. History and Society in the Thought of Saint Augustine* (Cambridge 1970), pp. 13–21.

156. See *De civitate Dei* X.20. Cf. G. Bonner, 'The Church and the Eucharist in the theology of Saint Augustine', *Sobornost* 7.6 (1978), pp. 448–61.

157. R. A. Markus, *Saeculum. History and Society in the Thought of Saint Augustine* (Cambridge 1970), pp. 61–2. The reference is to G. M. Hopkins, 'Spelt from Sibyl's Leaves', W. H. Gardner and N. N. Mackenzie, *The Poems of Gerard Manley Hopkins* (London 1967⁴), pp. 97–8.

158. See A. Nichols, O.P., 'Afanas'ev and the Byzantine Canonical Tradition', *Heythrop Journal* XXXIII (1992), pp. 415–25.
159. R. T. Wallis, *Neoplatonism* (London 1972), pp. 160–1.
160. E. Booth, *Aristotelian Aporetic Ontology in Islamic and Christian Thinkers* (Cambridge 1983), p. 77.
161. See P. E. Roram, 'Iamblichus and the Anagogical Method in Ps.-Dionysian Liturgical Theology', *Studia Patristica* 17 (1982), pp. 453–60; A. Louth, 'Pagan Theurgy and Christian Sacramentalism in Denys the Areopagite', *Journal of Theological Studies*, N.S. 37.2 (1986), pp. 432–8 where Dr Louth points out that for Denys the Liturgy itself is not so much a *theourgia* as a hymning of the divine *theourgiai, viz.* the divine saving actions and principally the Incarnation.
162. R. Roques, *L'Univers dionysien. Structure hiérarchique due monde selon le Pseudo-Denys* (Paris 1954; 1983), pp. 36–67.
163. P. E. Rorem, *Biblical and Liturgical Symbols within the Ps. Dionysian Synthesis* (Toronto 1984).
164. Denys, *De hierarchia ecclesiastica* II.1.
165. N. Afanas'ev, 'Dve idei vselenskoi Tserkvi', *Put'* 45 (1934), p. 19. Cf. pp. 4, 29, 34.
166. *De hierarchia ecclesiastica* I. 2.
167. Ibid., I. 4.
168. Ibid., I. 2.
169. A. Louth, 'Pagan Theurgy and Christian Sacramentalism in Denys the Areopagite', *Journal of Theological Studies*, N.S. 37.2 (1986), pp. 436–7.
170. *De hierarchia ecclesiastica* I. 3.
171. Cf. ibid., III.9; 11.
172. Y. Congar, 'Les saints Pères: organes privilégiés de la tradition', *Irénikon* 35 (1962), pp. 479–98. The basic meaning of 'fathers', according to Congar, is 'those who have determined something in the life of the Church, whether in regard to her faith, or in connexion with her discipline or action (*comportement*). Congar continues (p. 483): 'But there can be no authentic determination of the Church's life, without positing the special grace of the Spirit.'
173. The emergence of this tendency in Afanas'ev's thought is traced in A. Nichols, O.P., *Theology in the Russian Diaspora. Church, Fathers, Eucharist in Nikolai Afanas'ev, 1893–1966* (Cambridge 1989), pp. 62–93. First appearing in 'Dve idei vselenskoi Tserkvi', *Put'* 45 (1934), it was developed in *Tserkov' Dukha Sviatogo* (Paris 1971) and reached its most com-

bative statement in 'L'Eglise qui préside dans l'Amour', in N. Afanasieff *et al.*, *La primauté de Pierre dans L'Eglise Ortho-doxe* (Neuchâtel 1960).

174. Particularly stressed in the school of hermeneutics associated with H. G. Gadamer: v. *Wahrheit und Methode* (Tübingen 1960), pp. 185–228. An application to the New Testament situation may be found in F. Mussner, *The Historical Jesus in the Gospel of John* (Et: London 1967). For a statement in terms of fundamental theology, see A. Louth, *Discerning the Mystery. An Essay in the Nature of Theology* (Oxford 1983), pp. 17–44.

175. It is surprising that Afanas'ev draws so little on the copius pre-Revolutionary Russian patristic monographs described in C. Kern, *Les traductions russes des textes patristiques. Guide bibliographique* (Chevetogne 1957).

Chapter VII: The Dogma of the Image at Nicaea II

1. See H. Menges, *Die Bilderlehre des hl. Johannes von Damaskus* (Kallmünz 1937), 44–60; T. Nikolaou, 'Die Ikonenverehrung als Beispiel ostkirchlicher Theologie und Frömmigkeit nach Johannes von Damaskos', *Ostkirchliche Studien* 25, 1 (1976), p. 149. Notable here is not only John's *Orations on the Images* III.8–23, but also I.9–13.

2. For the fragments of Leontius's *apologia* for the images see Mansi, *Concilia* XIII, 43A–53C. See further, L. Barnard, 'The Theology of Images', in A. Bryer and J. Herrin (eds), *Iconoclasm* (Birmingham 1975), p. 8; N. Gendle, 'Leontius of Neapolis: a sixth-century defender of holy images', in E. A. Livingstone (ed.), *Studia Patristica* XVIII (Kalamazoo, Mich., 1985), pp. 135–40.

3. G. B. Ladner, 'The concept of the image in the Greek Fathers and the Byzantine Iconoclastic Controversy', *Dumbarton Oaks Papers* VII (1953), pp. 5–10; A. Grillmeier, 'Die Herrlichkeit Gottes auf dem Antlitz Jesu Christi. Zur Bild-Theologie der Väterzeit', in A. Grillmeier, *Mit ihm und in ihm. Christologische Forschungen und Perspektiven* (Freiburg, Basel, Vienna 1975), pp. 27–8.

4. G. B. Ladner, 'The concept of the image in the Greek Fathers and the Byzantine Iconoclastic Controversy', *Dumbarton Oaks Papers* VII (1953), pp. 10–16; G. A. Mahoney, *Man the Divine Icon. The Patristic Doctrine of Man made according to the Image of God* (Pecos, N. Mex., 1973); A. Grillmeier, *Mit ihm*

und in ihm. Christologische Forschungen und Perspektiven (Freiburg, Basel, Vienna 1975), pp. 2–30.

5. A. Grillmeier, *Mit ihm und in ihm. Christologische Forschungen und Perspektiven* (Freiburg, Basel, Vienna 1975), pp. 30–75. There is a crying need for a study which will show the relation of Christological trends to the use of the metaphor of the image in patristic theology. This would contextualise such a study as C. von Schönborn, *L'Icône du Christ. Fondements théologiques* (Fribourg 1976), in a broader setting, and offer an evaluation of the claims that Iconoclast theology has a rooting in the Christology of Origen as suggested by G. Florovsky, 'Origen, Eusebius and the Iconoclastic Controversy', *Church History* 19 (1950), pp. 77–96, or of Arius, as proposed by C. Murray, 'Le problème de l'iconophobie et les premiers siècles chrétiens', in F. Boespflug and N. Lossky (eds), *Nicée II, 787–1989. Douze siècles d'images religieuses* (Paris 1987), pp. 41–9. See R. P. C. Hanson, 'The Transformation of Images in the Trinitarian Theology of the Fourth Century', in E. A. Livingstone (ed.), *Studia Patristica* XVIII (Oxford 1982), pp. 97–115 for some useful remarks on the use of the icon analogy in Eusebius, Marcellus of Ancyra, Athanasius and Hilary, as well as in the Cappadocians.

6. Mansi, *Concilia* XIII, 373E–376C.

7. II Cor 4:4.

8. For this *horos* in its own conciliar context, see S. Gerö, *Byzantine Iconoclasm during the Reign of Constantine V* (Louvain 1977), pp. 53–110; for the response of the fathers in Nicaea II, see G. Dumeige, *Nicée II* (Paris 1978), pp. 130–6.

9. Mansi, *Concilia* XIII, 208D–216BD for the interpretation of the Johannine 'worship in spirit and truth' (Jn 4:23–4) in terms of liberation from adoration of the creature that the bishops of 754 offered. Had not Gregory Nazianzen called the confusion of the created with the Uncreated the 'ultimate and primordial evil'?: *Orations* 38, 12; PG.36, 325A, Iconodules were naturally aware that this was the heart of the Iconoclast position: for an Iconophile's insistence on the difference between 'image', *eikôn*, and 'idol', *agalma* or *zôdion*, see J. M. Mercati, 'Stephen Bostreni nova de sacris imaginibus fragments e libro deperdito *kata Ioudaiôn*', *Theologische Quartalschrift* LXXVII (1895), 663ff. After the Council of 787, Theodore of Studios would need to return to it in the 'second' Iconoclast period, see *Antirrheticus* II. 38; PG.99, 380B. The religious seriousness of con-

founding image with idol is brought out in the anonymous Iconophile, *Nouthesia gerontos peri tôn hagiôn eikonôn,* edited by the Russian Byzantinist, B. M. Melioranskij from its only extent manuscript, in Moscow. The distinction between image and idol is the key to interpreting a number of apparently anti-iconic statements in the early fathers, though difficulties remain in the case of the Council of Elvira, the context of whose 36th canon is uncertain, and of Epiphanius of Salamis. See C. Murray and P. Maraval, 'Epiphane: "docteur des iconoclastes",' in F. Boespflug and N. Lossky (eds), *Nicée II, 787–1989. Douze siècles d'images religieuses* (Paris 1987), pp. 51–62.

10. Eph 5:25–7.
11. Mt 28:20.
12. Jer 12:10.
13. Mansi, *Concilia* XIII, 376D–377B.
14. Ibid., 377C.
15. *'Horos* du Concile *Nicée II',* in F. Boespflug and N. Lossky (eds), *Nicée II, 787–1989. Douze siècles d'images religieuses* (Paris 1987), p. 33.
16. G. W. H. Lampe, *A Patristic Greek Lexicon* (Oxford 1961), pp. 678–9.
17. J. Mendham, *The Seventh General Council* (London 1849), p. 439.
18. See H. G. Thümmel, 'Neilos von Ankyra über die Bilder', *Byzantinische Zeitschrift* 71 (1978), pp. 10–21.
19. Mansi, *Concilia* XIII, 36A–D.
20. Ibid., XII, 1062A. Cf. 1063D.
21. F. van der Meer, *Early Christian Art* (London 1967), pp. 91–9.
22. E. Kitzinger, 'Byzantine Art in the Period between Justinian and Iconoclasm', in E. Kitzinger, *The Art of Byzantium and the Mediaeval West* (Bloomington, Ind., and London 1976), pp. 172–85, 191–5.
23. P. Huber, *Bild und Botschaft. Byzantinische Miniaturenzum Alten und Neuen Testament* (Zürich and Freiburg 1973).
24. E. Kitzinger, 'Byzantine Art in the Period between Justinian and Iconoclasm', in E. Kitzinger, *The Art of Byzantium and the Mediaeval West* (Bloomington, Ind., and London 1976), p. 199.
25. Cf. Clement of Alexandria, *Paedagôgos* I.1: Methodius of Olympus, *De autexusio* I.
26. See, for example, G. W. Stroup, *The Promise of Narrative Theology* (London 1984).

27. Cf. L. Barnard, 'The Theology of Images', in A. Bryer and J. Herrin (eds), *Iconoclasm* (Birmingham 1975): 'The difference between the ancient figure of the lamb and the new figure of Christ was apparently the emphasis on his humanity. It is possible that members of the Council had in their view quasi-Monophysite elements in the Church which tended to exalt Christ's divine nature in contrast to his humanity. But of that we cannot be certain. However, it is clear that the Trullo Council intended that images of Christ should be used to support Christological orthodoxy.'
28. For the legend cycle of this image, see E. von Dobschütz, *Christusbilder. Untersuchungen zur christlichen Legende* (Leipzig 1899), pp. 40–60, 123–134, 3–28.
29. Ibid., p. 12.
30. George Pisides, *De expeditione persica* I.145; *Patrologia Graeca* 92, 1908A.
31. Mansi, *Concilia* XII, 1144D.
32. Ibid., XIII, 40E–41A.
33. For the notion of metaphor as ontological disclosure resulting from a transaction between contexts, see P. Ricoeur, *La Métaphor vive* (Paris 1975), pp. 10–12, 221–399.
34. C. von Schönborn, *L'Icône du Christ. Fondements théologiques* (Fribourg 1976), p. 143.
35. *Oratio in Barlaam, mart* 3; PG.31, 489AB. Cf. Gregory of Nyssa, *Oratio laudatoria sancti ac magni martyris Theodori, Patrologia Graeca* 46, 757D.
36. *De sancti Felici natalita carmen* IX, 541ff; *Patrologia Latina* 61, 660C–661A.
37. Eph 9:208; 11:10.
38. *Oratio de deitate Filii et Spiritus Sancti, Patrologia Graeca* 46, 572C.
39. For Theodore's speech, see Mansi, *Concilia* XIII, 12A.
40. J. Bidez, *Philostorgius' Kirchengeschichte* (Leipzig 1913), p. 78.
41. Cited in N. H. Baynes, *Byzantine Studies and Other Essays* (London 1955), pp. 237–8.
42. See E. Kitzinger, 'The Cult of Images in the Age before Iconoclasm', in E. Kitzinger, *The Art of Byzantium and the Mediaeval West* (Bloomington, Ind., and London 1976), pp. 96–100.
43. Ibid., p. 197.
44. See C. Walter, 'The Origins of the Iconostasis', in C. Walter, *Studies in Byzantine Iconography* (London 1977), pp. 251–67 (especially p. 258).

45. S. Pfeilstücker, *Spätantikes und germanisches Kunstgut* (Berlin 1936), p. 138.
46. M. Mesnard, 'L'église irlandaise de Kildare d'après un texte du septième siècle', *Rivista di archeologia cristiana* IX (1932), pp. 37ff.
47. E. Kitzinger, *The Art of Byzantium and the Mediaeval West* (Bloomington, Ind., and London 1976), p. 200.
48. In connexion with the Iconoclastic iambic poems, a witness to primitive 'Leonine' Iconoclasm, as studied in S. Gerö, *Byzantine Iconoclasm during the Reign of Leo II* (Louvain 1973), p. 119.
49. Mansi, *Concilia* XII, 377E.
50. *De Spiritu Sancto* 18, 45.
51. G. Dumeige, *Nicée II* (Paris 1978), p. 120.
52. For Nicephorus, see P. J. Alexander, *The Patriarch Nicephorus of Constantinople: Ecclesiastical Policy and Image Worship in the Byzantine Empire* (Oxford 1959); for Theodore, J. Meyendorf, 'L'image du Christ d'après Theodore Studite', in *Synthronon. Art et archéologie de la fin de l'Antiquité et du Moyen Age. Receuil d'études par André Grabar et un groupe de ses disciples* (Paris 1968), pp. 115–119.
53. In his *L'Icône du Christ*.
54. E. Kitzinger, *The Art of Byzantium and the Mediaeval West* (Bloomington, Ind., and London 1976), pp. 210–12.
55. Ibid., p. 210; cf. p. 243.
56. E. Hammerschmitt, 'Eine Definition von *hypostasis* und *ousia* während des 7. allgemeinen Konzils Nikaia II, 787', *Ostkirchliche Studien* 5 (1956), pp. 52–5.
57. During the sixth session, as part of Epiphanius the Deacon's refutation of the *horos* of Hiereia; Mansi, *Concilia* XIII, 260E–261A.
58. E. Hammerschmitt, 'Eine Definition von *hypostasis* und *ousia* während des 7. allgemeinen Konzils Nikaia II, 787', *Ostkirchliche Studien* 5 (1956), p. 55.
59. See S. Schlossmann, *Persona und prosôpon im Recht und im christlichen Dogma* (Kiel 1906), pp. 37–8 (especially p. 38).
60. E. Levinas, *Totalité et infini* (The Hague 1961), pp. 173–4; E. Wyschogrod, *Emmanuel Levinas. The Problem of Ethical Metaphysics* (The Hague 1974), pp. 85–94. I am aware that Levinas himself rejects visual art for the reasons reminiscent of Plato's in the *Republic*: but, even apart from the crucial question of faith in Incarnation, it may be that an art which found its inspiration in the *horos* of Nicaea II would mediate,

not obfuscate, the call of the Face which he describes. There are suggestive hints along these lines in J. L. Marion, 'Le prototype de l'image', in F. Boespflug and N. Lossky (eds), *Nicée II, 787–1989. Douze siécles d'images religieuses* (Paris 1987), pp. 451–70, read in the light of three other works by Marion: *L'Idole et la Distance* (Paris 1976); *Dieu sans être* (Paris 1982); *Prolégomènes à la charité* (Paris 1986).

61. P. Evdokimov, *L'art de L'icône. Théologie de la beauté* (Paris 1970), p. 181.
62. T. S. Eliot, *The Idea of a Christian Society and Other Writings* (London 1939; 1982), p. 81. I have attempted such a retrieval of tradition in A. Nichols, O.P., *The Art of God Incarnate. Theology and Image in Christian Tradition* (London 1980).

Chapter VIII: St Thomas Aquinas on the Passion of Christ

1. J. A Weisheipl, *Friar Thomas d'Aquino. His Life, Thought and Works* (Oxford 1975), pp. 293–300.
2. *Summa Theologiae*, Ia, prologue.
3. Ibid., IIIa, prologue.
4. M.-D. Chenu, *Introduction à l'étude de Saint Thomas d'Aquin* (Montreal and Paris 1950), pp. 71–3.
5. Cited as testimony of the monks of Monte Cassino in P. Conway, *Saint Thomas Aquinas of the Order of Preachers (1255–1247). A Biographical Study of the Angelic Doctor* (London 1911), p. 6.
6. *Summa Theologiae*, IIIa, q.46, a.1.
7. His discussion of necessity turns on Aristotle's *Metaphysics* V.5, 1015a 20.
8. *Summa Theologiae*, q.46, a.2.
9. Ibid., ad iii: '*supremum et commune bonum totius universi*'.
10. Thomas takes his cue for this discussion from Augustine, *De Trinitate* XIII.10; *Patrologia Latina* 42, 1024.
11. *Summa Theologiae*, q.46, a.3.
12. Ibid., responsio '... *tanto aliquis modus convenientior est ad assequendum finem quanto per ipsum plura concurrunt quae sunt expedientia fini*'.
13. Citing Rom 5:8.
14. In dependence on 1 Pet 2:21.
15. The source Thomas uses here is 1 Cor 6:20.
16. Citing 1 Cor 15:57.
17. I have modified Thomas's arrangement of his *multa*, 'multiple considerations', so as to devote greater space to what is, in fact,

his *third* reason. He treats it only briefly at this point as he is preparing to deal with the theme at greater length in IIIa, q.48. Thomas's discussion there takes its rise from Augustine's commentary on Phil 2:9 ('Therefore God exalted Christ Jesus …') in tractate 104 *In Joannem, Patrologia Latina* 35, 1903, in the light of Jn 17:10 which speaks of Christ's glorification both in himself and his disciples. Thomas's account of Christ's receiving grace as *caput* of redeemed humanity follows on his remarks in IIIa, q.7, a.1, and ibid., q.8, aa.1–6.

18. Heb 12:2.
19. *Summa Theologiae,* q.48, a.2, ad i.
20. Ibid., q.49, a.3, ad iii.
21. Ibid., q.46, a.4.
22. Thomas's authority here is Augustine, *Liber octoginta trium quaestionum* 25; PL.40, 17.
23. See M.-D. Chenu, 'La Mentalité symbolique' and 'La Théologie symbolique' in M.-D. Chenu, *La Théologie au douzième siècle* (Paris 1957), pp. 159–209.
24. *In Christi resurrectionem* 11; *Patrologia Graeca* 46, 624.
25. Cf. Augustine, *Sermo 32 de Passione, Patrologia Latina* 39, 1808.
26. *Summa Theologiae,* q.84, a.7: the subject of Karl Rahner's extended meditation in *Geist in Welt* (Freiburg 1957²) (Et: London 1968, 1979).
27. *Summa Theologiae,* IIIa, q.46, a.5.
28. *Against* authenticity: A. Wilmart, 'La Tradition littéraire et textuelle de l'*Adoro te devote,*' in *Recherches de Théologie ancienne et médiévale* 1 (1920), pp. 21–40; 149–76. *For* authenticity: F. J. E. Raby, 'The Date and the Authorship of the poem *Adoro te devote*', *Speculum* 20 (1945), pp. 236–8, and F. J. E. Raby, *Christian Latin Poetry. From the Beginnings to the Close of the Middle Ages* (Oxford 1953 2), p. 410.
29. W. H. Gardner and N. H. Mackenzie (eds), *The Poems of Gerard Manley Hopkins* (London 1967⁴), p. 212.
30. *Summa Theologiae,* IIIa, q.46, a.6.
31. With reference to Chrysostom, *Homilia in Joannem* 22; *Patrologia Graeca* 59, 136.
32. Thomas's Christ suffers not so much in penal substitution, in our place, as in representative solidarity, on our behalf: cf. L. Hardy, *La doctrine de la rédemption chez saint Thomas* (Paris 1936), p. 111.
33. *Summa Theologiae,* q.46, a.7.

34. Ibid., a.8.
35. Ibid., ad i.
36. Ibid., a.9.
37. Ibid., a.10.
38. See R. L. Wilken, *John Chrysostom and the Jews. Rhetoric and Reality in the Late Fourth Century* (Los Angeles, Calif., 1988).
39. C.S.EL.
40. *Summa Theologiae*, q.46, a.9., ad iv; with a reference back to q.14, a.4, 'Utrum Christus omnes defectus corporales hominum assumere debuerit'.
41. Ibid., q.46, a.11.
42. *Homilia 87 in Matthaeum, Patrologia Graeca* 58, 770; *homilia 85 in Joannem, Patrologia Graeca* 59, 460.
43. A symbolic christology, whether broadly imaginative or more specifically narrative in style, cannot prescind from this ontological question. The holding together of the two is the test of the christologian's ability.
44. *Summa Theologiae*, q.46, a.12.
45. *Epistolae* 17; *Patrologia Graeca* 77, 121; cf. Mansi, *Concilia* IV, p. 1084. For the context and possible Apollinarian misconstrual of Cyril's letter, see W. H. C. Frend, *The Rise of the Monophysite Church. Chapters in the History of the Church in the Fifth and Sixth Centuries* (Cambridge 1972), p. 19.
46. Citing Theodotus of Ancyra, *Homilia 2 in nativitatem Salvatoris, Patrologia Graeca* 77, 1384; cf. Mansi, *Concilia* V, 216.
47. On argument from *conveniential congruentia*, see *Summa Theologiae* Ia, q.32, a.1, ad ii. Reason may be said to have (in theology) a twofold function; first, to establish a principle by sufficient proof; secondly, to show the congruity of certain effects with a principle previously established.
48. Bernard Gui, *Legenda sancti Thomas* 13, as translated in K. Foster, *The Life of St Thomas Aquinas. Biographical Documents* (London 1959), p. 36.
49. *Hystoria beati Thomae*, p. 34.
50. Ibid., p. 29.
51. J. Pieper, *The Silence of Saint Thomas* (Et: London 1957), pp. 45–7.

Chapter IX: Homage to Scheeben

1. See M. Schmaus, 'Die Stellung M. J. Scheebens in der Theologie des 19. Jahrhunderts', in *M. J. Scheeben, Der Erneuerer katholischer Glaubenwissenschaft* (Mainz 1935), pp. 31–54.

2. E. Paul, *Denkweg und Denkform der Theologie von Matthias Joseph Scheeben* (Munich 1970), pp. 1–28.
3. M. J. Scheeben, 'Die theologische und praktische Bedeutung des Dogmas von der Unfehlbarkeit des Papstes, besonders in seiner Beziehung auf die heutige Zeit', in *Das ökumenische Konzil* 3 (1871), pp. 432–7.
4. E. Paul, *Denkweg und Denkform der Theologie von Matthias Joseph Scheeben* (Munich 1970), pp. 29–33. See also L. Scheffczyk, 'Der Weg der deutschen katholischen Theologie im 19. Jahrhundert', *Theologische Quartalschrift* 145 (1965), pp. 273–306.
5. *Die Mysterien des Christentums* (Freiburg 1865), preface.
6. Mainz 1861.
7. Freiburg 1863.
8. Freiburg 1941 (Et: *The Mysteries of Christianity*, St Louis, Mo., 1946).
9. Freiburg 1873–1882. The works of Scheeben are now best consulted in the *Gesammelte Schriften*, edited by J. Höfer, published at Freiburg from 1949 to 1967. Additional materials are listed in E. Paul, *Denkweg und Denkform der Theologie von Matthias Joseph Scheeben* (Munich 1970), pp. xii–xiii.
10. *Matthias Joseph Scheeben. Un teologo tomista* (Rome 1988), preface.
11. *The Mysteries of Christianity* (St Louis, Mo., 1946), p. 4.
12. Ibid., p. 5.
13. H. U. von Balthasar, *Herrlichkeit. Eine theologische Aesthetik* I. (Einsiedeln 1961), pp. 98–110.
14. *The Mysteries of Christianity* (St Louis, Mo., 1946), pp. 762–70.
15. H. de Lubac, S.J., *Surnaturel: Etudes historiques* (Paris 1946).
16. *Matthias Joseph Scheeben. Un teologo tomista* (Rome 1988), p. 13.
17. See L. Klein, *Kreatürlichkeit als Gottebenbildlichkeit bei M. J. Scheeben* (Frankfurt 1975).
18. *Gesammelte Schriften* I *(Natur und Gnade)*, p. 403.
19. J. H. Newman, *The Dream of Gerontius* (London 1905), p. 52. Italics are, of course, added.
20. *Gesammelte Schriften* II *(Die Mysterien des Christentums)*, p. 366.
21. Ibid., V/1 *(Handbuch der katholischen Dogmatik. Drittes Buch)*, p. 402.

22. *The Mysteries of Christianity* (St Louis, Mo., 1946), pp. 431–65.
23. M. J. Nicolas, O.P. 'Le concept de maternité sponsale dans la théologie mariale de Scheeben', in *Matthias Joseph Scheeben. Un teologo tomista* (Rome 1988).
24. John of Damascus, *De fide orthodoxa* III.2.
25. Cited in H. U. von Balthasar, *The Office of Peter and the Structure of the Church* (Et: San Francisco 1986, p. 200). Balthasar compares Scheeben's teaching to the sermon of Cyril of Alexandria at Ephesus: 'Let us praise the ever-virgin Mary, and that means, indeed, the Holy Church, as well as her Son and immaculate Bridegroom', *Patrologia Graeca* 77, 996c.
26. W. H. Gardner and N. H. Mackenzie (eds), *The Poems of Gerard Manley Hopkins* (London 1967⁴), pp. 93–6.
27. Rom 12:1.

Index of Names

Tertullian 143–148, 154, 155, 156, 157, 169
Teresa of Avila 64
Theodore of Catana 187
Theodore of Jerusalem 186
Theodore of Mopsuestia 116
Theodore of Studios 189
Theodore of Tarsus 111
Theodoret 115
Theodosius I 170–171
Theodosius II 116, 117
Thomas Aquinas 12, 66, 192–214, 205
Tiberius II 185
Tirechàn of Tirawley 101
Trubetskoy, E. 123
Tugwell, S. 12
Tyrrell, G. 27

Ullmann, W. 143

Undset, S. 13

Valerian 154, 155
Victorinus of Aquitaine 102
Vigilius 117
Vogt, H. G. 149
Vokes, F. E. 129, 130, 131
Von Schönborn, C. 187, 189

Ware, K. T. 11
Westermann, C. 47, 60
Wheeler-Robinson, H. 44, 46
Wilfrid 109, 110, 111
William of St Thierry 66
William of Tocco 203
Wordsworth, W. 2

Zernov, N. 11
Zita, empress 9
Zizioulas, J. D. 113

DATE DUE